JAPAN

and the
Politics of
Techno-Globalism

JAPAN

and the
Politics of
Techno-Globalism

Gregory P. Corning

An East Gate Book

M.E.Sharpe
Armonk, New York
London, England

An East Gate Book

Library of Congress Cataloging-in-Publication Data

Corning, Gregory P., 1965–
  Japan and the politics of techno-globalism / by Gregory P. Corning.
    p. cm.
  An East Gate Book.
  Includes bibliographical references and index.
  ISBN 0-7656-0969-X (alk. paper)
  1. High technology industries—Japan. 2. Research, Industrial—Japan. 3. Technological
innovations—Japan. 4. Japan—Foreign economic relations. 5. Globalization. I. Title
HC465.H53C67 2004
338′.064′0952—dc22

                                                                    2003023979

Printed in the United States of America

BM (c)   10   9   8   7   6   5   4   3   2   1

To my mother and father

Contents

List of Tables and Figure

Tables

Figure

Acknowledgments

I was fortunate to study under a number of excellent teachers at Brown University and the University of Southern California. I would like to begin by thanking Terrence Hopmann and Jan Kalicki for first encouraging my interest in international relations. I would also like to thank a number of faculty at USC's School of International Relations for their guidance and support during my time in graduate school. I am grateful to Jonathan Aronson, Jerry Bender, Tom Biersteker, Chip Blacker, Roger Dingman, Steve Lamy, Abraham Lowenthal, and Bill Tow. Although they may have long forgotten me, I will benefit from their guidance for many years yet to come.

I also owe a deep debt of gratitude to all those who have helped this project evolve from a dissertation into a book. The staff of the Inter-University Center for Japanese Language Studies in Yokohama prepared me to conduct field research in Japan while Junko Kato kept a watchful eye on early research during my time as a visiting student at Tokyo University. It is not possible here to thank by name all of the people who provided data or agreed to be interviewed over the years. Nevertheless, the Human Frontier Science Program Organization, the Real World Computing Partnership, the IMS Promotion Center, and the IMS Inter-Regional Secretariat deserve special mention for providing introductions to many of these individuals and for supplying a wealth of research materials. A number of organizations also provided funding that was crucial to the completion of this project. A Department of Education FLAS Fellowship provided support for language training at the Inter-University Center while grants from the East Asian Studies Center at USC, the Center for International Studies at USC, and the Sanwa Bank Foundation allowed me to complete the dissertation. A Department of Education Fulbright-Hayes Fellowship and a Santa Clara University Junior Faculty Fellowship during Fall 2000 gave me time to begin revising the manuscript. I am particularly grateful to Kenneth Pechter for hosting me during this time at Tokyo University's Institute of Social Science.

My greatest professional debt in completing this book is to Mike Mochizuki, who has provided unwavering support over the years. I would also like to thank Takuyo Furukawa for research assistance, the anonymous reviewers for their advice on how to sharpen my analysis, and Richard Gunde for his expert copyediting. I am also indebted to my friends in the political science department at Santa Clara University who have provided a nurturing environment for me to grow as a teacher and researcher. On a personal level, I owe thanks to Shigeru Toma and my friends at Kameya Sushi and Tori Kago Yakitoriya, who taught me more about Japan than I could ever have learned in a classroom or library. I am also grateful for the support of family and friends who did not forget me during my years of traveling before I settled in the Bay Area. My greatest debts, both emotional and financial, are to my parents who have been my teachers for almost forty years. It is with love and thanks that I dedicate this book to them.

List of Acronyms

AIST	Agency for Industrial Science and Technology (METI National Institute for Industrial Science and Technology [after 2001])
ARC	Administrative Reform Council
ASET	Association of Super-Advanced Electronics Technologies
ASUKA	Advanced Semiconductors through Collaborative Achievement
ATP	Advanced Technology Program
CSTP	Council for Science and Technology Policy
DRAM	Dynamic Random Access Memory
ETL	Electrotechnical Laboratory (MITI)
ERATO	Exploratory Research for Advanced Technology Program
EUREKA	European Research Coordination Agency
FGCP	Fifth Generation Computer Project
GATT	General Agreement on Tariffs and Trade
HALCA	High-Performance and Agilent Cleanroom Association
HFSP	Human Frontier Science Program
HYPR	Hypersonic Transport Propulsion System Project
ICORP	International Cooperative Research Program (Japan)
IMEC	Inter-University Microelectronics Center (Belgium)
IMS	Intelligent Manufacturing Systems Initiative
ISMT	International Sematech
ITER	International Thermonuclear Experimental Reactor
JEITA	Japan Electronics and Information Technology Industries Association

JESSI	Joint European Submicron Silicon Project
JSPS	Japan Society for the Promotion of Science
JST	Japan Science and Technology Corporation
MEDEA+	Microelectronics Development for European Applications Plus
MESC	Ministry of Education, Science, and Culture
METI	Ministry of Economy, Trade, and Industry
MEXT	Ministry of Education, Culture, Sports, Science, and Technology
MIRAI	Millennium Research for Advanced Information Technology
MITI	Ministry of International Trade and Industry
MOF	Ministry of Finance
MOSIS	Metal Oxide Semiconductor Implementation Service
MOSS	Market-Oriented Sector-Specific
NEDO	New Energy and Industrial Technology Development Organization
NIH	National Institutes of Health
NIST	National Institute of Standards and Technology (U.S.)
NSF	National Science Foundation
OECD	Organization for Economic Cooperation and Development
OSTP	Office of Science and Technology Policy (U.S.)
SDI	Strategic Defense Initiative
RWC	Real World Computing
SELETE	Semiconductor Leading Edge Technologies
STA	Science and Technology Agency
STARC	Semiconductor Technology Academic Research Center
TLO	Technology Licensing Organization
USCAR	U.S. Council for Automotive Research
VLSI	Very-Large-Scale Integrated Circuit

JAPAN

and the
Politics of
Techno-Globalism

—— Chapter 1 ——

Introduction

In the 1980s, Americans perceived Japan as an economic juggernaut challenging U.S. dominance in a range of industries. Today, they see a country adrift in financial turmoil and political gridlock. After averaging growth of only 1 percent during the "lost decade" of the 1990s, the world's second largest economy saw growth come to a virtual halt in the early years of this decade.[1] Although Japanese leaders have been reluctant to take the painful steps necessary to reform the nation's ailing banking system, they have been far more decisive in strengthening the science and technology system. In response to the downturn of the 1990s, the government focused on traditional strengths and redoubled R&D efforts. In 1995, the Diet passed the Science and Technology Basic Law, which sought to revitalize Japanese R&D through two Basic Plans. By the end of the First Basic Plan (1996–2001), government R&D spending was double the level of 1992.[2] Under the Second Basic Plan (2001–2006), the government intends to increase R&D spending by an additional 40 percent. The Second Basic Plan also establishes government-wide research priorities for the first time and places new emphasis on increasing the efficiency of the science and technology system as part of the administrative reform of government that began in 2001.[3]

As Japan set out to strengthen its science and technology capabilities in the mid-1990s, Western academics remained skeptical about the chances of any meaningful opening in its national system of innovation. These doubts are rooted in Japan's long history of using neomercantilist policies to access and assimilate foreign technologies. For most scholars, Japan remains the "paradigmatic case of techno-nationalism." Beginning with the modernization drive of the mid-nineteenth century, Japanese bureaucrats and business leaders "fused industrial, technological, and security priorities."[4] This image of a techno-nationalist Japan became more entrenched in the West as economic frictions grew during the 1980s. Scholars pointed both to structural differences between Japanese and Western capitalism and to the Japanese government's deliberate moves to restrict foreign competition until Japanese firms became leaders in a particular industry.[5] Seeing the past in Japan's future, Mike Mochizuki predicted in the mid-1990s that "Japanese bureaucrats will continue to view technology as a long-term strategic asset. Techno-nationalism will survive."[6] Likewise, the National Research Council argued that Japan had proven unwilling to collaborate on reciprocal terms in defense-related technology.[7] As the 1990s ended, Edward Lincoln contended that R&D consortia sponsored by the Japanese government continued to perpetuate "the tradition of blurring government-industry boundaries, pursuing narrow nationalism, and devising new informal or opaque relationships—the kind of relationships that deregulation and administrative reform were presumably diminishing."[8]

As Japan's financial crisis continued into a new decade, many scholars remained doubtful that the pressures on the government and firms would weaken techno-nationalism or lead to increased opening of the economy. Japan showed no signs of moving away from industrial policies intended to build national competitiveness; bureaucrats continued to establish programs to promote industries including satellites, biotechnology, and semiconductors. Moreover, the results of restructuring in the private sector were far from clear. Japan has welcomed substantial foreign direct investment in industries such as automobiles and financial services, but foreign interests still represent only a tiny part of the Japanese economy. Even in the case of major investments, foreign control remains limited. All of the high-profile foreign investments in the Japanese auto industry, for example, have involved only minority stakes. Although Renault's 37 percent share of Nissan gives the firm veto rights on some corporate decisions, it is still far short of majority ownership.[9] The situation is even more ambiguous regarding the future of the *keiretsu*—the six corporate groups built on cross-shareholding arrangements and ties to a common bank—that were a central feature of the Japanese economy during the second half of the twentieth century. The stable share-holding arrangements and preferential business relationships among *keiretsu* members created a barrier to both foreign investment and imports. Although recent mergers among banks from different groups raised the possibility that *keiretsu* ties might be weakening, skeptics suggest that corporate relationships are simply re-forming around four consolidated *keiretsu*.[10]

While recognizing significant continuity in Japan's political economy, a second group of scholars argues that the pressures on Japan have already resulted in some opening despite the nation's continued commitment to techno-nationalist values. Among this more optimistic group, Ulrike Schaede and William Grimes describe Japan's managed globalization in terms of "permeable insulation." Faced with the hollowing out of the manufacturing industry and the need to create new business models based on innovative technologies, Japan has adopted a dual-track approach to managing globalization that allows for different degrees of opening and closure across sectors. The Japanese government will still try to insulate domestic firms from market forces when felt necessary, but a decline in the power of the state and the solidarity of private institutions such as *keiretsu* and trade associations has made this insulation more permeable. Schaede and Grimes contend that understanding Japan's dual-track policy requires a case-by-case evaluation of policy intent and outcome in different sectors.[11]

Likewise, Gerald Hane suggests that Japan's financial crisis has "put a dent in techno-nationalism." Efforts to deal with the economic downturn have increased both the foreign presence in the financial sector and the number of mergers and acquisitions in industries such as electronics and pharmaceuticals. In turn, these changes in the financial structure are creating an increasingly multinational innovation base. Hane acknowledges that these changes are not part of a fundamental philosophical shift to greater openness, but contends that Japan's techno-nationalism has nonetheless been compromised by the need to take advantage of a more open economic structure.[12] D.H. Whittaker agrees that Japan's commitment to techno-nationalism is unlikely to diminish soon, but concedes that "competing visions might weaken its effectiveness . . . [and that] techno-globalism, particularly in its corporate-interests-first form, might either supplement it, or be used to pursue it."[13]

In short, these cautious optimists agree that the nature—if not the goals—of Japan's technonogy policy may be changing as a result of both globalization and the nation's ongoing economic downturn. This book concurs that there has been a major shift in Japanese technology policy but argues that it began long before the severity of the nation's financial crisis became apparent. In 1989, Japan's Ministry of International Trade and Industry (MITI), the ministry most closely associated with Japan's postwar industrial policy, opened many of its large-scale research programs to foreign participation on more liberal terms than those offered even now by government technology programs in the United States and the European Union (see Table 1.1). The United States has no uniform rules that apply across different federal departments and agencies. The semiconductor industry's Sematech consortium remained closed to foreign participation until its government subsidy ended in 1996. The U.S. Council for Automotive Research (USCAR), which runs several government-subsidized projects, rejected Toyota's petition for membership despite the changes brought about by the 1998 merger of Daimler-Benz and Chrysler. Yet, many U.S. programs now offer conditional access to subsidiaries of foreign firms. For example, the Department of Commerce's Advanced Technology Program (ATP) is open to foreign-owned firms, domiciled in the United States, whose participation in ATP will be of benefit to the United States and whose home governments provide American firms with reciprocal access to R&D programs, as well as comparable investment opportunities and protection of intellectual property.

Table 1.1

Rules on Foreign Access to Publicly Subsidized R&D Programs

	Rules on Foreign Access
United States	
Sematech	Closed until 1996 when public subsidy ended
USCAR	Conditionally open
	• Requirement for "significant" local R&D facilities
	• Research must be done in the United States
ATP	Conditionally Open
	• Foreign firms' participation must be judged in the interest of the United States
	• Reciprocal national treatment in research opportunities, foreign investment, and protection of intellectual property
Europe	
Framework Programs	Conditionally Open
	• Local subsidiaries receive same treatment as firms from member nations.
	• Nondomiciled foreign firms from industrialized countries outside Europe allowed to participate in programs designated under bilateral science and technology agreements
	• No research subsidy from E.U.
EUREKA	Conditionally Open
	• Project must have participants from at least two member-nations whose governments participation
Japan	
MITI Programs	No general rules governing foreign access but roughly one-third of projects during the 1990s were unconditionally open
	• No requirement for local R&D facilities
	• No requirement for reciprocal national treatment
	• Full subsidy available to nondomiciled firms and research institutes

There is also some variation in rules between Europe's two largest research programs. In 1994, the European Union adopted uniform rules on foreign access to its Framework Programs in industrial technology. Domiciled foreign firms with substantial R&D facilities are treated the same as firms based within the European Union. Nondomiciled foreign firms may participate in collaborations permitted under bilateral science and technology agreements. However, firms from advanced industrialized countries—such as Australia, Canada, and the United States—are not eligible for European Union research subsidies. Access to projects under the umbrella of the European Research Coordination Agency

(EUREKA) is decided on a case-by-case basis. EUREKA is an industry-led program that helps match firms from member countries. Although participants must fund their own participation in EUREKA, many receive subsidies from their respective governments. Since the late 1990s, firms and research institutes from nonmember countries have been able to take part in EUREKA if invited to join a project with participants from at least two member states whose governments approve of the foreign participation.

Ironically, the most liberal membership terms have been offered by MITI programs. (In 2001, a reorganized MITI became the Ministry of Economy, Trade and Industry [METI]. This book uses the acronym MITI when discussing policies initiated before 2001). Since the early 1990s, fully subsidized participation in MITI R&D programs has been open to nondomiciled foreign firms and research institutes—not simply local subsidiaries with substantial research facilities. MITI called this policy of opening "techno-globalism."[14] Yet, this techno-globalism is circumscribed in two ways. First, like the United States, Japan never established general rules governing foreign participation in its programs. Thus, bureaucrats retained discretion in deciding which programs to open. Although the administrative reform of the Japanese government has weakened METI's influence over the day-to-day management of its affiliated research organizations, this is unlikely to result in any major shift in the current policy regarding foreign participation. Second, the ministry's budget for large-scale R&D collaborations is much smaller than that of research-funding agencies in the United States and Europe. Still, many programs have been opened to foreign participation. Like other advanced nations, Japan is now focused on assessing the results produced by publicly funded research. METI now subjects all its large-scale R&D programs to external evaluations. Of the sixty-six projects evaluated between 2000 and 2002, twenty-two included foreign participants.[15]

Assuming that the ministry's programs provide participants with valuable research opportunities, they do not seem to fit with the image of a resolutely techno-nationalist Japan. In examining the substance beneath the rhetoric of MITI's techno-globalism, this book is guided by two fundamental questions. Why did MITI open its research programs to foreign participation? And has this opening provided meaningful opportunities for foreign firms and research institutes? The case studies discussed in this book suggest that bureaucratic politics and techno-national ideology have not played a decisive role in internationalization. Most of MITI's international programs have fallen squarely within the ministry's regulatory domain and so have generated little conflict with other ministries. The programs are also not the efficient mechanisms for accessing and indigenizing foreign technologies that an understanding based on techno-national ideology would seem to suggest. In the context of the global movement toward more open forms of technology promotion, MITI's policy of techno-globalism appears much less cynical than techno-nationalist analyses of Japan suggest. Although often overlooked by political scientists, leveraging complementary resources and capabilities has often been an important factor driving the opening of MITI programs. In this view, MITI's techno-globalism has been a self-interested response to the same forces driving the internationalization of corporate R&D and the opening of publicly subsidized programs throughout the triad. That MITI was the first to seize the rhetorical high ground in opening its research programs is a function of both the foreign pressure on Japan to contribute more to the international community and the insulation of Japanese bureaucrats from domestic political pressures in developing technology policy.

Of course, the opening of MITI programs would mean very little if Japanese firms saw them of minimal value and took part only to placate bureaucrats who could make life more difficult on other issues. Therefore, in addition to discussing the forces driving internationalization, this study also addresses the related debate over the effectiveness of MITI research programs. Although the perceived success of the Very-Large-Scale Integrated Circuit (VLSI) project in the late 1970s generated enthusiasm in the West for the "Japanese model" of collaborative R&D, MITI failures during the 1980s appeared as examples of anachronistic, top-down industrial policy pushed on indifferent and even reluctant firms. However, MITI learned from its mistakes and adapted to the role of promoting frontier research from a position of greatly diminished influence over Japanese firms. With increased breadth and flexibility in research goals, MITI programs during the 1990s provided a better complement to the needs and interests of Japanese firms—especially as the nation's protracted economic downturn forced firms to slash funding for long-term research. Depending on the technologies involved, these programs also offered important opportunities for foreign participants who were given the freedom to choose their own research themes and the same rights to intellectual property as their Japanese counterparts. While METI remains committed to advancing Japan's science and technology base, changes in the nation's relative technological position and the nature of research and development have altered the means available to pursue this goal.

Contending Explanations of Japan's Techno-Globalism

Leading scholars of Japan's national system of innovation provide a number of frameworks for understanding MITI's decision to open its research programs to foreign participation. Opening can be explained as a result of bureaucratic politics, techno-national ideology, foreign pressure, or the same technological and financial motives that drive firms to enter strategic alliances. In order to build a more solid foundation for science and technology collaborations with Japan, it is important to evaluate the different explanations of opening, and the potential value of these collaborations to corporate and university researchers both in Japan and abroad. The Japanese government is currently taking steps to maximize the returns on publicly funded research and placing renewed emphasis on promotion of several high-tech sectors including semiconductors, biotechnology, nanotechnology, and environmental technology. Cursory dismissal of MITI's techno-globalism as an attempt to siphon foreign technology, or as a token response to foreign pressure, could blind foreign firms and governments to genuine opportunities for balanced exchange.

Chalmers Johnson emphasizes the primacy of bureaucratic politics in the formation of Japanese technology policy. In his view, foreign pressure and technological change provide only "opportunities and constraints that indirectly influence" bureaucrats whose prime motivation is advancing the interests of themselves and their ministry.[16] The internationalization of MITI research programs coincided with the ministry's move toward more basic research involving university researchers. From a bureaucratic politics perspective, the decision to internationalize research programs would be diplomatic cover for MITI to expand its turf relative to that of the Ministry of Education, Science, and Culture (MESC) and the Science and Technology Agency (STA). MITI's recruitment of academics to participate in its more basic, international research programs should have produced significant conflict with MESC, which oversees the university research system, and with STA, which oversaw large-scale international collaborations in basic science before being absorbed by MESC in 2001. In short, if bureaucratic politics explains MITI's decision to open its research programs, then these programs should have generated significant bureaucratic friction because they reflected MITI's drive to maximize its regulatory powers vis-à-vis rival ministries.

Richard Samuels contends that techno-national ideology fundamentally shapes Japanese technology policy. He describes this ideology in terms of three core policies: indigenization of foreign technologies, diffusion of these technologies throughout the national economy, and nurturing of domestic capabilities to innovate and manufacture.[17] Following the thrust of Samuels's argument, one would have to conclude that MITI's decision to internationalize research programs is simply the latest manifestation of an ideological drive to access and indigenize foreign technology. If techno-national ideology does explain MITI's decision to open its research programs, then the initial proposals for these programs should reflect a systematic effort to maximize the potential inflow of technology, especially in areas where Japan trails the state of the art.

Foreign pressure provides a third possible explanation for MITI's techno-globalism. During the 1980s, the United States pressed MITI to open its research programs to foreign participation. The first request to open these programs came in the Market-Oriented Sector-Specific (MOSS) talks during 1985–86. The request was repeated much more forcefully during the renegotiation of the U.S.-Japan Science and Technology Agreement in 1988.[18] That MITI began to open research programs shortly after the signing of this agreement led many to think foreign pressure was the decisive force driving the ministry's policy of techno-globalism. If foreign pressure does explain MITI's decision to open its research programs, then there should be a correlation in the timing of specific applications of pressure and the opening of these programs. In order to gauge the effect of foreign pressure, it is also necessary to specify the range of potential outcomes. If foreign pressure is very effective in producing opening, then MITI programs should reflect foreign preferences on research priorities and terms of collaboration. If foreign pressure is only partially effective, then MITI might simply open projects of little interest to foreigners or make participation in important projects too burdensome to be worthwhile.

A fourth explanation of MITI's decision to internationalize research programs points to the rapid growth in strategic alliances between firms headquartered in different nations and the conditional opening of publicly subsidized research programs in the United States and European Union during the mid-1990s. This view suggests that MITI was responding to the same forces driving corporate alliances and the opening of research programs throughout the triad. These forces include the rising costs and risks of high-tech research as well as the desire to leverage complementary scientific or technological capabilities.[19] If these forces explain MITI's decision to open its research programs, then these programs should be characterized by high costs and risks or by a clear opportunity to leverage the complementary capabilities of international partners.

Testing Techno-Globalism in MITI Research Programs

At the end of the 1980s, Japan's science and technology bureaucracy was just beginning to increase its ties with the West. The MESC expanded programs for the international exchange of researchers at universities and national research institutes and the STA assumed a major role in megascience collaborations such as the Space Station and the International Thermonuclear Experimental Reactor. MITI efforts stood out, however, because they were Japanese initiatives in organizing large-scale, international research projects. In examining the motivation behind these efforts and the results they produced, this book first weighs the role of bureaucratic politics, techno-national ideology, foreign pressure, and complementary scientific and technological capabilities in explaining MITI's decision to open its research programs to foreign participation. It then assesses the utility of these programs for both Japanese and foreign participants in terms of both research results and potential for meaningful international collaboration. The analysis focuses on case studies of the three most controversial MITI programs launched between 1989 and 1995: the Human Frontier Science Program (HFSP), the Intelligent Manufacturing Systems Initiative (IMS), and the Real World Computing (RWC) program (see Table 1.2).

Consistently cited in MITI reports as "models" of international collaboration, these three projects generated greater fears of Japanese techno-nationalism than any other initiated in the first half of the 1990s.[20] Varying in research focus, scope, and level of interest to the West, they also represent three distinct responses to the forces driving the internationalization of research and development. The HFSP is a grant program funded chiefly by Japan but managed by a foundation that leaves all research and funding decisions to an international committee of scientists. The IMS Initiative began as a Japanese proposal to fund an international program on next generation manufacturing technology but developed into a multilateral effort to organize R&D on a global scale. In contrast, the RWC program was an open, national project in which Japan decided the basic research objectives and management structure before opening the program to foreign partners. While the HFSP and IMS stand as unique experiments in international collaboration, RWC is representative of most open, national programs, including the hypersonic jet engine, micromachine, and semiconductor projects discussed in chapter 7.

The HFSP is a nonprofit organization established in Strasbourg in 1989 that funds international teams and individual fellows conducting research on the complex mechanisms of living organisms. Since the mid-1990s, its annual budget has hovered around $50 million, with roughly 65 percent of the total provided by Japan. The HFSP makes a particularly revealing case study because, first, the proposal to create the program stirred significant controversy out of fear that MITI was targeting Western strengths in biotechnology. Second, as MITI's first international research initiative, the HFSP provides unique insight into the forces propelling the opening of research. Third, as a grant program for academic researchers, the HFSP provides an important test of the bureaucratic politics argument and a different perspective on internationalization than the other cases, which focus on industrial technology.

Table 1.2

Overview of the Case Studies

	HFSP	IMS	RWC
Research focus	Basic interdisciplinary research on molecular-level biological functions in living organisms	Management of extended, global enterprises; process technologies like virtual manufacturing	Parallel and distributed computing; software and hardware for processing ambiguous multimedia info
Structure	*International Grant Program*: Management and project selection by an international committee of scientists	*Umbrella for International Consortia*: International management structure led by industry; multiregional consortia define own research agenda	*Open National Consortium*: MITI and Japanese firms decided basic objectives and organization; one central lab and 19 distributed labs
Participants	International teams of university researchers	More than 400 firms, institutes, and universities from Asia, Europe, and North America	15 Japanese firms, 4 foreign research institutes
Budget	About $50 million per year, 65% from Japan	About $40 million per year; funding arrangements decided on a regional basis	About $60 million per year, 100% from Japan
Time period	1989–2007	1995–2005	1992–2001
Initial international interest	High academic, low government	High academic, high corporate	High academic, low corporate

Like the HFSP, IMS also evolved from a Japanese initiative into a unique, multilateral program. All funding decisions are made within IMS "regions," and management responsibilities are distributed among Australia, Canada, the European Union, Japan, South Korea, Switzerland, and the United States. The IMS program encourages the development of consortia across the entire spectrum of manufacturing activities from process issues such as the development of autonomous manufacturing modules to management issues such as the coordination of production in the extended, global enterprise. IMS is also industry led, with firms developing their own consortia within the broad parameters of the program. Firms and universities are able to submit expressions of interest in IMS projects to a secretariat in their respective region. The secretariats then exchange and circulate this information, giving interested parties leads on potential research partners. Project proposals, which must have members from at least three IMS regions, are then evaluated by an international panel of judges. More than just a test of MITI's techno-globalism, IMS is the first attempt to coordinate industry-led R&D consortia on a global scale. IMS began in 1995 and is scheduled to end in 2005, although discussions are underway about extending the program. At the end of 2002, the IMS portfolio included 14 completed projects, 23 ongoing projects, and 16 proposals awaiting endorsement. The ongoing projects brought together 234 partners—60 percent of them firms—and committed funding of roughly $229 million.[21]

Launched in 1992, the ten-year RWC program was a $600 million effort to develop a range of next-generation computer technologies. As MITI's largest electronics program during the 1990s, the RWC provides an important illustration of changes in the ministry's innovation policy over that decade. The program's flexible research agenda and organization were a significant departure from earlier MITI computer consortia such as the Fifth Generation Computer Project (FGCP). Rather than following a rigid plan to develop one prototype system, the RWC program was organized around a loose grouping of research themes. Firms chose both the themes in which they wished to participate and the topics they wished to research within those themes. The RWC program was also the first MITI computer consortium to offer full membership to foreign firms and research institutes. Four research institutes from Germany, Holland, Singapore, and Sweden joined the RWC program as full partners. Concerned that Japan would benefit disproportionately from U.S. participation in the broader RWC program framework, Washington proposed a Joint Optoelectronics Project within the RWC program as a more limited, "brokered" collaboration in the prototyping of optoelectronic devices. Although fully open to foreign participation, RWC is best characterized as an "open national project" because the research plan and management structure were developed largely by Japan and opened on terms decided by Japan.

The analysis of these cases—and other Japanese, American, and European projects discussed throughout the book—draws on a range of materials including government documents, newspapers, trade journals, and reports issued by the various project secretariats. To supplement and cross check these written sources, the analysis also incorporates information from more than one hundred interviews conducted during 1994–96 and 2000–2, which cover a variety of national and organizational perspectives on each project.

The Argument in Brief

The initial negotiations concerning the HFSP, IMS, and RWC suggest that bureaucratic politics and techno-national ideology were not very important in driving the opening of these programs. The attempt to nurture university-industry collaboration that began in the 1980s helped to mitigate conflicts with the MESC over MITI's recruitment of university researchers for its large-scale projects. Factors such as the freedom of foreign partners to choose their research themes, the distribution of research at members' own labs, and changes in intellectual property rules all reduced concerns about Japanese techno-nationalism.

With rising criticism of Japan's "free-ride" in basic research during the bubble economy of the late 1980s, foreign pressure played a key role in pushing MITI to open its research programs. There is, however, no simple relationship between the application of foreign pressure and the way MITI opened projects. In the HFSP, the ministry ignored foreign preferences and pushed ahead with its own priorities. In RWC, it opened a project of little interest to the West. And in IMS, it responded directly to foreign efforts to harness complementary technological skills. Although less apparent at the outset of the RWC program, attempts to leverage the complementary capabilities of partners from different countries have often encouraged internationalization.

Beyond the HFSP and IMS programs, complementary capabilities have played an important part in attracting foreign partners to projects in areas such as aerospace, new materials, micromachines, and energy technologies. In these instances, MITI's techno-globalism can be understood as a response to the same forces driving the internationalization of corporate R&D and publicly subsidized research programs throughout the triad. Nonetheless, MITI's renewed promotion of the semiconductor industry since the mid-1990s has been interpreted by many as evidence of the ministry's continued techno-nationalism. It is true that the ASET and MIRAI semiconductor projects illustrate the limits of techno-globalism in certain technologies, but these and many other semiconductor consortia throughout the triad have been drawn into significant international collaboration.

Western analysts have tended to dismiss the opportunities offered by MITI's techno-globalism because of rigid assumptions about the nature of Japanese industrial policy. After the disappointing results of several frontier research initiatives during the 1980s, MITI moved away from a top-down model of industrial policy and experimented with more flexible programs that provided a better complement to the needs and interests of firms. Although the funding for these programs was very small in comparison to the R&D budgets of member firms, the subsidies were still important in supporting basic research that was being cut from corporate budgets during the slow economy of the 1990s. Moreover, many of these programs offered foreign participants nondiscriminatory terms for collaboration, funding, and sharing of results.

With the dominance of American firms in the information and telecommunications sectors, however, there is now much less urgency in the United States about accessing Japanese technology. And while METI continues to open national research programs in the absence of foreign pressure, it has not proposed any more innovative collaborations such as the HFSP and IMS. Today, discussions about collaboration in industrial technology continue but with a much lower profile. In 2000, for example, the Joint U.S.-Japan Dialogue Group–a bilateral committee of distinguished scientists from industry and academia—recognized that the possibility for leveraging complementary capabilities still exists in several areas including energy, environmental technology, and nanotechnology.[22] To make these opportunities more attractive to the West, however, Japan needs to make greater progress in strengthening its R&D infrastructure.

The struggle to revitalize the Japanese science and technology system began in the mid-1990s with a range of initiatives including breaking down barriers to collaboration among government, academia, and industry and requiring more rigorous external evaluations of government projects. Revitalization initiatives became even more focused with the launch of the Second Science and Technology Basic Plan and the administrative reform of government that reorganized the science and technology bureaucracy in 2001. The Second Basic Plan takes a more strategic view of research than the First Plan by establishing four priority themes for funding: life sciences, information and communications technology, environmental technology, and nanotechnology. Parts of this agenda dovetail nicely with themes identified by the Joint Dialogue Group as most promising for international collaboration. Furthermore, one of the major goals of the administrative reform of MITI has been to make the research system under METI more responsive to the needs of industry by transforming the Agency for Industrial Science and Technology (AIST) into a quasi-private institution with greater operational and financial independence. The new AIST has already begun to recruit foreign researchers to lead research projects, and to hold symposia overseas to promote joint research with foreign firms. Such attempts to obtain greater benefits from publicly sponsored research present the West with its best opportunity to engage Japan where opening provides a practical and politically expedient response to forces globalizing research and development throughout the triad.

Perhaps, the most important obstacle to increased opening and industrial collaboration with Western partners is an apparent weakening of the Japanese government's commitment to invest in basic research with applications beyond a five-year time horizon. Frustrated by more than a decade of anemic growth, the government seems to be looking for a quick technological fix for the nation's economic woes. In 2003, Japan launched the government-wide R&D Project for Economic Revitalization which includes $489 million in subsidies for projects that are likely to create new markets within three years. METI initiated forty-two projects with a total FY 2003 budget of $359 million in the four fields established by the Second Basic Plan.[23] With their focused goals and short time horizons, many of these projects fund work conducted by small groups of firms or even individual firms. Although the move to shorter and more applied projects could make identifying appropriate foreign partners easier, it seems more likely to reduce the number of opportunities for international collaboration.

With the trend toward more open forms of government technology promotion throughout the triad, METI's techno-globalism is by no means exceptional. Although METI programs offer subsidized participation to nondomiciled foreign firms, the ministry has not adopted formal guidelines on foreign access to research programs and its research budget, while growing, is smaller than that for comparable funding agencies in the United States and the European Union. In short, the opening of METI research programs is only a very small step in the opening of Japan's national system of innovation. Yet, attributing this opening to techno-national ideology marginalizes the importance of programs that often present foreign firms and universities with meaningful, nondiscriminatory research opportunities.

—————Chapter 2—————

Techno-Globalism in the Triad

In the mid-1980s, major multinational corporations began to invest more heavily in R&D labs outside their home countries. Although the United States, the European Union and Japan have been eager to attract foreign investment in local research facilities, they have been more cautious about welcoming foreign participation in publicly subsidized research programs. Surprisingly, Japanese programs have tended to offer less restrictive terms on foreign participation than industrial research programs in either the United States or Europe. Yet, Japan has failed to establish general guidelines governing foreign access to its programs, and funding for these programs—while consistent with that for closed programs during the 1980s—remains below that in the West.

The Internationalization of Corporate R&D

The internationalization of R&D has been neither a persistent nor a generalized phenomenon; its pace has varied by sector, corporate nationality, and time period.[1] The pioneers in establishing an international R&D presence were large firms such as Asea Brown Bovari, Philips, and Ericsson based in small European markets with limited R&D resources.[2] For the most part, the surge in internationalization of R&D that began in the 1980s was limited to larger firms in the United States, the European Union, and to a lesser extent Japan. In a study of 353 overseas R&D labs established by leading multinationals in the 1980s, Robert Pearce and Satwinder Singh found that 181 were located in the United States, 68 in the United Kingdom, and 50 in Germany; taken together these labs represented nearly 85 percent of all those in the sample.[3] As these figures show, multinationals have been most eager to establish overseas R&D facilities in the United States.

According to data compiled by the U.S. Department of Commerce, "R&D expenditures by foreign-owned companies in the United States tripled from $6.5 billion in 1987 to $19.7 billion in 1997, and accounted for nearly 15 percent of total company-funded R&D."[4] There were 715 foreign-owned R&D facilities operated by 375 parent companies in the United States at the end of 1998.[5] The majority of these facilities were managed by firms from

Japan (251), Germany (107), the United Kingdom (103), France (44), and Switzerland (42). Nevertheless, the total research expenditure of Japanese-owned facilities was less than that for countries with fewer U.S. R&D centers. Switzerland and Germany ranked first in R&D expenditures by foreign companies in the United States, each spending $3.3 billion in 1997. They were followed by Japan ($3.2 billion) and the United Kingdom ($3.1 billion). Industries with the largest foreign R&D presence in the United States include drugs and biotechnology (116), chemicals and rubber (115), computer software (54), automobiles (54), and medical devices and instrumentation (53). European investments in U.S. R&D facilities are concentrated in the drugs and chemicals industries, and Japanese investments, in the automotive and electronics industries.

Japanese firms began to establish overseas research facilities during the 1970s. Forty-three percent of new R&D labs set up by Japan's top thirty high-tech firms during the 1970s were established overseas, with the figure rising to 84 percent in the 1980s.[6] By 1990, about 20 percent of all patent applications in the United States and about 15 percent of those in Europe were submitted by Japanese applicants.[7] Although Japanese-funded R&D in the United States experienced the most rapid rate of growth over the years 1982 to 1997, Japan's share of U.S. patents remained relatively stable at about 20 percent.[8] The Japanese research presence in California has been particularly conspicuous. Of the 188 foreign-owned R&D facilities in California in 1997, almost 60 percent were owned by Japanese multinationals. Like Japanese firms that have been active in expanding R&D operations in the United States, American firms have also increased their research presence in Japan, albeit to a more modest degree. Of 186 R&D facilities operated by U.S. multinationals overseas in 1997, a total of 43 were located in Japan—substantially more than in the United Kingdom (27), Canada (26), France (16), Germany (15), or Singapore (13).[9]

Major multinationals in the information technology and automotive industries have been especially active in the cross-Pacific internationalization of R&D. IBM established the earliest presence in Japan; by the mid-1980s it had three R&D labs in Japan, the largest of which employed more than three thousand people. IBM's lead was followed by Digital Equipment (1982), Eastman Kodak (1985), and Texas Instruments (1991), all of which invested in major labs in the Tokyo metropolitan area. By the early 1990s, Fujitsu, Hitachi, Matsushita, NEC, and Sony had all established both corporate and divisional labs in the United States. As the decade ended, four of the fifteen largest foreign R&D centers in the United States were operated by Honda, Nissan, Sony, and Toyota.[10]

Alan Pearson argues that no single variable can explain the role of overseas R&D facilities because firms do not approach the internationalization of R&D by identical strategies in all markets.[11] In some cases, ownership of an overseas lab may be the result of a merger or acquisition rather than deliberate R&D planning. More commonly, the creation of overseas R&D facilities is part of an evolutionary process that reflects the growing market scope of a firm's products. According to typologies of R&D internationalization offered in several studies, foreign research facilities are initially established to support technology transfer to factories overseas and to monitor technological developments abroad. Over time, the facilities become full-fledged labs developing new products and technologies as part of a globally integrated research network.[12]

The internationalization of R&D by Japanese firms has been shaped by reliance on export-based strategies for penetrating international markets and Japan's experience as a technology follower.[13] Japanese firms first established overseas labs in the United States and Europe as listening posts. Moving production offshore more recently than their U.S. and European counterparts, Japanese firms also tended to establish wholly owned labs with highly focused mandates and strong functional linkages with labs in Japan.[14] For Japan's largest firms, however, the role of overseas labs became more sophisticated and independent in the late 1980s, during the bubble economy. Examples include the basic research labs established in the United States by NEC in 1989, and by Canon and Mitsubishi Electric in 1991. The confidence of Japanese firms during these years coupled with U.S. pressure to contribute more to the American research base made this shift in the nature of overseas R&D a practical move in both business and political terms. Yet, as economic stagnation during the 1990s pushed firms to emphasize applied research, and as the boom in the U.S. economy reduced political pressure on Japan, the move by Japanese multinationals to establish more independent R&D facilities in the United States slowed. However, this return to a more centralized R&D strategy was not unique to Japanese firms. In the mid-1990s, fiscal consolidation in R&D activities in almost all of the OECD nations produced a streamlining of distributed R&D networks that had become too unwieldy. Firms like IBM and Siemens also moved toward a strategy of multiple centers of learning with one dominant center of coordination.[15]

Although analysts have traditionally stressed the importance of demand factors, such as better meeting the needs of local customers, in driving the internationalization of corporate R&D, a number of recent studies have pointed toward the growing importance of supply factors, especially gaining access to complementary capabilities. In a 1996 survey of 200 foreign-affiliated labs in the United States, respondents rated the following as their central activities: developing new product ideas (87 percent), obtaining access to high-quality researchers (74 percent), and obtaining information on scientific and technological developments in the United States (72 percent).[16] During the 1990s, the need to develop new ideas and access local research talent became particularly important for Japanese firms wanting to tap American creativity in the development of multimedia technologies. In 1995, for example, Mitsubishi Electric, Sharp, Matsushita, Olympus Optical, and Casio Computer established digital and telecommunications technology labs in the United States.[17] The primacy attached to developing new product ideas suggests that foreign-affiliated labs in the United States enjoy a fair degree of autonomy in managing their research agendas. However, Japanese multinationals typically have a more centralized system of R&D management than their European counterparts. For example, Hitachi uses a system of "liaison persons" in which a "mentor" at the corporate R&D headquarters deals directly with a Japanese director or "gate-keeper" at a foreign lab. These two individuals manage the internal planning network while a citizen of the host country serves as a "leader" or liaison with the local research community and market.[18]

A 1998 survey by the Ministry of Education asked Japanese multinationals the reasons for establishing R&D centers overseas. According to the more than one thousand respondents, the objectives of these facilities included developing products tailored to local needs (71 percent), accessing local research talent (38 percent), acquiring vital non-R&D information such as on national policies (25 percent), and gaining quicker access to excellent R&D achievements (20 percent). The primary objectives of these centers were applied research near the final product stage (80 percent), basic research (24 percent), and collaboration with universities and national research centers (13 percent). Indeed, 88 percent of Japan's top fifty R&D spenders have outsourced research to foreign universities and public organizations.[19] Despite the continuing economic downturn at home, a growing number of Japanese companies have been establishing R&D centers in other countries since the late 1990s. While most of these are located in the United States, a growing number are in Asia—particularly in China. These new Asian R&D centers concentrate on software and electrical machinery.[20]

Although multinationals from every nation continue to establish overseas R&D centers, the evidence remains mixed as to what contribution these labs make to host economies. Edward Graham and Paul Krugman have found that, despite a greater propensity to import, the behavior of foreign affiliates in the United States does not differ markedly from that of American firms, and in certain respects, such as R&D per worker in the manufacturing sector, actually surpasses the performance of American firms.[21] Likewise, Richard Florida has found foreign-affiliated labs in the United States to be reasonably innovative; his sample of 200 labs produced "2,469 patent applications,

1,068 patents, 669 copyrights, and 1,812 published articles in 1994."[22] Yet, Pari Patel and Keith Pavitt contend that the contribution made to host economies has been exaggerated. Consolidating U.S. patent data under the names of parent firms, they found that, with the exception of firms in the pharmaceuticals industry, the world's 700 largest multinationals use their home base for the bulk of patent-creating research.[23] However, this does not mean that foreign R&D labs are simply free-riding on the relative strengths of host countries. John Cantwell has found that experienced multinationals tend to locate R&D in all markets where they are major participants.[24] Moreover, these firms tend to locate R&D labs abroad in areas that share their core areas of strength. In their survey of the 220 firms with the highest volume of patents outside their home countries between 1992 and 1996, Pari Patel and Modesto Vega found that more than 75 percent located labs abroad in areas that shared their core strengths, while only 10 percent went abroad to exploit the technological advantages of the host country in areas of relative weakness at home.[25]

One of the primary forces pulling the internationalization of R&D is competition among governments to host innovative activities. Using tax and other incentives, governments compete for internationally mobile capital and highly skilled labor. As John Dunning has observed, relations between governments and multinational firms have shifted from conflict over issues of sovereignty and exploitation to cooperation because governments now see the presence of foreign firms as increasingly important for generating and sustaining competitive advantage.[26] Although governments may welcome investment by foreign firms in local research facilities, they have been slower to welcome foreign firms or their local affiliates in publicly subsidized research programs.

The Politics of Opening Government-Subsidized R&D Programs

Disagreement over the relevance of corporate nationality in a global economy, and the extent to which national governments can influence the structure of interdependence, is at the heart of a debate over the place of foreign firms in national technology programs. On one hand are "techno-globalists" who emphasize the gains accruing to states that allow unconditional participation in open R&D programs. On the other hand are "techno-nationalists" who identify conditional national treatment by foreign governments and performance requirements for foreign firms as the minimum prerequisites for the opening of R&D programs. During the 1990s, these ideal types defined academic and policy discussions of international technology collaboration. For example, the division of American policy makers between these two camps is clearly visible in the National Research Council's 1997 report *Maximizing U.S. Interests in Science and Technology Relations with Japan.*[27] Today, analysts are more ready to acknowledge that the technology policies of all triad nations reflect a mixture of the two views. The question is the balance between these views in different nations and how or why this balance might change. Techno-nationalism may grow during periods of economic uncertainty or heightened foreign competition, while techno-globalism may grow during times of high economic growth or new technological challenges. It may also be that some nations, such as Japan, are inherently more techno-nationalist than others. This section examines the core techno-globalist and techno-nationalist arguments, the growing acknowledgment of how these ideas are combined in practice, and how MITI attempted to seize the rhetorical high ground in policy debates with its advocacy of techno-globalism in the early 1990s.

Techno-Globalism and Techno-Nationalism

Techno-globalists agree that government attempts to contain technological advance within national borders are not only increasingly difficult, but also ultimately self-defeating. They are divided, however, as to the wisdom of government funding of technology programs to bolster competitiveness. Eschewing strategic trade and technology policies, Robert Reich has argued that the idea of a "national" economy, product, or technology is meaningless because corporations have become disconnected from their home nations. He cites the fact that by 1990 more than a quarter of U.S. exports bore the labels of foreign-owned companies, with Japanese firms alone accounting for more than 10 percent of total American exports. In a world where firms operate globally and enter strategic alliances with foreign counterparts, national technology programs are inherently leaky. The practical result is that taxpayer money is subsidizing the research of foreign firms. Reich concludes that governments would be most prudent to invest in their own labor force, the one factor of production that is relatively immobile internationally.[28]

Other techno-globalists advocate a more activist role for the state. Beyond simple investment in education, they see a need to nurture partnerships between universities and industry that enhance the ability to draw on an increasingly globalized technology base.[29] David Mowery argues that the critical weakness of both American and European firms has been the translation of R&D advances into commercial products. Rather than limiting access to the results of publicly funded R&D, government policy should aim to improve the domestic adoption of new technologies developed both at home and abroad. In other words, policy needs to achieve a better balance between support for technology creation and technology adoption.[30]

A third group of techno-globalists advocates an even more activist role for the state; they see state support of industrial technology programs as necessary to deal with technological change and increased globalization. At the same time, they believe such programs should be unconditionally open to foreign participation. In this view, the balance between the domestic and overseas activities of firms cannot be determined by government performance requirements that make substantial local research activities a prerequisite for membership in national research programs. They consider such measures as destructive of economic efficiency and harmful to the economy of the implementing nation by poisoning the climate for foreign investment. This variant of techno-globalism also opposes requirements for conditional national treatment on the basis that it might lead to retaliation by foreign governments. Among this breed of more activist techno-globalists, Richard Florida has advocated greater international collaboration in high technology, citing MITI programs like IMS and RWC as models.[31]

For techno-nationalists, corporate nationality matters. They argue that techno-globalism exaggerates the disconnection between firms and their home nations. Even most large corporations continue to do most of their R&D at home and thus these activities are heavily influenced by the national system of innovation. Only large firms from a few European nations such as Belgium and Holland perform more than half of their R&D activities abroad.[32] That large firms have operations in several nations does not mean each of these nations is of equal importance to them. Distribution of assets and employees, ownership and control, as well as legal and tax considerations all give the firm a center of gravity in the nation where it is headquartered.[33] Even when overseas operations exceed 50 percent in aggregate, this percentage is divided among a number of host nations with the likely result that most assets and employees are based in the home nation, under the jurisdiction of the home government. Thus, economic strategies are not generated by multinational corporations that stand outside a home base, but within particular institutional arrangements that shape the choices open to firms.[34]

Techno-nationalists acknowledge that national systems of innovation have become increasingly interconnected but contend that techno-globalism does not address how market processes, and government manipulation of those processes, shifts power between nations.[35] Alan Tonelson argues that techno-globalists forget that terms like interdependence and cooperation describe complex relationships where one party may enjoy a relatively advantageous position.[36] Globalization does not necessarily mean convergence in the capabilities of national systems of innovation; in fact, it often means an increase in sectoral specialization, which can lead to winners and losers in terms of economic growth.[37] In this view, sovereignty does not fade away as globalization advances. Governments must deal with the twin goals of globalization and national responsiveness.

A major part of this task is recognizing where national responses must be strongest. Steven Weber and John Zysman draw a sharp distinction between the kinds of policies appropriate for science and for technology. Scientific knowledge is expressed in basic theories that can be easily communicated in a common language. Therefore, the international flow of scientific information between open research institutions like universities is extensive. Technology, however, is very different. "Technological knowledge accumulates in local institutions in the form of learned know-how."[38] Performance requirements and conditional national treatment become important for controlling the diffusion of such learned know-how. Techno-nationalists reject unconditional opening of national technology programs as akin to unilateral disarmament. In 1998, Michael Borrus concluded it was no longer desirable to exclude foreign firms from publicly subsidized R&D programs because they often contribute important know-how and assist U.S. innovations in being adopted as global standards. He cautioned, however, that foreign participation should be conditional in order to maximize the potential benefits to the U.S. economy. Washington should insist that potential foreign partners bring complementary capabilities, agree to launch innovations in the United States, and form strong production links with local suppliers.[39]

As the policy debate on access to national R&D programs moved toward a middle ground between the ideal types of techno-globalism and techno-nationalism, academic studies also began to recognize the existence of such compromises in national technology policies. In their edited volume examining the impact of the Asian financial crisis on the institutions of science, technology, and innovation in the region, William Keller and Richard Samuels identify the "techno-hybrid" as an intermediate category between techno-globalist and techno-nationalist states. Hybrids embrace limited techno-globalism in order to win a share of added value in multinational production networks. These states invest heavily in the domestic infrastructure for technology research and education while pursuing strategic industrial policies that attract foreign investment by high-tech multinationals. Keller and Samuels see Taiwan and parts of China's technology system as hybrids that fall between techno-globalist Singapore and techno-nationalist Japan.[40]

In contrast to the view that certain small nations might be described as hybrids, Atsushi Yamada suggests that all major states are being pushed toward a more open but still self-serving "neo-techno-nationalism." This policy consists of four basic elements: expanded state commitments to promote innovation at home; increased reliance on private initiative and public-private partnerships; greater openness to collaboration with foreign firms and universities; and renewed attention to international rule making in areas such as intellectual property rights.[41] The techno-nationalist aim of state promotion remains the same, but the means to bolster national competitiveness are changing. Unable to keep up with the pace of innovation, bureaucrats are forced to rely more on private initiative; and with ever tighter budget constraints, they are pushed to maximize the returns on publicly funded research by fostering relationships among universities, government institutes, and firms. They also welcome greater foreign investment in R&D labs and greater foreign participation in national technology projects in order to nurture state-of-the-art capabilities at home. Each of these elements is clearly visible in MITI's muted techno-globalism during the 1990s.

MITI and the Rhetoric of Techno-Globalism

The concept "techno-globalism" first gained prominence as the theme of a March 1990 symposium organized by the Technology and Economy Program of the Organization for Economic Cooperation and Development (OECD). Shortly afterward, MITI embraced the concept, at least on a rhetorical level, as the philosophical underpinning of its technology policy. As with much policy jargon, "techno-globalism" lacks a precise definition. It has been used to describe the global exploitation of technologies produced on a national basis, the global generation of technology within a multinational corporation, and global R&D collaboration among multinationals based in different countries.[42] MITI set forth its philosophy of techno-globalism in a series of reports issued by the Industrial Technology Council, an advisory group that brings together representatives from industry and academia to develop recommendations on the future direction of Japanese technology policy.[43]

MITI explained techno-globalism as a response to the changing demands of research and development, and to Japan's obligation to contribute more to the international scientific community.[44] It characterized the opening of research programs as a practical step toward resolving the incongruity between "borderless" corporate research activities and closed national technology programs. The ministry also cited the familiar examples of AIDS and environmental degradation as global challenges that necessitate greater cooperation among governments.

MITI's conception of techno-globalism was tied closely to the need for Japan to bolster basic research capabilities. The need to do more basic research was explained as both a technological necessity and an international responsibility. The ministry described a growing "resonance" between science and technology whereby advances in one lead to advances in the other. As research in microelectronics advances to the atomic scale, for example,

researchers must have a fundamental understanding of the physics of electron behavior. Concomitantly, advances in microelectronics make new research techniques possible.[45] MITI acknowledged that Japan could not be
a credible advocate of techno-globalism without making contributions to
international science and technology that were more in line with its financial and technological resources. This admission of unmet responsibilities
stood in stark contrast to decades of defensive rhetoric in explaining Japanese trade surpluses.

From 1992 to 1998, the most recent period for which figures are available, nondefense R&D expenditures as a percentage of GDP were higher
in Japan than in any other industrialized nation. Yet, as both a source of
R&D funds and a performer of R&D, the Japanese government played a
smaller role in its economy than the American, French, German, and British governments did in their economies (see Table 2.1). The share of R&D
performed by industry ranges from just over 70 percent in Japan and the
United States to between 60 percent and 70 percent in Germany, France,
and the United Kingdom. Industry accounts for roughly 73 percent of total
R&D funding in Japan, 67 percent in the United States, 64 percent in Germany, 54 percent in France, and 47 percent in the United Kingdom.[46] Although it accounts for 15 percent of world GNP, Japan remains a net importer
of basic science technologies from the United States and Europe.

In 1994, MITI declared that Japan "must stimulate creative activities in
science and technology and facilitate international distribution and transfer
of their results with the aim of maximizing the benefits that science and
technology will bring to mankind."[47] It proposed to increase Japan's contribution to global science and technology through two policies: first, to create
"centers of excellence" that enhance Japan's research infrastructure and in
so doing provide more attractive facilities for visiting, foreign researchers;
and second, to play a leadership role in promoting greater international collaboration in precompetitive industrial technologies. This "strategic use of
joint research" in projects like IMS and RWC was seen as a means to counter
"technology protectionism" abroad and to produce new technologies through
the fusion of Japanese and foreign capabilities.[48]

In some respects, these plans reflected a lingering headiness from the
years of the bubble economy. By the second half of the 1990s, plans to
bolster the Japanese science and technology base were justified by a more
pessimistic assessment of Japan's performance in information technology,
biotechnology, and other high-tech fields. In 1995, the Diet passed the Science and Technology Basic Law (*Kagaku gijitsu kihon-hō*), which was explicitly intended to increase government R&D expenditures, bolster the
creativity of Japanese researchers, and achieve a better balance between

Table 2.1

Comparative National R&D Expenditures (1998)

	Japan	USA	France	Germany	UK
Nondefense R&D (US$ billions)	89.0	187.0	25.0	40.0	20.0
Nondefense R&D (% of GDP)	3.0	2.2	2.0	2.2	1.6
Source of R&D funds (%)					
Government	19.3	28.6	37.3	33.8	31.1
Industry	72.6	66.9	53.5	63.5	47.3
Higher education	7.2	2.3	0.9	0.0	0.8
Private nonprofit	0.7	2.2	0.9	0.3	4.0
Abroad	0.3	N/A	7.4	2.4	16.8
Performer of R&D (%)					
Government	9.2	11.2	18.6	14.3	13.4
Industry	71.2	73.9	62.3	68.6	66.0
Higher education	14.8	11.6	17.6	17.0	19.5
Private nonprofit	4.7	3.3	1.5	0.0	1.3

Source: National Science Board, *Science & Engineering Indicators 2002*, Appendix Tables 4–40 and 4–42, pp. A4–77 and A4–80. Nondefense R&D expenditures in billions of constant 1996 dollars. Total R&D includes both defense and nondefense expenditures.

basic and applied research. The government set about realizing these goals in two five-year Basic Science and Technology Plans. The First Basic Plan (1996–2001) committed $150 billion to R&D over five years, a figure that doubled the level of investment over that in 1992 and brought the government's share of total national R&D investments more in line with those of other G-7 governments. The Second Basic Plan (2001–2006) aims to boost R&D expenditures by an additional 40 percent and concentrate funding on four priority themes.

Along with these changes, Japan embarked on a major restructuring of its national system of innovation. In 2001, as part of the administrative reform of the government, a reorganized MITI became the Ministry of Economy, Trade, and Industry (METI). Today, METI is playing a leading role in forging stronger links among government, industry, and academia in order to enhance Japan's capabilities as a technological innovator. While this is framed mostly in terms of achieving sustainable economic growth, the Second Basic Plan emphasizes the importance of international research collaboration in achieving such growth.[49] In line with this basic outlook, METI continues to open research programs to foreign participation. Yet, how much substance lies behind the ministry's techno-globalism? Answering this question requires a closer look at American, European, and Japanese policies on the internationalization of publicly subsidized research programs.

Rules on Foreign Access to Government-Subsidized R&D Programs

Although the Uruguay Round of the General Agreement on Tariffs and Trade (GATT) established rules regarding the permissible levels of government subsidies for research performed under contract with national governments, the development of multilateral rules on foreign access to government-funded technology programs has proved difficult. Rules differ from program to program, even within the same country or regional economic group. Sylvia Ostry and Richard Nelson believe that a limited notion of reciprocity regarding intellectual property rights and membership rules for government-supported R&D programs is feasible but that full reciprocity in terms of unconditional access and national treatment is unlikely.[50] In many programs, access decisions are based on criteria that include reciprocal treatment and local exploitation of results. Reciprocity requires that domestic firms receive comparable access to technology programs in a foreign firm's home country, while exploitation criteria require participants to pursue any project-related development and manufacturing in the host country.[51]

According to a 1998 OECD study based on data from 404 R&D programs operating in member countries during 1996, only 4 percent of the programs continued to restrict participation to nationally owned firms. Approximately 79 percent of the programs were open to domiciled foreign firms with a substantial local R&D presence, while only 7 percent were open to all firms of any nationality, irrespective of a local R&D presence.[52] Thus, by the mid-1990s, the norm for OECD members was to allow domiciled foreign companies to participate on a basis almost equivalent to that for nationally owned firms. However, access to R&D programs, and especially access to public subsidies, remained restricted for nondomiciled firms.

As of 2004, rules on foreign access to R&D programs in each leg of the triad remain different. While several government-subsidized technology programs in the United States remained closed to foreign participation through the mid-1990s, most have now been opened on a conditional basis. The European Union treats domiciled firms with foreign owners the same as firms from member nations; it also allows nondomiciled firms from several advanced industrial countries to participate in specific technology programs designated under bilateral science and technology agreements—though without any subsidy from Brussels. Ironically, METI programs offer the most flexible terms of participation within the triad. Fully subsidized participation in several METI programs is open to foreign firms without any requirement for local research facilities. However, METI has not adopted a general policy on foreign access and the funding for its programs—though consistent with funding levels during the 1970s and 1980s—is much lower than that for many comparable American and European programs.

U.S. Programs

Washington funds a wide variety of research programs in academic, government, and industrial settings. The rules on foreign access to these programs have ranged from prohibition to complete openness. Research labs at American universities are open on a competitive basis to students from all over the world. Moreover, many of the unclassified research programs at government labs like the National Institutes of Health are also open on a competitive basis to visiting fellows from abroad. Beginning in the mid-1980s, Washington also allowed increased participation by domiciled foreign firms in research accords between industry and national laboratories known as Cooperative Research and Development Agreements (CRADAs). Between 1986 and 1997, for example, 41 of the 475 CRADAs involving the National Institutes of Health included foreign participation.[53] Nonetheless, foreign participation can still spark controversy. In 1998, for example, Democratic Senators Joseph Lieberman and John Rockefeller questioned the decision to include the German semiconductor maker Infineon Technologies in an Intel-led CRADA developing next-generation lithography.[54]

Advisory bodies like the National Academy of Engineering argue that membership rules for government-subsidized technology programs should be guided by the extent to which a firm contributes to the American economy. Such programs should not discriminate among firms on the basis of corporate nationality provided there is sufficient reciprocity.[55] Currently, however, the United States has no uniform rules on foreign access to technology programs sponsored by different federal agencies. Because of the decentralized management and funding structure of government research, there are also no comprehensive data on overall foreign participation in these programs. The wide range of U.S. policies on foreign access can be seen in industrial technology programs such as Sematech, the United States Council for Automotive Research (USCAR), and the Advanced Technology Program (ATP). With different sponsors, goals, and organizational structures, these programs have adapted to the internationalization of R&D in very different ways.

Sematech

Established in 1987, Sematech brought together the U.S. government and fourteen U.S.-based semiconductor manufacturers with the goal of regaining American leadership in semiconductor manufacturing technology. From 1988 through 1995, the Department of Defense provided matching annual funds of up to $100 million to support the work of Sematech. During this time, the consortium initiated limited international collaboration with foreign counterparts but did not allow foreign chipmakers to become members. Sematech's first international collaboration evolved from informal discussions with European firms prior to their launching the Joint European Submicron Silicon Initiative (JESSI) in 1989. Sematech provided advice on various issues including the management of contracts with supplier companies and intellectual property rights. In 1990, Sematech and JESSI began a study of the competitive positions of the U.S., European, and Japanese semiconductor industries, as well as a feasibility study aimed at adopting common semiconductor standards. Yet, there was no cross funding of research, and information sharing was limited to university research and discussion of standards. As long as the government subsidy lasted, membership in Sematech was restricted to U.S.-based firms. When AT&T announced the sale of NCR Microelectronics to Korea's Hyundai Electronics in February 1995, for example, Sematech required NCR to leave the consortium by the end of the year.

This experience helped push Sematech to become more flexible in responding to changing market conditions. Both American chipmakers and suppliers had regained strength and market share. In addition, the increasing number of cross-national, strategic alliances in the semiconductor industry, and the anticipated costs of conversion to larger silicon wafers, were making it harder to sustain a closed, national consortium. As a result, Sematech decided to end its financial relationship with the U.S. government and cautiously began to expand its portfolio of international collaborations. In 1995, Sematech established the International 300 mm Initiative (I300I) to develop tool standards and specifications for 300 mm silicon wafers. I300I included six U.S. firms and seven foreign firms from Europe, South Korea, and Taiwan. In 1998, Sematech established a subsidiary called International Sematech (ISMT) that expanded the involvement of these foreign firms in Sematech's research on 300 mm technologies and processes. According to Sematech managers, technological hurdles rather than foreign competition had become the main challenge confronting U.S. chipmakers.

At first, the participation of foreign firms was circumscribed by political pressures. Even though the government subsidy had ended, some policy makers in Washington worried that the results achieved by Sematech over the previous decade would spill over to the members of ISMT. As a result, the foreign firms had to obtain written permission to use technical data and license patents generated during the time Sematech received government support.[56] Japanese chipmakers were also noticeably absent from ISMT. As discussed in chapter 7, there is disagreement as to whether this was a reflection more of U.S. or Japanese preferences. Although its collaboration with

Japanese firms was still limited mostly to information sharing and coordination in setting standards, Sematech continued to become more international in membership and outlook. In 2000, Sematech became International Sematech by merging its domestic and international activities into one consortium and making foreign-based firms full members.

Despite its increasingly international membership and linkages, the consortium may still be subject to occasional techno-nationalist pressure from Washington. In July 2002, ISMT announced a five-year, $320 million joint program with the State University of New York at Albany to accelerate the development of next-generation lithography. Before deciding on Albany as the location for the new venture, ISMT also considered foreign locations, including a promising site in Belgium. ISMT officials acknowledge that the Department of Defense, among others, expressed concern about locating the facility overseas but insist that this did not influence their final decision.[57]

Since becoming ISMT, the consortium has moved aggressively to execute programs on a global basis by broadening ties with its Japanese and European counterparts. In 2001, ISMT joined Japan's Semiconductor Leading Edge Technologies (SELETE) in a project to standardize e-manufacturing guidelines. In the same year, it signed a research agreement with the Inter-University Microelectronics Center (IMEC) in Belgium that based ISMT consignees overseas for the first time. Although two foreign members—Hyinx and STMicroelectronics—withdrew from ISMT for financial reasons, the consortium forged relationships with several foreign firms in extreme ultraviolet (EUV) lithography and mask technology. EUV lithography uses extremely short wavelengths of light to etch circuit patterns on a silicon substrate; masks are the quartz plates that serve as the negatives from which microchips are made. In its first joint development contract with a Japanese toolmaker, ISMT announced in January 2003 that it would work with Lasertec to develop an inspection tool for EUV mask blanks.[58] Six months later, it signed an agreement with Asahi Glass, which dispatched scientists to the consortium's Albany facility to work on advanced mask technology and materials for EUV lithography.[59] ISMT North is also likely to collaborate with Tokyo Electron, which will become its neighbor following the construction of a $300 million R&D facility at SUNY Albany.[60]

USCAR

As with Sematech, the United States Council for Automotive Research (USCAR) has faced the challenge of promoting national interests in an increasingly global economy. Confronting stiff Japanese competition and government regulations that required the development of safer and more environmentally friendly vehicles, the Big Three automakers came together in 1988 to form the Automobile Composites Consortium. The success of this endeavor led to the formation of consortia addressing other generic challenges. Foreign participation, however, was limited. In 1991, for example, the U.S. Advanced Battery Consortium (USABC) set out to develop a more viable battery for electric cars. According to the Department of Energy's Transportation Technology Lab, the main condition for participation in the USABC was that all manufacturing be done in the United States. The consortium favored U.S. firms to develop technology but would try to get the best technologies from wherever it could.[61] Toyota asked to join the consortium but was turned down.[62] In later years, however, Hydro-Quebec worked as a subcontractor for 3M and the German firm Varta as a subcontractor for Duracel.

In 1992, General Motors, Ford, and Chrysler established USCAR to manage their collaborative research. In 1993, USCAR joined with the federal government to form its most high-profile collaboration, the Partnership for a New Generation of Vehicles (PNGV), with the aim of developing a midsized sedan comparable in cost and performance to the vehicles of the time but with three times the fuel economy. The 1998 merger of Daimler-Benz and Chrysler to form Daimler-Chrysler raised serious questions about the role of the new firm in federally funded USCAR research. USCAR decided in April 1999 to open itself to "any firm with significant research and development in the United States" that was "willing to fully contribute technology to the partnership." The definition of "significant" R&D presence proved controversial.

Toyota argued that it qualified for membership in USCAR. A technology leader in the auto industry, Toyota operates a research center in Michigan and had just signed a research agreement with General Motors. Nevertheless, Toyota was denied membership. According to Daimler-Chrysler, only the three existing members satisfied the condition of "significant" U.S. research.[63] USCAR was particularly cautious about the question of foreign participation in PNGV. Already labeled as misguided industrial policy by critics in Congress, PNGV ran into even more criticism as consumer tastes moved toward less fuel efficient sport-utility vehicles. With the rationale for PNGV already in question, USCAR was reluctant to aggravate critics by allowing any further foreign participation in the program. According to a 1999 statement by Daimler-Chrysler, expanding PNGV to include other foreign companies would be "problematic."[64]

In January 2002, President Bush announced that PNGV would be replaced by the new Freedom Car program to develop hydrogen-based fuel cells. In

January 2003, the administration announced plans to commit $1.7 billion to the initiative over five years, and six months later, it signed an agreement with the European Union to cooperate in seven areas of fuel cell research in order to minimize duplication and overcome technical obstacles more quickly.[65] Although no specific plans for collaboration with Japan have been announced yet, all G-8 members pledged during summer 2003 to work more closely on fuel cell and hydrogen technologies.[66]

Advanced Technology Program

The Advanced Technology Program (ATP) features the clearest and most consistently applied guidelines on foreign participation of any U.S. technology program. The National Institute of Standards and Technology (NIST) established the ATP in 1990, a time when many feared that the United States was losing the technology race to Japan. The ATP soon became the cornerstone of the Clinton administration's civilian technology policy and the focus of conservative critics who attacked the program as "corporate welfare."[67] The goal of the program is to assist industry in the development of enabling technologies with strong commercial potential. In order to be eligible for ATP funding, a firm must be incorporated in the United States or be a sole proprietorship or partnership established in the United States. From 1994 to1998, the bulk of ATP funding was dedicated to focused technology programs in areas such as digital video information networks, tissue engineering, and manufacturing composite structures. Since 1998, firms have been free to propose projects in any area. In addition to taking the initiative in proposing ATP projects, firms share in the costs of research with government. A small or medium-sized enterprise working alone can receive up to $2 million over three years to cover direct project costs while a Fortune-500 firm working alone must cover at least 60 percent of total project costs. A joint venture between at least two firms is eligible for funding of up to 50 percent of total project costs for a period of up to five years. Between 1990 and 2003, the ATP received 5,451 proposals requesting $11.7 billion in funding; it awarded almost $2 billion in matching funds to 649 projects involving more than 1,336 participants.[68]

All project proposals are evaluated on the basis of five criteria: scientific and technical merit, potential economic benefits to the United States, plans for commercialization of results, level of commitment and organizational structure, and experience and qualifications.[69] In order to take part in an ATP project, U.S. subsidiaries of foreign-owned companies must also satisfy several additional criteria. To begin, the home nation of the firm's parent company must provide American firms reciprocal access to R&D programs similar to ATP, local investment opportunities comparable to those available to foreign firms in the United States, and effective protection of intellectual property rights. In addition, the firm must be judged to make a significant contribution to R&D, manufacturing, and employment in the United States. Furthermore, the firm must agree to perform its share of project research and to promote the manufacture of any product resulting from the project in the United States.

The ATP conducts a foreign eligibility finding when a U.S. subsidiary of a foreign-owned company seeks to join an ongoing ATP project, or is part of a project proposal selected as a finalist in an ATP competition. It also conducts a foreign eligibility finding when a foreign firm or individual becomes the majority owner of an American firm participating in an ATP project. Between 1990 and 1997, the most recent period for which data are available, the ATP carried out fifty-one foreign eligibility findings. Of these, only two were negative. Both of these findings applied to Japanese firms, which were denied participation in ATP based on the national policies of Japan rather than any problems with the proposed role of the firms in their respective projects. Of the 842 participants in ATP projects up to 1997, a total of 33 participants in 29 projects were U.S. subsidiaries of firms headquartered in twelve countries: Belgium (1), Canada (3), Finland (1), France (4), Germany (2), Israel (1), Italy (1), the Netherlands (6), Norway (1), Sweden (1), Switzerland (4), and the United Kingdom (5).[70] The ATP represents one of the main venues for U.S. subsidiaries of foreign firms to receive federal government subsidies, but the future of the program is uncertain.

The opening of the ATP to foreign participation has been less controversial than the program itself. Since its inception, the ATP has been a favorite target of Republicans on Capitol Hill. Believing that most ATP awards went to companies in districts represented by Democrats, House Science Committee Chairman Robert Walker led a campaign to abolish the ATP during the mid-1990s.[71] Although the program survived, the budget dropped steadily from a peak of $340.5 million in FY 1995 to $178.8 million in FY 2003. In 2002, the Bush administration proposed six changes in the program including a greater role for universities and an annual royalty of 5 percent on gross revenues from every ATP project until it had paid back five times its grant amount. Congressional proponents of ATP feared the cost-recovery provision was an administration attempt to sabotage the program because it would encourage ATP managers to favor lower-risk projects that would make the program an easy target for budget cutters.[72] These reforms were shelved, but then the White House set about eliminating the program altogether. It requested only $27 million in funding for the program during FY 2004, enough to cover "administrative and other expenses needed to terminate ATP."[73]

European Programs

In response to both Europe's sagging competitiveness and the rise of Japan as a major technological competitor, European nations embarked on several collaborative technology programs during the mid-1980s. The European Union established the ESPRIT program to encourage research collaboration between firms and universities in a range of information technologies, and the RACE program to lay the foundation for a new generation of optical fiber communications systems. The perceived success of these programs and closer political integration under the Single European Act of 1986 led to the consolidation of European Union research activities under a series of so-called Framework Programs. In addition, France took the initiative in establishing a looser and more bottom-up mechanism for inter-European collaboration in the European Research Coordination Agency (EUREKA).

Financially, these initiatives are relatively modest. By the mid-1990s, European Union spending on R&D still accounted for only 4 percent of the total European Union budget—about one-tenth the amount spent on agricultural programs. Even when spending on the Framework Program, EUREKA, and the European Space Agency is added together, it totals less than 13 percent of total public sector spending on R&D.[74] This is largely because basic science and support for university research remain the province of national governments. Nevertheless, spending in the Framework Program and EUREKA exceeds $4 billion each year. These are the largest and highest-profile industrial technology R&D programs in Europe.

European Union Framework Program

The Fifth Framework Program (1998–2002) was divided into two parts: the $14.9 billion Research Technological Development and Demonstration (RTD) program and the $1.4 billion EURATOM program, which addressed nuclear research and training. Of this total, however, only 34 percent went to industry. The RTD program included four thematic and three horizontal programs. The former focused on quality-of-life and management-of-living resources ($2.6 billion), user-friendly information society ($3.9 billion), competitive and sustainable growth ($2.9 billion), and energy and sustainable development ($2.3 billion). The horizontal programs concentrated on confirming the international role of community research ($517 million), promoting innovation by SMEs ($396 million), and improving the socioeconomic base ($1.4 billion).[75] The Framework Program supports 50 percent of the cost of industrial R&D. Rights to intellectual property arising out of work carried out as part of such cost-sharing contracts are shared by the European Commission and the partners in a project.

Until 1994, there were no official rules regarding access to the Framework Program, although foreign firms were permitted to take part on a case-by-case basis as long as both the research and the first application of any resulting technologies took place in Europe. The implicit requirement in these conditions was that foreign firms have research facilities in a European Union nation.[76] A number of European affiliates of American firms such as AT&T, Dow Chemical, DuPont, Honeywell, IBM, and ITT were able to meet these conditions and took part in the First, Second, and Third Framework Programs.[77] Yet, the more general opening of the Framework Programs to foreign participation was slow and cautious. As late as 1990, the nations of the European Free Trade Association were denied full participation. With rising numbers of petitioners from both inside and outside Europe, however, it became easier to adopt formal rules than to review each case individually. By the mid-1990s, policymakers had also become more comfortable with the view that European firms would have to collaborate and compete globally in order to remain competitive.[78]

For the Fourth Framework Program (1994–98), the European Parliament and the European Commission adopted formal guidelines on foreign participation. The European Union no longer places formal restrictions on the participation of domiciled foreign companies in its R&D programs; they are subject to the same rules relating to access, finance, and exploitation of results as firms based in member nations. Participation by nondomiciled foreign firms is possible in certain programs if bilateral agreements exist, or if the participation of an individual firm is considered crucial to the success of a particular project. However, eligibility for funding depends on the country where the organization is legally registered. Firms from developed countries such as Australia, Canada, and the United States are not eligible for European Union support. Firms from nations such as Iceland, Liechtenstein, and Norway, which contribute financially to the Framework Program, are eligible to receive Framework subsidies. Most nonmember states from Central and Eastern Europe that do not contribute to the Framework Program are eligible to receive subsidies from a special fund set aside for international collaboration.

The Fourth Framework Program made the first attempt to organize all R&D collaboration with nonmember countries and international organizations under one umbrella—the International Cooperation (INCO) program. INCO operates a dedicated program funding cooperation with mostly Eastern European and developing nations, and promotes greater participation of non-European industrialized nations in the thematic and horizontal programs of the RTD program through the negotiation of science and technology agreements. The total budget for INCO was approximately $517 million in the Fifth Framework Program. The distribution of this budget clearly reflected political priorities close to home. The main beneficiaries of INCO funds under the Fourth Framework Program were Central and Eastern European nations, followed by the newly independent states of the former Soviet Union, and the developing nations of Northern Africa. Industrialized countries from outside Europe accounted for a very small number of proposals under the INCO program. In fact, more than 60 percent of the proposals from this group came from Israel.[79]

INCO negotiates two types of agreements. Under association agreements, the European Union provides funding for partners from a nonmember country in return for a contribution to the Framework Program. In 1996, Israel became the first, and up to now only, country from outside Europe to sign such an agreement. By 2001, Israel had contributed 1.2 percent of total funding for the Fifth Framework Program, and Israeli firms and universities had taken part in more than 240 projects.[80] Under cooperation agreements, the European Union establishes target themes for collaboration with third countries as well as the basic mechanisms for collaboration including guidelines on intellectual property and reciprocal access to programs. Between 1994 and 2001, the European Union signed over twenty agreements with countries around the world. Although it is too early to offer a complete assessment of these agreements, they seem to have significantly strengthened scientific and technological collaboration between the European Union and non-European Union countries, including Australia, Canada, and the United States.[81]

Australian firms and research organizations took part in thirty-seven projects launched during the Fourth Framework Program in areas such as medical and marine science. This comprised 40 percent of the international projects launched by the Australian Research Council during this time. In 1999, the cooperation agreement with Australia was revised to expand collaboration in projects at large-scale facilities and to open all the thematic research under the Fifth Framework Program. Canadian firms and research organizations were part of 307 research proposals received under the Fourth Framework Program, 76 of which received funding. And as with Australia, the cooperation agreement with Canada was broadened to include all of the thematic research under the Fifth Framework Program.

The level of American participation in the Fourth Framework Program was comparable to that of Canada. Of 237 proposals involving U.S. firms and research organizations, 74 were approved for funding, mostly in information and telecommunication technologies and the life sciences. With the signing of a bilateral cooperation agreement in 1998, the level of American participation increased by almost half; U.S. entities took part in 110 projects approved for funding during the Fifth Framework Program.[82] In 2000, the European Union began discussions with Japan on the possibility of signing a bilateral science and technology agreement. Neither side expected a rapid conclusion to the discussions since the European Union had yet to finalize the details of the Sixth Framework Program, and the administrative reform of Japanese government, launched in January 2001, changed the interlocutors on the Japanese side. In June 2003, the European Council authorized the negotiation of a scientific cooperation agreement with Japan that would allow Japanese participation in the remainder of the Sixth Framework Program (2002–6). Until such an agreement is concluded, collaboration continues on an ad hoc basis under the bilateral Forum in Science and Technology established in 1994.[83]

The European Union has budgeted $17 billion for the Sixth Framework Program, an increase of about 8.8 percent over the Fifth Framework Program when adjusted for inflation. As in the past, over half of this funding will go to universities and research institutions. Large firms will receive about 18 percent and SMEs about 16 percent of total funding. Unlike earlier programs, however, the Sixth Framework Program will emphasize projects that require the cooperation of the entire European Union. Practically, this will mean a smaller number of larger and more heavily funded projects.[84] While striving to ensure that research complements broader foreign policy objectives, the Sixth Framework Program also emphasizes the creation of networks among researchers. In part this will involve attracting more of the world's top scientists to Europe, and providing European firms and research institutes with better access to knowledge and technology generated outside Europe. In order to accomplish these objectives, the European Union acknowledges it will have to increase the level of research collaboration with third countries by negotiating more bilateral science and technology agreements and exploiting more fully the opportunities existing agreements offer. To maximize the efficiency of these efforts, the European Union will also have to do a better job of coordinating R&D priorities at the national and European levels.[85] As responsibilities for education, training, and basic science remain largely at the national level, the European Commission will continue to depend on national governments for developing much of the infrastructure for international collaboration.

EUREKA

French President François Mitterand proposed EUREKA in 1985 as an alternative to European participation in Ronald Reagan's Strategic Defense Initiative. France, Germany, and the United Kingdom also saw EUREKA as a way to direct more resources toward national priorities and regain some of the initiative lost to the European Commission in ESPRIT and the Framework Program.[86] Although Mitterand initially envisioned a program of grand projects, EUREKA evolved into an umbrella organization for mostly smaller-scale R&D collaborations. The objective of EUREKA is to encourage firms from at least two member states to collaborate in the development of high-tech, civilian products, processes, or services. Unlike the European Union Framework Program, which took shape around existing regional institutions, EUREKA developed as an ad hoc, intergovernmental bargain. In contrast to the Framework Programs, EUREKA is characterized by near-market R&D, bottom-up project generation by partners and decentralized funding. EUREKA began with twenty members, including the nations of the European Community and the European Free Trade Association, Turkey, and the European Commission. Over time EUREKA has grown to include fourteen additional members, mostly from Central and Eastern Europe. More than $14.8 billion was invested in a total of 1,051 projects completed by 2001. At the end of 2002, an additional $2.2 billion was invested in 723 ongoing projects. The latter group brought together more than 3,000 different organizations from across Europe, roughly two thirds of them from industry.[87]

Day-to-day activities are managed by a small secretariat of civil servants seconded from EUREKA member states. The secretariat collects and disseminates information on projects, helps locate partners for projects, and provides access to funding sources in member states. It has no policy responsibilities; project approval and funding depend entirely on national governments. Within the same projects, some partners may be subsidized by their respective governments while others may not. Only a few member nations have budgets earmarked for EUREKA, and most of these are quite small. Member governments usually fund EUREKA projects from an array of national funding mechanisms, which can lead to serious coordination problems for project partners applying to programs with different rules and time frames. Although there are no official figures for total spending of member governments on EUREKA, unofficial estimates place spending at an average of about 35 percent of direct costs for most projects.[88]

For over a decade, EUREKA had no formal rules concerning the participation of foreign firms; decisions were made on a case-by-case basis. Foreign firms were only admitted to a EUREKA project if their "unique expertise" was seen as essential to the success of a project already planned by firms from member states. As a result, foreign participation was very limited. With increased political pressure in the 1990s to extend membership to Eastern European nations, EUREKA was forced to develop clearer criteria for participation by firms from nonmember states. Yet, it did not make a concerted effort to expand non-European participation until the mid-1990s. Globalization became a major theme under the chairmanship of Britain during 1996–97, which organized a major brokerage event to bring together European and American firms interested in working on environmental technologies. At this time, EUREKA also reached consensus on new and more transparent rules for nonmember participation. A firm or research institution from a nonmember country can participate in a EUREKA project from the outset if that project has participants from at least two member states and the government of each of the EUREKA partners agrees to its participation. By one estimate, roughly 8 percent of EUREKA projects during the mid-1990s included non-European participation.[89] In 2003, however, only thirty-two organizations from nonmember countries—the United States (10), Ukraine (7), Canada (4), China (3), Japan (1), and others (7)—were taking part in the 723 projects underway.[90]

Japanese Programs

From basic industries in the 1950s to information technology in the 1990s, almost all Japanese government R&D in industrial technology was overseen by the Ministry of International Trade and Industry (MITI), later slightly reorganized as the Ministry of Economy, Trade, and Industry (METI). The implications of this reorganization for international R&D collaboration are addressed more fully in chapter 8. This discussion focuses on the unfolding of MITI's policy of techno-globalism during the 1990s.

Although MITI stood at the center of the Japanese government's industrial R&D program, its share of the national research budget remained fairly small. The ministry consistently ranked third in terms of its share of the budget. During most of the 1990s, the Ministry of Education received between 40 percent and 45 percent of the annual R&D budget, the Science and Technology Agency roughly 25 percent, and MITI between 12 percent and 18 percent.[91] MITI's R&D activities included both the work of research institutes organized under the Agency for Industrial Science and Technology (AIST) and contract R&D with the private sector. AIST operated fifteen research institutes with approximately 2,500 researchers, over 40 percent of them holding doctorates.[92] These institutes participated in researcher exchanges and small-scale research projects with counterpart institutes in other countries. Although much of this collaboration was with developing countries, AIST also maintained significant relationships with advanced industrial countries. At the end of the 1990s, a total of thirty-five research projects were underway with research organizations from developed countries. Working with the U.S. Department of Commerce, for example, AIST designated six themes for joint projects involving both firms and research organizations in Japan and the United States.[93]

The more significant dimension of MITI's international research activity was the opening of large-scale research programs conducted on a contract basis with the private sector. The formal internationalization of these programs began in 1989 following the passage of the Law for Consolidating

Research and Development Systems Relating to Industrial Technology. The various research associations managing these projects reported to either MITI's Machinery and Information Industries Bureau, AIST, or the New Energy and Industrial Technology Development Organization (NEDO). About 45 percent of MITI's R&D budget funded large-scale programs in industrial and energy-related technology, which constituted the main venue for international collaboration.[94] Energy-related programs absorbed about half of the budget for large-scale research during the 1990s. This left about 23 percent of MITI's research budget in any given year to fund R&D on the entire range of industrial technologies from aerospace to robotics to semiconductors.[95] This level of funding may seem modest, but funding of large-scale programs actually grew—along with MITI's entire R&D budget—as these programs became open to foreign participants.

As Table 2.2 illustrates, during the 1990s MITI opened a wide range of large-scale research programs to foreign participation. Although some projects attracted the interest of only smaller firms or research organizations, several projects attracted major foreign firms such as BASF, General Electric, and Intel. As it opened research programs, MITI also revised guidelines on intellectual property rights for projects with foreign partners so that the government would share rights on a fifty-fifty basis with project participants. By the end of the 1990s, it had revised these guidelines again and turned over ownership of all intellectual property produced in its projects to the firms or institutes that generated the results. And most important, MITI offered foreign partners research subsidies without any requirement for local research facilities. This made the terms for foreign partners in these programs far more concessionary than, for example, the Framework Program and the ATP, which make subsidies available only to domiciled foreign firms. Yet MITI never adopted any general rules governing foreign access to its programs. In other words, MITI had discretion to decide which programs were open and the degree of foreign participation that might be acceptable. Thus, the ministry certainly pursued a muted form of techno-globalism.

MITI's largest single research undertaking is the New Sunshine Program. Launched in 1993, the program merged research initiatives on new energy and energy-conservation technologies that began in the 1970s. Several North American firms and research institutes have taken part in this program, particularly in the work on hydrogen-conversion approaches to clean energy. MITI also opened projects within its flagship program in industrial technology. Until 1993, AIST administered three major research programs. The National R&D Program, established in 1966, focused on large-scale systems and industrial plants. The Basic Technologies for Future Industries Program,

Table 2.2

Foreign Participation in MITI/METI Research Programs

Project	Foreign participants
Hypersonic jet engine (1989–96)	General Electric, Rolls Royce, SNECMA (France), United Technologies
High-performance materials (1989–98)	Crucible Materials (U.S.)
Nonlinear photonics materials (1989–98)	BASF
New model for software architecture (1990–97)	SRI International (U.S.)
Advanced chemical processing (1990–98)	SRI International
Biological production of hydrogen (1991–98)	Eniricerche (Italy)
Complex carbohydrates (1991–2000)	Pharmacia (Sweden)
Quantum functional devices (1991–2000)	Motorola
Silicon-based polymers (1991–2000)	University of Kent, University of Colorado
Micromachine technology (1991–2001)	IS Robotics (U.S.), SRI International, Royal Melbourne Institute of Technology
CO_2 high temperature separation technology (1992–2001)	University of Warwick
Real World Computing (1992–2001)	GMD (Germany), ISS (Singapore), SICS (Sweden), SNN (Holland)
Ultimate manipulation of atoms and molecules (1992–2001)	Texas Instruments, Dupont, Motorola, Samsung
Network system using a wide range of energy sources (1993–2000)	SRI International, University of Wales
Photovoltaic power generation technology (1993–2000)	Czech Academy of Sciences, Julich Research Center, University of Neuchatel
Synergy ceramics (1994–2003)	University of Cambridge, Swedish National Ceramics Center, Hamburg Institute of Technology, Limerick University, Dow Chemical
Accelerated biofunctional construction technology (1995–98)	Virus Research Institute (UK), University of Sheffield, University of Zurich
Jet engine for small aircraft (1995–2001)	General Electric

(*continued*)

Association of super-advanced electronics technologies (1995–2001)	Intel, Merck, Motorola, Samsung
Novel high-functional materials (1996–2001)	Amersham Biotech (U.S.), University of Cyprus
Smart materials and structures (1998–2002)	Daimler-Chrysler, University of Washington
Genome informatics technology (1998–2002)	University of London, Max Planck Institute
Frontier carbon technology (1998–2002)	University of Sussex, Vienna University of Technology, Fraunhofer Institute
Superconductive application basis technology (1998–2002)	DuPont, SRI International
Twenty-first century light (1998–2003)	Agilent Technologies
Environmentally compatible propulsion system for next generation supersonic transport (1999–2003)	General Electric, Rolls Royce, SNECMA, United Technologies
Advanced high temperature air combustion technology (1999–2003)	CNRS (France), German Aerospace Center
Millennium research for advanced information technology (2001–8)	Intel, Samsung

Source: www.meti.go.jp/policy/tech_evaluation/e00/eh130004.html, project evaluation reports (no. 50-121). Also Rutchik, *Japanese Research Projects and Intellectual Property Laws*, p. 61.

which began in 1981, focused on component technologies such as new materials. Finally, the smaller Medical and Welfare Technology Program started in 1986. In 1993, these three programs were reorganized into the Industrial Science and Technology Frontier Program (ISTF), which emphasized eight areas: superconductivity, new materials, biotechnology, information and telecommunication technology, machinery and aerospace, natural resources, medical technology, and technology for new living environments. In the late 1990s, nondomiciled foreign entities were taking part in thirteen of the twenty-one ISTF projects. They included eighteen firms, ten universities, and five research institutes.[96]

In addition to opening the ISTF, MITI also invited foreign participation in projects sponsored by the Japan Key Technology Center. The center was founded in 1985 as a special corporation to facilitate collaborative R&D on fundamental technologies between firms and research institutes affiliated with either MITI or the Ministry of Posts and Telecommunications. At the end of the 1990s, both Hewlett-Packard Japan and Hoechst Japan were taking part in Key Technology Center programs. Although the Western pressure to open research programs decreased substantially during the 1990s as Japan's economy slowed, MITI continued its policy of techno-globalism. Today, METI does not track, or at least does not release, statistics on foreign participation in its programs. Yet, it is possible to gather this data from project evaluation reports. Like all nations in the triad, Japan is now focused on assessing the results produced by publicly funded research. Consequently, METI now subjects all its large-scale R&D programs to external evaluations. Of the sixty-six projects evaluated between 2000 and 2002, twenty-two included foreign participants.[97]

Conclusion

The 1980s witnessed a dramatic expansion in the international R&D operations of multinational corporations throughout the triad. Multinationals from both Japan and Europe have been most eager to establish R&D labs in the United States. Japanese firms in the auto and electronics industries have been particularly active in expanding their research presence in the United States. American firms have also been internationalizing their R&D operations. By the end of the 1990s, U.S. firms had established more labs in Japan than in Canada or any single European nation. This growing internationalization of corporate R&D activities sparked a debate about the effectiveness of national R&D programs in a global economy. Techno-globalists contend that government efforts to contain technological advances within national borders are not only increasingly difficult, but also ultimately self-defeating. Techno-nationalists counter that corporate nationality matters and that sovereignty does not fade away as globalization advances. As a result of the tension between these two views, the opening of government-subsidized R&D programs proceeded much more slowly than the internationalization of corporate research activities. Nevertheless, over the course of the 1990s, governments in each leg of the triad moved toward a muted techno-globalism or conditional opening of programs.

The many U.S. departments and agencies that manage R&D programs have not adopted uniform rules governing foreign access. During the 1990s, however, several programs moved toward conditional opening to local subsidiaries of foreign firms with significant research facilities in the United States. Like the United States, Japan failed to adopt clear guidelines on foreign access to its R&D programs. Nonetheless, a third of the large-scale projects evaluated by MITI/METI between 2000 and 2002 offered subsidized participation to nondomiciled, foreign firms and universities. In 1994, the European Union adopted the clearest guidelines on foreign access within the triad. European subsidiaries of firms with foreign parents are treated as European firms with full privileges in the Framework Programs. Nondomiciled entities from advanced industrial countries, whose governments have signed scientific and technical agreements with the European Union, may participate in all activities allowed by those agreements—although without any subsidy from Brussels.

Thus, a comparison of rules on foreign access to government-subsidized, industrial research programs reveals the surprising result that MITI programs launched in the early 1990s offer more liberal membership terms than programs in either the United States or Europe. However, the lack of conditionality in this area is balanced by a more selective opening of programs, especially compared to the European Union. So how different is MITI's techno-globalism from that in other parts of the triad? Did it evolve as a means to deflect foreign pressure, as part of a broader techno-nationalist strategy to access Western technologies, or as a response to the financial and technological forces that have produced opening throughout the triad? Moreover, do American and European firms stand to gain from participating in the ministry's open programs? It is to these questions that we turn next.

———Chapter 3———

Explaining and Evaluating
MITI's Techno-Globalism

Leading approaches in the study of Japan's political economy offer very different explanations for MITI's decision to open its research programs to foreign participation. Case studies of the HFSP, IMS and RWC suggest that foreign pressure and complementary capabilities have played a more important role in driving internationalization than bureaucratic politics and techno-national ideology. Nonetheless, the relative importance of these two factors has varied by program. These cases also suggest that MITI research programs during the 1990s represented a departure from earlier efforts in the flexibility of research objectives and management structures. As the catch-up era ended in the late 1970s, MITI initiated several bold initiatives such as the Fifth Generation Computer Project (FGCP) that sought to catapult Japanese firms ahead of their Western counterparts. The meager results led MITI to reassess its approach to technology policy. The more flexible approach adopted in programs ranging from IMS to the RWC and the Hypersonic Transport Propulsion System Project (HYPR) show how MITI learned from past mistakes and adapted to the role of promoting frontier research from a position of dramatically decreased influence over Japanese firms. These programs were more responsive to the needs of Japanese firms than programs during the 1980s and, depending on the technologies involved, offered important opportunities to foreign firms and research institutes.

Explaining MITI's Techno-Globalism

Bureaucratic Politics

In addition to furthering the mission of the ministry, support for R&D programs can be interpreted as a survival strategy for bureaucrats themselves. Dr. Junichi Shimada, research director of the RWC project, explains the creation and funding of research associations as a way for MITI officials to further both their bureaucratic and postbureaucratic careers.

> It is too naive to assume that MITI's only goal is promoting Japanese industry. Egoism is at the base of MITI projects. MITI officials want credit,

either personal or organizational. One way to get credit in MITI's world is the creation of postretirement or *amakudari* jobs in industry. This is now a major issue at MITI because these posts are harder to find. There are two basic ways to do this. One is to create new organizations, which provide jobs or require new laws. The other is to give money to companies and receive *amakudari* posts in return.[1]

For Shimada, organizations like the Real World Computing Partnership satisfy both of these conditions. The quasi-governmental research associations that manage MITI's large-scale R&D projects provide jobs for MITI officials and research funding for firms. In addition to promoting the interests of individual MITI officials, support for R&D programs has also promoted the interests of MITI in its competition with other ministries over budget allocations and regulatory authority.

Chalmers Johnson explains Japanese policymaking in high technology as a product of rivalry among ministries. In a country "always more preoccupied with domestic developments than with external events," technological developments and foreign pressures "only supply opportunities and constraints that indirectly influence the primary motivations of domestic protagonists."[2] For Johnson, these protagonists are bureaucrats and their primary motivation is the promotion of self-interest through the protection of ministerial autonomy and jurisdictional boundaries. According to this argument, MITI's interest in the promotion of high-tech industries of the future created two types of conflict with other ministries.

The first involves technologies where traditional bureaucratic domains overlap as in the so-called Telecom Wars. During the 1980s, for example, MITI came head-to-head with the Ministry of Posts and Telecommunications (MPT) concerning the regulation of computer networks linked via phone lines. The technological merging of MITI's regulatory domain in computers and MPT's regulatory domain in telecommunications services created a battle for regulatory control over these networks. Such bureaucratic rivalries have been common in policymaking for high technology; MITI continued to clash with MPT during the 1990s over rival policy visions for multimedia technologies.[3]

The second area of conflict arose in the late 1980s with MITI's shift to the funding of more basic research programs. Several factors drove this policy change. Tensions generated by Japanese trade surpluses with the United States pushed MITI away from programs in applied research and development. Meanwhile, the increased resources and competitiveness of leading Japanese firms made the support of MITI less important to corporate research strategies than was the case during the catch-up era. Such changes forced

MITI to adopt a more entrepreneurial role in supporting *mokuteki kiso kenkyū* or "oriented basic research." This is research undertaken with commercial applications in mind but with a time horizon of up to ten years. According to bureaucratic politics arguments, MITI's entry into more basic research increased the likelihood of conflict with MESC, which oversees the university research system, and with STA, which conducted basic research at a network of national institutes and public corporations before being absorbed by MESC in 2001. For example, MITI and STA established rival consortia in the late 1980s during the research boom in high-temperature superconductivity.[4]

The bureaucratic politics approach suggests that MITI's efforts to enlist academic researchers in its more basic research programs would meet resistance from MESC. Hiroyuki Odagiri detects such resistance in MESC's rigid personnel management practices. For example, national universities have frowned on professors taking leave to participate in MITI projects because MESC does not allow them to hire temporary replacements. In addition, academics taking leave would temporarily lose their pension benefits. Odagiri and colleagues consider such inflexible rules as the primary reason that no university researchers joined MITI's Fifth Generation Computer Project during the 1980s.[5] Scott Callon argues that MESC was far more aggressive in seeking to protect its bureaucratic turf. He suggests that some academics were even told that research grants from MESC, the primary means of support for university research, might not be available to individuals who chose to participate in MITI projects.[6]

Although bureaucratic politics unquestionably plays a role in the competition between ministries for research funds, it was not a decisive factor in MITI's decision to internationalize research programs in the late 1980s. To begin, the plans for the RWC program and IMS fell squarely within the traditional regulatory domain of MITI's Machine and Information Industries Bureau rather than in the contested domain of an emerging technology. Only the HFSP in basic research on biological functions fell outside MITI's traditional policy domain. Even in this program, however, conflict with other ministries was minimal. This absence of bureaucratic friction surrounding MITI's international programs is the result of more than a lack of conflict with the research priorities of bureaucratic rivals. Interministry relations began to evolve in response to Japan's move to the science and technology frontier during the 1980s. This changing dynamic was especially clear in the evolution of MESC attitudes regarding the participation of academics in joint research projects with industry, including projects sponsored by MITI.

Until the 1970s, the left-wing politics of many Japanese academics precluded the possibility of research collaboration with industry. Concerned that the fruits of scientific research might once again be applied to military aims, university scientists prized academic autonomy. The linkages between academia and industry were in recruitment rather than research. Even without this ideological wall, however, research collaboration was still proscribed by MESC, known traditionally as one of Japan's most conservative ministries. Indeed, until the early 1980s researchers at national universities were prohibited from undertaking any joint research with private companies. MESC relaxed these restrictions in order both to strengthen the academic research infrastructure and to respond to increasing pressure from firms and other ministries that wished to promote links to the best university labs.

Revised guidelines issued in 1982 allowed joint research projects, including the assignment of corporate researchers to university labs and corporate endowment of university chairs or *kōza*.[7] Still there remained major obstacles to meaningful collaboration. Until the late 1990s, myriad government regulations continued to limit interactions between industry and employees of national universities. Although firms could provide funds or in-kind assistance such as equipment to universities, they had no say in how such support was used. Professors at national universities were also prohibited from employment by firms or from serving on corporate boards. They were also barred from starting a company or joint venture to commercialize their research. In addition, there were barriers to the transfer of intellectual property. No university had an office to file patent applications or to license patents to industry.[8]

Japan's endeavor to strengthen the connections between academia and industry mirrored efforts in the United States that began with the Bayh-Dole Patent Act of 1980, which allowed universities to own patents resulting from government-funded, faculty research. The U.S. government hoped this would maximize returns from federal research support by accelerating the diffusion of new technologies from university labs to industry, through both licensing and the creation of new start-up firms.[9] Within two years of the passage of the Bayh-Dole Act, MESC began the Program for Joint Research with the Private Sector. However, the fostering of greater industry-university collaboration did not gain real momentum until the economic slowdown of the 1990s. In 1995, the Basic Law for Science and Technology set the stage for increased linkages between academia and industry. Over the remainder of the decade, the government moved to improve incentives for joint research, to remove barriers to the mobility of researchers between sectors, and to facilitate greater technology transfer from universities to firms.

The first reforms gave professors at national universities greater freedom to work with industry. Initial results were impressive. Between 1994 and 1996, "the number of joint-projects increased over 30 percent from 2,586 to 3,714, with the funding increasing almost fourfold, from 6.6 billion yen to 23.3 billion yen."[10] In 1998, the government passed additional laws to further facilitate joint research. The Law for Promoting Research Cooperation (*Kenkyū kōryū sokushin-hō*) allowed companies setting up joint research facilities on university campuses to receive a 50 percent reduction in rent while the Law for Reinforcing Industrial Technology (*Sangyō gijutsuryoku-hō*) allowed national universities to receive corporate funding in multiyear arrangements.[11] With changes like these, the number of cooperative projects continued to grow. At the end of 2002, it had reached more than 5,200—a 30 percent increase over that in 2001.[12] To put these numbers in perspective, one must note that Japanese industry still contributes only a very small percentage of all research funds used by Japanese universities. Even for a premier research institution such as Tsukuba University, firms contributed only 9 percent of research funds in fiscal 2000.[13]

The reforms also sought to make it easier for university researchers to begin business ventures. Japanese bureaucrats looked jealously at a growing list of major U.S. companies such as Cisco Systems and Genentech that were established by academic entrepreneurs. In 1995, Japanese university researchers initiated only five venture enterprises compared to 169 started by American university researchers. Although new ventures in Japan grew to thirty-four in 2000, the gap had widened dramatically with the United States, where 368 new enterprises were established. To improve Japan's performance, the government relaxed regulations that made it difficult for researchers at national universities and institutes to serve concurrently as executive officers of firms.[14] This also had a substantial impact. In 2002, the number of university-related venture companies reached a total of 453, an increase of 65 percent over 2001.[15]

A third effort to strengthen the linkages between academia and industry came with the passage of the Technology Transfer Law (*Gijutsu iden kikan-hō*) in 1998. The law authorized the formation of Technology Licensing Organizations (TLOs) at universities to promote the commercialization of patents held by professors. It also authorized government support to TLOs for up to five years and financing to encourage joint projects with industry at these centers. Although TLOs were quickly established at several major universities, they failed to convince many analysts that they would soon replace informal mechanisms of technology transfer such as professors transferring patents to firms in exchange for research equipment or materials.[16] The TLO program did make some headway. Between 1998 and 2002, Japanese universities established a total of twenty-six TLOs. During this period, the TLOs submitted 1,145 patent applications and handled 1,954 patent licensing requests. By comparison, the 142 TLOs established in the United States since 1980 have submitted 5,623 patent applications and handled 10,802 licensing requests. According to a 2002 survey of leading Japanese firms, only 8.5 percent had used the services of a TLO even though 64.3 percent expressed an interest in doing so in the future.[17] The TLO system has been severely constrained by the fact that professors at national universities are government employees. As a result, intellectual property produced in industry collaborations with national universities may be owned jointly by government and industry. Such an arrangement is often problematic for firms because it makes cross-licensing difficult. Thus, firms have been cautious about collaborating with national universities. The real potential of the TLO system will not be realized until after April 2004 when national universities are scheduled to lose their government status as part of the ongoing administrative reform.[18]

Despite the government's efforts, Walter Hatch sees little evidence that research conducted by Japanese universities will play an important part in Japanese innovation in the foreseeable future. He suggests that Japanese firms are more likely to outsource research to U.S. universities.[19] In the short term, he may be right. In 2002, while ranking Japan second behind the United States in the overall quality of its science and technology system, the Swiss-based International Institute for Management Development ranked Japan forty-first in terms of cooperation between university and industry.[20] Japan clearly faces substantial work if it wants to obtain a greater return on public investment in the university research system. The problems facing TLOs in the early part of this decade reveal that bureaucratic politics are far from dead in Japanese technology policy. Even with the many obstacles that remain, however, progress during the past two decades suggests that both MITI and MESC made substantial headway in breaking down the barriers to greater collaboration between academia and industry. As attitudes shifted beginning in the 1980s, MESC began to allow greater academic participation in MITI research programs. Although MESC chose not to actively support the HFSP, it allowed Japanese academics to play a leading role in the design of this program. MESC also permitted more active academic participation in RWC and IMS. University labs participated as paid subcontractors in the RWC program and as full partners in the research consortia of the IMS. These changes in MESC policy are not a simple surrender to MITI on international projects, but part of a broader commitment to improve the infrastructure for frontier research by fostering greater cooperation between industry and academia.

Techno-National Ideology

Numerous, compelling studies document the Japanese government's use of neomercantilist policies to access and assimilate foreign technologies. Such studies offer examples ranging from the mid-nineteenth century to the present.[21] In the most influential of these studies published during the 1990s, Richard Samuels argues that techno-national ideology has been a fundamental force shaping Japanese technology policy. According to Samuels, Japanese beliefs about national security and technological independence constitute an ideology that guides decisions about general industrial structure, technology transfer, and economic growth. This ideology consists of three basic elements: indigenization of foreign technologies, diffusion of these technologies throughout the national economy, and the nurturing of domestic capabilities to innovate and manufacture.[22] Focusing on the development of the Japanese arms and aircraft industries, Samuels argues that there is a fundamental continuity in technology policy from the Meiji Restoration of 1868 to the present.

Samuels contends that "the struggle for technological autonomy did not slacken once Japan emerged as a technological superpower in the 1980s."[23] He acknowledges, however, that Japan's strategic use of foreign partners was complicated during the 1980s by increased American sensitivity to the leakage of technology to Japan, as well as greater American interest in gaining access to Japanese technology. These changes, he suggests, pushed the Japanese aircraft industry to pursue a two-pronged strategy of collaboration with foreign partners and renewed commitment to indigenous development. The former strategy would maintain access to foreign technology, while the latter would help both to reduce dependence on foreign technology and to increase Japan's bargaining power in future international projects.[24]

Although Samuels does not address directly MITI's decision to internationalize research programs, one can extrapolate from his argument that this policy is the latest manifestation of an ideological drive to access and indigenize foreign technology. In essence, Samuels argues that the ideology that propelled the industrial development of the Meiji era also explains MITI's decision to internationalize research programs more than a century later. This argument is troubling because it presents techno-national ideology as a constant while it relegates politics and technology to the role of situational constraints that alter only the means to achieve the goals of that ideology. This framework makes it virtually impossible to determine where ideological continuity might end and discontinuity might begin. It is also troubling because techno-national ideology is made to account for a wide range of policy outcomes. Like Samuels's earlier theory of "reciprocal consent" in the government-business relationship in Japan, the concept of techno-national ideology lacks the nuance to explain the variety of responses to the same situational constraints.[25] During the 1990s, for example, MITI opened more than half of the projects in its Industrial Science and Technology Frontier Program to foreign participants. Assuming for the moment that these programs continue to have value for domestic participants, this policy seems quite a departure for the ministry at the heart of Japan's postwar trade and industrial policy.

According to Samuels, the core of techno-national ideology, and the defining feature of Japanese strategies of technology collaboration, is the imperative to indigenize foreign technology. Thus, if techno-national ideology is to explain MITI's internationalization of research programs, these programs should reflect a systematic attempt to maximize the potential inflow of technology in areas where Japan trails the state of the art. MITI's initial proposals for research programs during the 1990s, however, did not reflect such a simple pattern. The first incarnation of the HFSP proposal that emerged from domestic discussions envisioned a central research facility with an international staff applying research on the brain and nervous system to the development of software and intelligent robots. While MITI continued to push for an applied research program on the biofunctions of living organisms, the initial proposal made to the international community was by no means a clear reflection of techno-nationalism. MITI left the actual design of program management and the specification of the research agenda to an international group of scientists. The result was a basic research program that uses a peer review system to select proposals submitted by international teams of researchers. Thus, there is no direct channel for technology indigenization.

The IMS program generated substantial interest among American and European firms and so brought the most cautious reaction from their national governments. MITI proposed the establishment of an IMS organization with 60 percent of its budget coming from Japan and a central research facility to be located in either the United States or Europe. The IMS proposal called for the development of better manufacturing technology through the fusion of Japanese capabilities in factory automation with American capabilities in network technology and European capabilities in precision machinery. Many in the United States and Europe were suspicious that the proposal was a Trojan horse hiding the real intent of tapping foreign expertise in systems integration and software. Western governments were particularly troubled by the fact that Japan made direct overtures to private organizations rather than working only through official channels. Yet, as in the HFSP program, the initial MITI proposal left the responsibility for project design and management to an international committee. More than four years of sporadic negotiations followed before the official launch of the IMS program in which groups of firms develop their own consortia.

As an open national project, the RWC program appeared to be a more likely expression of techno-national ideology. The research objectives and management structure of the RWC program were decided by Japan and the program initially focused on several technologies in which Japan trailed the state of the art. However, several aspects of program design made the RWC program a less-than-efficient mechanism for indigenizing foreign technology. First, foreign partners were allowed to choose the themes in which they participated and so were not locked into unwanted collaborations. Second, the distributed network of RWC labs limited interaction and potential information exchange between the central lab in Tsukuba and the overseas labs of foreign partners. Indeed, the foreign partners agreed that the distributed structure of the program limited the benefits of internationalization for all parties. Third, the system of brokered collaboration in the U.S.-Japan Joint Optoelectronics Project, which came under the umbrella of the RWC program, was designed by the United States and clearly reflected the American preference for "technology access without acquisition" rather than a Japanese strategy of technology indigenization. Thus, the role of techno-national ideology in the RWC program was not as strong as it might appear at first glance.

In short, MITI's initial proposals for the HFSP, IMS, and RWC programs did not reflect a systematic effort to access and indigenize foreign technology. Neither did proposals for other open, national projects like HYPR and the Micromachine Consortium, which shared the distributed structure of the RWC. Even in semiconductor consortia like Millennium Research for Advanced Information Technology (MIRAI), where members share a common clean-room facility, foreign partners have minimal concerns about Japan reaping greater relative gains from collaboration.[26] Although the substantial evidence of Japanese indigenization of foreign technologies lends credence to the notion of techno-national ideology, the concept is unwieldy as an explanation of MITI's decision to open its R&D programs. Samuels posits an ideology that, by its own assumptions, explains all Japanese initiatives in international research collaboration as motivated by technology indigenization. Rather than assuming that techno-national ideology explains policy, research must show that the designs of MITI's initial proposals reflect a systematic attempt to access and indigenize foreign technology, and that this attempt is something qualitatively different from the goal of matching complementary technological assets—which is one of the most common motivations for forming strategic alliances.

Maintaining access to foreign technologies is undeniably an important component of Japanese technology policy. Indeed, stemming the tide of techno-nationalism in the United States and Europe has been an openly acknowledged goal of MITI's techno-globalism. It is possible, then, that MITI's opening of research programs may only be part of a broader techno-nationalist strategy geared to keeping the American and European research systems open to Japan. In other words, MITI opened select programs with fairly basic research agendas in order to disarm Western critics. Yet, even this degree of opening poses a challenge to Samuels's notion of continuity in Japan's techno-national ideology. If the price of continued access to foreign technology is the subsidizing of foreign firms and the sharing of research results with them, contemporary MITI policy diverges sharply from that in earlier eras. Japan's move to the technological frontier and the pressure for Japan to contribute more to the international community so changed the means available to access and indigenize foreign technology that even MITI's initial proposals for international research programs did not clearly reflect the goal of technology indigenization. The goal and not simply the means of accessing foreign technology has been so impacted by new circumstances as to represent a major discontinuity with the techno-national ideology of the catch-up era.

Foreign Pressure

Western academics and journalists' widespread use of the Japanese term *gaiatsu*, or foreign pressure, suggests the appeal of this explanation for internationalization. Reflecting the increasing complexity of the U.S.–Japan relationship, foreign pressure explanations of Japan's internationalization became more sophisticated in the 1990s. At one time, foreign pressure was seen primarily as a means of offering Japanese bureaucrats political cover to pursue liberalization policies unpopular with sectors long sheltered from foreign competition. More recently, Leonard Schoppa has illustrated the use of foreign pressure as a tool for manipulating policy debates in Japan by energizing interest groups and identifying policy alternatives more sympathetic with foreign goals.[27]

Adding credibility to foreign pressure explanations of opening is the acknowledgment by leading Japanese policymakers of how they were pushed to liberalize the economy. According to former MITI Vice-Minister Naohiro Amaya, whose ideas formed the nucleus of MITI policies governing the shift of industrial structure during the 1970s, "almost all liberalization policies effected in Japan in the postwar period were implemented due to foreign pressure."[28] There is disagreement among academics, however, concerning the explanatory power of foreign pressure. Political economists such as Peter Cowhey and Jonathan Aronson tend to argue that MITI liberalized membership rules for consortia "only under massive pressure from the United States."[29] Yet, Japan specialists as diverse in approach as Frances Rosenbluth and Chalmers Johnson share skepticism about the relationship between foreign pressure as cause and internationalization as effect. According to Rosenbluth, "foreign diplomatic pressure is effective only when market forces have already altered domestic costs and benefits or when there is a perceived threat of retaliation."[30] Thus, assessing the role of foreign pressure in the internationalization of MITI research programs requires consideration of the timing of specific applications of foreign pressure, including threats of reduced access to foreign science and technology.

There has been pressure on Japan to open its markets to foreign goods and services since the 1960s. The literature on trade relations abounds with cases where Japan has done its utmost to avoid true opening. Yet, the pressure for MITI to open its R&D programs to foreign participation went unnoticed by both Japanese voters and politicians. It failed to generate interest among voters because opening presented no adjustment costs, and among politicians because MITI's R&D programs offered no opportunity for political pork.[31] With the notable exception of Prime Minister Nakasone's personal interest in the HFSP, the internationalization of MITI research programs was entirely a bureaucratic concern. The issue was far more political in the United States.

The American interest in the internationalization of MITI research programs reflected more than general dissatisfaction with the asymmetry in access to the two economies. The announcement of MITI's FGCP in 1982 worried many Americans and Europeans who attributed Japan's rising share of the global semiconductor market to the success of MITI's VLSI Project. American firms like Control Data and AT&T were vocal in demands for the opening of government-supported research programs and decided to channel their grievances through the U.S. government. Access to Japan's science and technology system first became an issue in U.S. government trade strategies during the early 1980s. In response to the rising trade deficit and threats by Congress to pass Senator John Danforth's "reciprocity bill," the Reagan administration organized new strategy sessions on Japan policy. Secretary of Commerce Malcolm Baldridge directed his department to develop a comprehensive plan more intent on achieving results than previous initiatives. Calling for greater coordination of science and trade policies, the plan recommended that the access of Japanese researchers to U.S. government labs should be reviewed in light of restrictions on the participation of American firms in Japanese government research programs. The proposal never became policy, however, on account of opposition within the U.S. government. The Treasury Department and the Council of Economic Advisors thought the proposal violated free trade principles while the State Department objected to any linkage of threats.[32]

Access to Japanese research programs did not formally appear on the U.S. trade agenda until the MOSS negotiations of 1985–86. Driven by frustration with a lack of progress in trade talks, the Reagan administration began an intensive series of negotiations to reduce trade barriers in four sectors where competitive, and often superior, American goods were largely shut out of the Japanese market: forest products, telecommunications, medical equipment, and pharmaceuticals. As part of the MOSS talks on electronics, U.S. negotiators requested that American firms be allowed to participate in government-sponsored research projects and to license patents from the Japanese government. According to Laura D'Andrea Tyson, these requests produced little more than token responses. The Japanese government granted limited access to its computer-related patents and invited U.S. firms to participate only in the Sigma Project in computer software, an area where America was far ahead.[33] Although U.S. pressure in MOSS produced few tangible results, acknowledgment of the need to improve access to research programs was beginning to be expressed, at least on a rhetorical level, by Japanese scientists and political advisory groups like the Maekawa Commission.

In the autumn of 1985, Prime Minister Nakasone appointed Haruo Maekawa, former governor of the Bank of Japan, as chair of a seventeen-member panel known informally as the Maekawa commission. After five months of debate, the commission issued an eleven-page report calling for changes in Japan's export-oriented industrial structure that would help reduce the nation's current account surplus. The report dealt mostly with macroeconomic policies but made some general recommendations about the need to promote more basic research and greater international cooperation in science and technology.[34] A second report issued the following year called for Japan to become a leader in initiating large-scale international programs such as the newly proposed HFSP.

Although indicative of the fledgling internationalism under Nakasone's leadership, the Maekawa commission was a private body and so its recommendations lacked any binding force. As implied by its official name, Advisory Group on Economic and Structural Adjustment for International Harmony, the commission was largely a response to foreign pressure for change. Issued two weeks prior to a summit meeting between Nakasone and Reagan, the Maekawa report was interpreted in both the Japanese and American press as a means to deflect foreign criticism of Japan's growing trade surplus.[35] Yet, by late 1987, the question of access to government-supported research moved from being simply one item on a crowded diplomatic agenda to the focus of negotiations on the renewal of the U.S.–Japan Science and Technology Agreement.

The first umbrella science accord between the two countries was signed by President Carter and Prime Minister Ohira in 1980. Limited in scope and short on detail, the 1980 agreement was viewed on the American side as having little impact on the course of bilateral science and technology arrangements. The expiration of the initial accord was, thus, considered by the United States as an opportunity to create a more balanced relationship in science and technology. The main principle guiding the American approach to renegotiation was "equitable responsibilities and reciprocal research opportunities."[36] There was broad consensus in the U.S. government that structural differences in the American and Japanese national systems of innovation had produced an untenable imbalance in mutual access. In the late 1980s, the U.S. government accounted for roughly 47 percent of national R&D expenditures, including those on defense, while the Japanese government accounted for only 22 percent of national R&D spending.[37] Thus, a much larger share of Japanese R&D was proprietary research conducted by industry and so less accessible to foreign researchers.

This structural imbalance was exacerbated by the fact that American universities and national labs were more attractive destinations for Japanese researchers than Japanese research facilities were for American researchers. In 1986, over three hundred Japanese earned positions as postdoctoral fellows or visiting researchers at the U.S. National Institutes of Health alone, while a total of only one hundred American researchers worked as visiting researchers in all Japanese government labs put together.[38] Although recognizing that part of the imbalance stemmed from the language barrier confronting American researchers, the United States called for increased Japanese funding for visiting foreign researchers and greater access to government-supported R&D consortia.

A significantly revised Science and Technology Agreement was signed in June 1988. The agreement called for shared responsibilities and benefits commensurate with respective strengths and resources. More specifically, it called for "comparable access to major government-sponsored or government-supported [research] programs" in a framework that guaranteed adequate protection and equitable distribution of intellectual property rights.[39] In addition to setting forth these goals, the agreement aimed to limit technology leakage by urging that cooperative projects be undertaken only in fields where each nation has "strong complementary or counterbalancing research and development skills."[40] The agreement listed seven broad categories of research as the initial target areas for cooperation: life sciences including biotechnology; information science and technology; manufacturing technology;

automation and process control; global geoscience and environment; joint database development; and advanced materials including superconductors.

The signing of the revised Science and Technology Agreement in June 1988 followed by the opening of the first MITI research programs less than a year later suggests a strong causal relationship between foreign pressure and internationalization. The relationship appears even stronger in view of the fact that MITI's flagship international programs—HFSP (life-science), RWC (information technology), and IMS (manufacturing)—represent three of the areas designated by the 1988 agreement. Nonetheless, the link between foreign pressure as cause and opening as effect is much less straightforward than might at first appear. Foreign pressure for Japan to contribute more to basic research in the life sciences did not produce the intended results. American threats to cut off Japanese access to data from the Human Genome Project were intended to increase the Japanese government's financial support for that program. MITI and STA ignored these threats and continued to place priority on funding for the HFSP. Japan also resisted American pressure to steer the research agenda of the HFSP toward tropical diseases and other developing-world issues. Ultimately, the origins of the HFSP lay more in Prime Minister Nakasone's desire to launch a program with the high profile of Reagan's Strategic Defense Initiative (SDI) and Mitterand's EUREKA than in foreign demands for Japan to increase funding for basic research in the life sciences.

In contrast to the pressure on Japan to contribute more to life-science research, there was hardly any pressure to open a computer project like the RWC. With the widely perceived failure of the FGCP and the American lead in many areas of RWC research, U.S. firms had little interest in RWC. The opening of the RWC program was essentially a token response to the more generic U.S. pressure for internationalization. Foreign pressure played the most direct role in the IMS program. The American desire to establish bilateral collaboration in manufacturing technology set the stage for the IMS program, and both Washington and Brussels played a major role in reshaping Japan's initial IMS proposal.

Complementary Capabilities

The voluminous literature in business and management studies on the formation of strategic alliances between firms has identified several factors that drive such alliances, including sharing the costs and risks of research, coping with the intersectoral nature of new technologies, achieving economies of scale, and reducing innovation time.[41] International alliances may also be motivated by political obstacles such as government trade and investment barriers or rules on local research content. When governments rather than firms initiate international collaboration, there is a greater likelihood that the collaboration is motivated by political rather than technological imperatives. In MITI's internationalization of research programs, however, this linkage has been assumed rather than demonstrated by systematic study.

Japan may be the paradigmatic case of techno-nationalism, but this does not preclude the possibility that its national system of innovation is changing in response to the same forces driving corporate alliances and the opening of government-subsidized research programs throughout the triad. The notion of MITI opening consortia so rapidly in response to the demands of R&D may seem suspicious in view of what most American and European observers see as Japanese intransigence in opening markets to foreign goods and services. Yet, internationalizing research programs is much easier than opening markets for consumer products because the adjustment costs are so low. The change in government research policies neither compromised the preferential investment and supplier relationships among Japanese firms nor posed any threat of dislocation to Japanese workers. In addition, many leading firms that would be likely to take part in MITI programs were already forming their own strategic alliances with foreign companies. Opening research programs was a technocratic rather than political issue.

The initial studies of strategic alliances established in the late 1980s emphasized the sharing of costs and risks as the key motivation for high-tech R&D collaborations. At the same time that each successive generation of technology becomes more expensive to develop, the contraction of the product cycle leaves less time to amortize costs. To remain competitive in the semiconductor business during the early 1990s, for example, firms had to increase R&D and manufacturing investments at a rate of about 20 to 30 percent per year.[42] Collaboration provided a way to reduce the costs and risks of such investments. In most industries, however, gaining access to complementary skills and knowledge has been more important in the collaborative strategies of firms than reducing costs and risks.

The Maastricht Economic Institute on Technology and Innovation (MERIT) compiled information on nearly ten thousand technology cooperation agreements signed in a range of high-tech industries between 1980 and 1989. According to MERIT data, the most frequently mentioned motives for collaboration are exploitation of technological complementarity, reduction of innovation period, and promotion of influence over market structure. With the exception of the aviation, heavy electrical equipment, and telecommunications industries, for which the creation of new generations of technology is particularly expensive, the motivation to reduce costs and risks played only a limited role.[43] A 1991 survey conducted by the Japan Management

Association also suggests that the main motivation behind collaborative R&D for Japanese firms is seeking complementary capabilities rather than reducing costs and risks. Of the nearly five hundred firms responding to the survey, more than 65 percent thought technological complementarity was driving increased research collaboration while only 13 percent cited reducing risks and 10 percent reducing costs.[44] Likewise, Mariko Sakakibara found gaining access to complementary knowledge to be the most important objective of participants in 237 R&D consortia sponsored by the Japanese government between 1959 and 1992. The sharing of costs and risks ranked as one of the least important objectives.[45]

The search for complementary technological knowledge or capabilities is sometimes part of what Fumio Kodama calls "technology fusion": the combining of technologies from different sectors into hybrid technologies. The development of optoelectronics during the 1970s, for example, required the matching of innovations in laser and semiconductor technologies with innovations in optical fibers. During the same decade, the field of biotechnology developed from synergistic collaboration between the food, pharmaceutical, and chemicals industries. In the 1980s, technological fusion between the ceramics and machinery industries produced the field of fine ceramics while collaboration between the ceramics and chemicals industries brought about the field of new materials.[46] By the late 1990s, technological fusion between the computer and telecom industries had made possible the development of handheld, wireless devices for internet access.

Technological fusion is also evident in the internationalization of MITI research programs. It is increasingly difficult for any firm to develop mastery across the range of complex technologies necessary to succeed in even its core business. The need for such capabilities may lead to collaboration among firms based in different countries when the necessary skills cannot be accessed domestically.[47] Thus, technological fusion can also explain Japan's drive to access complementary technologies as part of a universal phenomenon without reference to techno-national ideology. The need for multi-technology capabilities in fields like optoelectronics and mobile Internet access encourages firms everywhere to acquire the required technologies through domestic and international strategic alliances.

Kodama suggests that the growing importance of technology fusion is supported by statistics on both the focus of R&D spending by Japanese industry and the composition of MITI consortia. Although the data on R&D spending require some qualification, the data on MITI consortia are fairly clear cut. During the 1980s, all major Japanese industries diversified R&D spending into technologies outside their core businesses. For example, the electronics and communications equipment industries spent an average of

35 percent of R&D expenditures outside their core businesses.[48] A strategy of technology fusion does not, however, explain all cases of diversification in R&D spending. Although Kodama interprets the dramatic shift in the focus of R&D spending by the textile and steel industries during the late 1980s in terms of technology fusion, these changing R&D priorities also reflect the shifting of investment from sunset industries to entirely new areas of business. Moreover, some of the diversification during the 1980s can be attributed to the flush financial positions of firms during the bubble economy. The R&D spending of many Japanese firms became much more streamlined during the 1990s. Kodama's data on the changing composition of MITI consortia reflect more directly the increasing collaboration between industries. Since 1970, the average number of industries represented in MITI research associations has been increasing, while the number of participating companies per industry has been decreasing. In other words, MITI consortia have been attracting firms from different industries rather than simply different firms from the same industry.[49] Lee Branstetter and Mariko Sakakibara confirm that MITI and other ministries have tried in their R&D consortia to bring together firms with complementary research assets.[50] This intersectoral dynamic is evident in programs such as the RWC, IMS, and the Micromachine Consortium.

Nevertheless, the financial or technological necessity of international collaboration is not equally clear for all of MITI's international programs. These programs do not usually involve huge capital investments in central research facilities; most research is done by firms at their own existing labs. The need for international collaboration to reduce costs and risks was particularly weak in the case of the RWC program and the various semiconductor consortia that began in the mid-1990s because Japan provided 100 percent of project funding. The cost-sharing rationale is more compelling for IMS, in which hundreds of firms and universities from across the developed world are taking part in consortia that average more than twenty members each.

The possibility of leveraging complementary scientific and technological capabilities provides a stronger rationale for the internationalization of MITI programs than the sharing of costs and risks. The potential for leverage is, of course, not the same in all programs. Domestically, the RWC program reflected a strategy of technology fusion in optical computing technologies. For the first time a MITI computer consortium included among its members optical fiber firms like Furukawa Electric, Nippon Sheet Glass, and Sumitomo Electric in addition to major computer firms like Fujitsu and NEC. As an "open national program," however, the RWC program was less responsive to foreign interests than either the HFSP or IMS. Although research institutes from Singapore and Europe joined the RWC program as full partners, foreign firms believed there was more to lose than gain from participation in the program. The complementarity rationale was stronger in other open, national projects such as HYPR and the Association of Super-Advanced Electronics Technologies (ASET) but strongest in the HFSP and IMS programs, both of which were conceived as fully international undertakings.

The international panel of scientists that developed the HFSP proposal aimed to make emerging networks of collaboration in life-science research more efficient. According to Sir James Gowans, the first secretary-general of the HFSP Organization, the increasing complexity of research in the life sciences encourages greater collaboration among researchers. Even though the most appropriate collaborators are often researchers in other countries, traditional grants from national agencies place heavy restrictions on the use of funds that can inhibit meaningful international collaboration. Much less restrictive HFSP grants allow international teams of researchers the flexibility to plan and coordinate research projects more efficiently.[51] HFSP grants institutionalize, at least temporarily, informal international collaborations among researchers.

Of the three case-study programs, IMS offers the most convincing evidence of leveraging complementary national capabilities through international collaboration. The initial IMS proposal suggested that the program might fuse Japanese expertise in hardware technology like industrial robots and numerically controlled machine tools with European expertise in complex precision machinery and American expertise in software and network technology.[52] Although the initial proposal raised suspicion in foreign governments as to Japanese motives, it also generated considerable interest among major firms like Rockwell, United Technologies, and Asea Brown Bovari. The clearest indication that complementary technological interests played an important role in launching IMS is found in the fact that foreign firms and governments tried to build on the Japanese proposal rather than simply dismissing it as a ploy to access superior Western technologies.

The Changing Role of MITI Programs

The opening of MITI research programs to foreign participation would have little meaning if the programs lacked value for domestic participants. Thus, evaluating MITI's techno-globalism requires an understanding of the research opportunities these programs offer. Analysts are divided on the benefits that consortia have provided in the past. The most sympathetic studies believe consortia raise the level of Japanese technology but do not produce revolutionary advances. Less enthusiastic evaluations see the contribution of consortia in providing secondary benefits such as training and socialization of researchers rather than advancing technology. The most critical literature depicts the programs of the 1980s as misguided attempts to force an anachronistic industrial policy on reluctant firms. In any case, during the 1990s, MITI began to experiment with different forms of collaboration and revised rules on intellectual property rights that offered new incentives and opportunities for Japanese participants and nondiscriminatory terms for foreign participants. In short, the programs initiated beginning in the early 1990s represent a departure from the consortia of the 1980s in terms of flexibility and breadth of research goals, corporate interest, and academic participation.

Positive Evaluations

According to a 1989 survey of firms conducted by Keidanren, the Federation of Economic Organizations, MITI "research associations" were the most beneficial of all policy instruments used by the Japanese government to promote technological advance.[53] Although there is disagreement on the precise benefits of MITI consortia, a number of scholars agree that these consortia have helped to overcome market imperfections that lead to underinvestment in research. In a study of the five major electronics consortia organized by MITI during 1976–91, Martin Fransman argues that MITI leadership reduced the transactions costs of organizing collaborative research and compensated for the "bounded vision" of firms by subsidizing the development of core technologies with only long-run commercial prospects. He contends that even though the government's share of total R&D expenditures in Japan is low relative to that in other industrialized countries, it has, nevertheless, been important for the long-run development of particular technologies. During the 1980s, for example, MITI provided approximately 20 percent of the research budget of a leading Japanese industrial electronics firm for projects with a time horizon of ten years or more.[54]

Based on case studies of consortia in superconductivity and engineering ceramics during the 1980s, Gerald Hane concurs that MITI subsidies represented a significant share of private expenditures on frontier research despite the growing resources of leading Japanese firms. Furthermore, he argues that these subsidies enhanced rather than displaced R&D investment by firms. Hane finds that private-sector R&D on superconducting devices and systems such as Josephson Junctions and magneto-encephalographs preceded the formation of MITI consortia in these technologies, and that the latter worked primarily to accelerate private-sector investment.[55]

Hane is also more specific than Fransman about the dynamics of MITI consortia and the results they produce. For example, he concludes that in all of the MITI consortia in superconducting devices and systems, incremental innovations raised the level of technology from where Japan lagged behind the international frontier to where it rivaled or even surpassed the state of the art. Despite this, he argues that the dynamic driving these consortia was "procompetitive coordination" rather than "precompetitive cooperation."[56] According to Hane, MITI designed consortia around three or four core firms that it assigned to develop competing prototypes. Rather than sharing advances with competitors, the firms were able to gauge their relative progress based on insights gained from national labs that evaluated the advances of each company. The interaction between firms and national labs provided the transparency necessary to spur competition among the firms.[57]

Although neither Fransman nor Hane argue that MITI consortia produce revolutionary technological advances, both agree that these programs helped to raise the level of Japanese technology. Consistent with the predictions of the theoretical literature on research consortia, Branstetter and Sakakibara have found that Japanese consortia are more successful when the level of potential R&D spillovers is higher and when the projects pursue more basic research.[58] In a survey of 237 government-subsidized R&D consortia between 1959 and 1992, Sakakibara found participants believed the merits of projects exceeded their demerits. Yet, she found no clear link between the existence of R&D consortia and industry competitiveness, despite the fact that participation in consortia increased private R&D investment in target areas by an average of 38 percent.[59] Like Sakakibara, many other analysts see the benefits of MITI consortia as rather indirect. The National Research Council cites the training of young researchers and the cultivation of a "culture of exchange" as the major benefits of MITI consortia.[60] Similarly, Sully Taylor and Kozo Yamamura suggest that national projects are most useful in helping to overcome traditional barriers separating researchers in the less fluid Japanese labor market and in compensating for the lack of capital markets in Japan to fund high-risk research.[61] Of course, such secondary benefits would not provide any incentive for foreign firms to join MITI consortia.

Negative Evaluations

Scholars have questioned the effectiveness of MITI consortia in two main ways. Microlevel analyses of consortia organization and outputs raise questions about the opportunity costs and the efficiency of MITI consortia dating back to the 1960s. Macrolevel analyses suggest that Japan's emergence as a technological and economic power in the late 1970s created tensions between MITI and Japanese firms that undermined the effectiveness of consortia as a policy tool. Daniel Okimoto argues that even during the 1970s, when MITI's ability to implement industrial policy was stronger, several consortia such as the 3.75 Series Computer Development Project failed to achieve even modest objectives, let alone revolutionary breakthroughs. Okimoto further suggests that the Japanese information industry was poised to make a leap forward at the same time the VLSI project seemed to produce MITI's greatest success. He believes the same results would have been achieved in roughly the same time frame even without a MITI consortium.[62] Wakasugi and Goto also argue that the effectiveness of MITI research programs during the catch-up era has been exaggerated. Using the ratio of patents to research expenditures as a measure of productivity, they found the productivity of MITI research associations to be lower on average than that of the industries they represent.[63]

Scott Callon challenges the efficiency of MITI consortia with the argument that producing marketable technologies rather than simply patents provides the real test of the effectiveness of these programs. Whereas Hane would endorse as successful consortia that achieve technical breakthroughs, Callon argues that technical excellence is essentially irrelevant if it cannot be linked to marketable products. Callon also moves beyond the microlevel analysis of consortia organization and outputs to analyze the broader political and economic context of MITI consortia during the 1980s.[64] He contends that as the resources and competitiveness of Japanese firms grew, the incentives decreased for these firms to cooperate with MITI and with each other. By the 1980s, MITI accounted for only 1 percent of total Japanese R&D expenditures, and Japanese firms began to see domestic rivals rather than foreign firms as their foremost competitors. Callon also discusses how Japan's move to the technology frontier, and the consequent shift to funding more basic research, further strained MITI's relations with both firms and other ministries.

According to Callon, firms bitterly criticized the FGCP as totally divorced from their own needs and interests. Although firms had contributed more than 50 percent of the research budgets for earlier catch-up programs like the VLSI consortium, they refused to make any direct financial contribution to MITI's more esoteric projects. Without the financial contributions of firms, MITI was unable to keep pace with the increasing costs of leading-edge research. As a result, it was forced to make more focused technological bets that ran a much higher risk of failure. Callon also argues that the conflict between MITI and firms paralleled increased tensions between MITI and the Ministry of Education. The shift of consortia to a more basic focus made university researchers more appropriate partners, in many respects, than corporate researchers. Callon's research suggests that MESC nevertheless bitterly opposed academic participation in MITI programs. In short, Callon contends that MITI consortia during the 1980s were plagued by conflict and so failed to leverage government-firm and inter-firm cooperation for international competitive advantage.

Programs Since the Early 1990s

As Japan's leading firms grew larger and more independent of government support and guidance, MITI consortia became far less important in their research strategies than during the 1960s and 1970s. Even so, the programs of today's METI can provide useful research opportunities for Japanese firms. Although Callon offers an accurate picture of MITI's industrial policy during the 1980s, he presents only a snapshot of policy during that time. MITI learned from the mistakes of the 1980s and started to come to terms with its decreased influence over firms. The result was far more flexible programs that allowed firms to choose research themes that complemented their own research priorities. The more modest programs of the 1990s also minimized the earlier problem of focused technological bets because they researched multiple technologies rather than aiming to develop a single marketable product. In short, these programs were not examples of a top-down industrial policy thrust upon reluctant firms but experiments in new forms of more flexible and open research collaboration.

For decades, the R&D budgets of Japan's major firms have dwarfed the amount of funds available to them from MITI. With the nation's prolonged economic downturn, however, government subsidies took on new importance for firms forced to consolidate their manufacturing and research operations and to focus on short-term business rather than long-term research. In the late 1990s, for example, NEC and Toshiba merged their satellite operations while Hitachi and NEC merged most of their DRAM operations. At the same time, research subsidies from MITI encouraged these same firms to do research that they might not otherwise have been prepared to undertake. Although government funding represented only 1–2 percent of Hitachi's R&D budget during the late 1990s, R&D managers believe this support was much more valuable than a decade earlier, allowing them to expand research in information technology as well as to move into new areas such as genome informatics.[65] The major layoffs announced in the early years of this decade by firms including Fujitsu, Toshiba, and Hitachi provide even further evidence of the difficulties facing Japan's leading high-tech firms. Despite the pressures on corporate R&D budgets, however, Marie Anchordoguy suggests that the issue is not simply money. At a time when many of the institutions that promoted social and economic stability over the postwar period were weakening, firms still looked to MITI for guidance and leadership in the transition to a more creative society.[66]

Just as MITI's R&D programs evolved during the 1990s, METI's programs are likely to evolve in response to changing circumstances during the current decade. As the nation's economic downturn hit the ten-year mark, the Japanese government began scrambling to find new ways to restore growth. In 2002, as part of the Focus 21 initiative, METI announced sweeping plans to slash funding for programs unlikely to produce commercial results and to boost funding for a range of applied R&D projects intended to create new markets within three years.[67] In the short run, at least, Japan's commitment to basic research appears to be fading. The design and organization of consortia may be changing as well because many of these more focused projects are conducted by small groups of firms. Although such changes could make identifying appropriate foreign partners easier, they seem more likely to reduce the number of opportunities for foreign firms and universities to join future projects.

Conclusion

Although foreign pressure and complementary capabilities have always played a more important role in the internationalization of MITI programs than bureaucratic politics and techno-national ideology, the relative importance of these two factors has depended on the program and technologies in question. The more flexible R&D strategy adopted by MITI in the early 1990s suggests that it learned from the failures of the 1980s and adapted to the role of promoting frontier research from its position of decreased leverage over Japanese firms. The next three chapters explore these arguments in greater depth through detailed case studies of the HFSP, the IMS, and the RWC program.

———Chapter 4———

The Human Frontier
Science Program

The Human Frontier Science Program (HFSP) is a nonprofit foundation located in Strasbourg, France that funds molecular-level research on biological functions in living organisms. Established in 1989, the HFSP is unique in that it is the only program in the life sciences that funds multinational and interdisciplinary teams of researchers without specific criteria on the nationality of those researchers. It is also unique in that it was established, and continues to be funded, largely by Japan. The HFSP was the Japanese government's first experience as initiator of an international science or technology program. As such, it offers an excellent opportunity to study both the domestic and international forces at work in the planning and execution of Japanese science policy.

The role of bureaucratic politics in driving the HFSP proposal was minimal because of the personal involvement of Prime Minister Nakasone and the need for MITI to minimize foreign doubts about the program by enlisting the support of the STA. The role of techno-national ideology was also limited, in this case by Japan's decision to leave responsibility for HFSP planning to an international group of scientists. Similarly, the role of foreign pressure was limited; there was certainly pressure on Japan to contribute more to the international scientific community, but MITI largely ignored the preferences of foreign governments while planning the HFSP. Although not clearly articulated in early MITI discussions, the importance of complementary capabilities became clear in discussions among scientists.

MITI has played a hands-off management role in the HFSP premised on "giving money, not advice"—*kane wa dasu ga kuchi wa dasanai*.[1] As with project planning, the ministry depoliticized the HFSP by placing primary responsibility for management in the hands of an international group of scientists. The HFSP also helped push Japan along the learning curve of internationalization. Survey data on HFSP applicants and grantees, discussed later in this chapter, demonstrate the unique funding opportunities available in the program.

An International Grant Program

The philosophy of the HFSP is that research that explores "issues common to all humanity should be developed by marshaling scientific wisdom, on a global scale."[2] In practical terms, this involves the funding of multinational and interdisciplinary research teams as well as fellowships for individual researchers visiting foreign labs. In keeping with the theme of openness, the HFSP makes no claim to intellectual property arising from the work it supports. All intellectual property rights remain vested in the inventors or their institutions.[3] During its first decade, the HFSP-funded research in two general areas. About 70 percent of research funding went to the elucidation of biological functions at the molecular level, such as energy conversion or the expression of genetic information. The remaining 30 percent went to the elucidation of brain functions in areas such as perception and cognition, memory, and learning. In response to developments in biology during the 1990s, the HFSP decided in March 2001 to consolidate these two research areas under the single theme of complex mechanisms in living organisms.

The basic administrative organization of the HFSP was first outlined in the March 1988 report of the International Feasibility Study Committee (IFSC). Designed to place primacy on the views and active participation of scientists from around the world, the HFSP comprised three main bodies: the Board of Trustees, the Council of Scientists, and the Secretariat. The first, which consists of two government officials from each member nation, is responsible for overall program policy and functions as a liaison with sponsoring institutions in member nations and in countries wishing to join the program. The Council of Scientists, composed of two representatives from each member nation and the Commission of the European Communities, decides the basic principles of program management including allocation of funds and selection of priority research areas. Members of the council are practicing research scientists nominated by their peers and approved by the Board of Trustees. The council meets annually to make final proposals to the board concerning awards, and also selects the members of the review committees who make the initial ranking of all grant and fellowship applications. The secretariat is responsible for the routine management of the program, including finances and the processing of applications and awards. At least two of the full-time staff have traditionally been seconded from the Japanese bureaucracy.

The HFSP gives three types of awards: research grants, fellowships, and funding for workshops. The most distinctive of these are the research grants given to international teams of up to four researchers, with a principal researcher based in an HFSP member nation.[4] Between 1990 and 2003, the HFSP awarded 597 research grants that involved a total of 2,415 scientists. These grants are unique in the degree of intercontinental collaboration they make possible. During the program's first eight years, for example, 80 percent of the grants linked labs on two or more continents, with more than 30 percent linking labs on three or more continents. The national distribution of grant recipients during this time was as follows: United States (32 percent), Japan (16 percent), the United Kingdom (11 percent), Germany (9 percent), France (9 percent), other European Union (7 percent), Switzerland (5 percent), Canada (4 percent), Italy (2 percent), and others (5 percent).[5]

In 2000, the HFSP modified its grant program out of concern that the relatively modest size of the grants might make it difficult to begin a truly new research project, and that a success rate of only 13 percent for applicants might discourage many qualified scientists from even applying. It began by raising the annual award limit to $450,000 per team. As a result, the average amount for grants rose from $230,000 to $350,000 per year by 2003. The HFSP then introduced a two-tiered application process beginning with a first round of abstract proposals followed by a limited number of full-length, invited proposals. Teams invited to submit full-length applications have a 30–50 percent chance of receiving a grant. To increase the interdisciplinary nature of research teams, the HFSP also began to reach out to professional societies in the physical and mathematical sciences. This proved successful. Between 2001 and 2003, the proportion of researchers from outside the life sciences increased from 3 to 20 percent. Along with these changes, the HFSP inaugurated a Program for Young Investigators to support novel collaborations among scientists who are within the first five years of establishing their own laboratories.[6]

In addition to the research grants, the HFSP also awards fellowships to finance individual research at foreign institutions. If the researcher is a citizen of a member nation, the location of the host lab is not considered. For applicants not from member nations, however, the host lab must be located in a member nation. From 1990 to 2003, the HFSP received 8,490 applications for long-term fellowships and made 1,814 awards. As shown in Table 4.1, the nationality of fellowship recipients during the first ten years was as follows: Japan (17 percent), other European Union (15 percent), France (13 percent), Germany (10 percent), the United Kingdom (8 percent), Canada (7 percent), the United States (6 percent), Italy (4 percent), Switzerland (3 percent), and others (17 percent).[7] A striking aspect of these figures is that a very small number of U.S. scientists were awarded fellowships considering the large pool of potential applicants from the United States. In large part, this is because very few U.S. scientists choose to apply, feeling that their professional prospects would be better served by postdoctoral positions in the United States.

Table 4.1

HFSP Long-Term Fellows, 1990–2000: Nationality and Host Country

Fellow	Canada	France	Germany	Italy	Japan	Switzerland	UK	USA	Other EU	Other	Total	
						Host Country						
Canadian	0	7	8	0	0	2	17	63	4	1	102	7%
French	7	0	15	1	0	11	25	137	5	2	203	13%
German	6	10	0	0	3	11	11	115	4	2	162	10%
Italian	2	4	6	0	0	4	5	37	1	0	59	4%
Japanese	7	8	22	0	1	3	27	198	4	0	270	17%
Swiss	2	0	3	0	0	0	4	30	2	1	42	3%
British	5	4	3	2	2	2	0	103	3	1	125	8%
American	9	17	19	1	3	8	27	0	3	2	89	6%
Other EU	7	15	13	0	1	9	27	152	5	2	231	15%
Other	14	15	24	3	2	9	29	166	6	1	269	17%
Total	59	80	113	7	12	58	172	1,001	37	12	1,552	100%
	4%	5%	7%	0%	1%	4%	11%	65%	2%	1%	100%	

Source: Human Frontier Science Program Organization.

The overwhelming popularity of the United States as a destination for fellowship recipients suggests that many non-American fellows feel the same. For example, over 70 percent of long-term fellows in 2000 chose to use their fellowship in the United States. Although this is of major benefit to the United States and the fellows themselves, it became worrisome to many HFSP countries because a major percentage of fellows are slow to return to their home countries. Only 47 percent of fellows who received awards before 1995 had returned to their home countries, even two years following the end of their fellowships. Moreover, 70 percent of those fellows still remaining in the host country were in the United States.[8] In order to combat a "brain drain" of young scientists to the most advanced nations, the HFSP reorganized its fellowship program in 2000 to encourage the seeding of scientific talent more evenly across the globe. First, HFSP fellows are now eligible for a third year of funding. This can be used to extend the stay in the host laboratory or to support a year of research following return to their home country. Second, the HFSP initiated a competitive Career Development Award for fellows who return to their home countries.

Beyond long-term fellowships, the HFSP provides funding for a small number of short-term awards of up to three months that are intended to facilitate initial contacts between researchers, allow former long-term fellows to follow up on previous collaborative work, or to provide training in new equipment and techniques. Finally, the HFSP also accepts applications for funds to sponsor a few international workshops. In April 1995, the HFSP modified the format of workshops to emphasize closed-group meetings in Strasbourg with subsequent publication of the proceedings.

Forces Driving Internationalization

Major frameworks used in explaining Japanese science and technology policy provide very different interpretations of the motivations in proposing and managing the HFSP. The bureaucratic politics approach would interpret the HFSP as an attempt by MITI to expand its bureaucratic turf at the expense of MESC and STA, both of which were far more active in funding basic research in the life sciences. This framework suggests that MITI would seek to create a program that serves primarily to maximize its own regulatory powers and research capabilities vis-à-vis rival ministries. The techno-national ideology explanation would interpret the HFSP in terms of the strategic use of foreign partners to enhance Japanese capabilities in bioscience. It suggests that MITI would seek to create a program that maximizes the potential flow of information to Japan. The foreign pressure explanation would posit that the HFSP was motivated mainly by foreign criticisms that Japan should contribute more to international science and that the program should reflect foreign preferences in organization and research objectives. Finally, the complementary capabilities perspective would interpret changes in the demands of life-science research as the force behind Japan's HFSP proposal. Although bureaucratic politics and techno-national ideology played a minimal role in the HFSP, foreign pressure was a key motivation for establishing the program. Ultimately, however, the HFSP took shape as a result of scientists' interest in nurturing interdisciplinary and intercontinental networks of collaboration.

Overcoming Bureaucratic Conflict in a Sōri Puroguramu

The history of the HFSP shows little of the conflict suggested by a bureaucratic politics explanation of Japanese science and technology policy, despite the ample opportunity for such conflict to develop.[9] Although both MITI and STA had certain self-interested motives for working together, the primary factor supporting cooperation was the personal role of Prime Minister Nakasone in initiating the HFSP as an international project. The potential for conflict with MESC arose with MITI's recruitment of academics to participate in the planning of the HFSP. Although MESC neither participated in HFSP planning nor supported the program financially, it also made no effort to restrict academic participation. Finally, the initial opposition of the Ministry of Finance (MOF) to the HFSP resulted from a fear of a spiraling financial commitment more than any disagreement with the substance of the program. With the help of Nakasone's personal endorsement of the HFSP, MITI eventually won MOF's endorsement of the program by supporting that ministry's plans for a new consumption tax.

Until 2001, when STA was absorbed by the Ministry of Education, the HFSP was jointly managed by MITI and STA, with over 60 percent of Japanese funding coming from STA. This arrangement was unusual both because of the precedent of MITI's involvement in a joint project in the life sciences, and the seemingly leading role played by STA. The balance of responsibilities in this arrangement and the high level of cooperation in the partnership could be traced to early direction given to the program by Prime Minister Nakasone and the mutual benefits for MITI and STA in joint administration of the HFSP.

Rather than emerging through the usual process of bottom-up planning, the HFSP began at the initiative of the prime minister. Nakasone's hope was to establish a program that would rival the scale and financial commitment of the SDI in the United States and EUREKA in Europe. Nakasone also set the basic direction of the HFSP by calling for an interministry program in bioscience. Earlier in his career, the prime minister had played an important role in establishing an ongoing program in cancer research administered jointly by STA, MESC, and the Ministry of Health and Welfare.[10] He now hoped to establish a similar program on an international level. Nakasone envisioned more of an applied technology program than that which actually developed. In early discussions about the program, he would use the example of real-time translation machines as one of the potential applications of the research.[11]

The call for proposals was directed to both MITI's Agency for Industrial Science and Technology (AIST) and STA via the prime minister's Council on Science and Technology. As AIST prepared its proposal for a Human Frontier Program, STA began work on its proposal for a Human and Earth Science Program. Larger in scope, the STA proposal also addressed environmental issues. After hearings on each proposal in February 1986, the Council on Science and Technology opted for the AIST proposal, but asked for the cooperation of AIST and STA in the execution of the program. According to Tateo Arimoto, the key STA bureaucrat involved in the first days of this joint program, the two main reasons the AIST proposal was chosen over that of his own agency were, first, Nakasone considered earth science too mundane and better left to conventional forms of collaboration, and second, the STA proposal involved more than simple lab research. It was believed that the larger scale of the proposal would make organizing the program more difficult. Even several senior officials in STA felt strongly that choosing a manageable framework for the project was the most important consideration for Japan's first international initiative—even more important, perhaps, than the theme of the research itself.[12] A slightly more cynical explanation is offered by a former MITI bureaucrat who suggested that the STA proposal was essentially recycled ideas put together in a rush to challenge the AIST proposal. He notes that STA did not even assemble a study group, which is a standard feature of the consensus-building procedure in preparing any major proposal.[13]

Once the AIST proposal had been chosen as the basis for further discussions of the HFSP, the challenge was to define more clearly the structure of the program and gain the support of the international community. This second phase of planning is notable for the close coordination between MITI and STA. If ministries compete for bureaucratic turf as fiercely as the bureaucratic politics argument suggests, why would MITI and STA seek each other's cooperation after the MITI proposal had been chosen over that of STA? The answer lies in Nakasone's support for the program, MITI's desire to win foreign approval of the program, and STA's desire to expand the role of the Council on Science and Technology.

The HFSP proposal took on added weight for both MITI and STA because it was a *sōri puroguramu* or prime minister's program.[14] For this reason, it differs from cases like research in high-temperature superconductivity, in which the two ministries established rival consortia during 1988. Consensus between MITI and STA was reached under the guidance of Dr. Michio Okamoto, Nakasone's close friend and chairman of the Policy Committee of the Council on Science and Technology. Okamoto was a leading medical researcher who had gained respect in political circles as chairman of a committee on reform of the college entrance system. Okamoto helped shape the HFSP proposal further by pushing for a more basic research program that put the ideas of scientists first.

Feeling pressure from Nakasone to collaborate with STA, MITI also had its own reasons for making the HFSP a joint effort. First, the HFSP was touted as "basic science" and was therefore outside MITI's traditional domain; cooperation with STA would help to legitimize MITI's activity in this area. Second, MITI feared its reputation abroad would undermine acceptance of the program and thus it was eager to include other ministries in the administration of the HFSP.[15] As part of this plan, a seven-ministry panel was formed, but this group played only a minor role in recommending scientists for the domestic feasibility study committee. The core relationship was that between MITI and STA. The joint endeavor allowed MITI to draw on STA's large research budget and gave STA's Council on Science and Technology added prestige. STA saw an opportunity for the Council to step out from its role as an advisory body to play a prominent role in coordinating interministerial discussions on the HFSP.

Rivalry between MITI and MESC presented a second area of potential conflict in the development of the HFSP proposal. MESC oversees all scientific research in universities and affiliated research institutions. According to the bureaucratic politics argument, any move by MITI to enlist academic researchers in a high-profile international program would be interpreted as an incursion into MESC's domain. Despite the leading role played by Japanese academics in the planning of the HFSP, MESC never chose to become involved in the program. The official rationale for this decision was that the focus on life science was too narrow.[16] According to Katsuhiko Umehara, deputy director of planning for the HFSP at MITI, the official position of MESC reflects elements of both *honne* (true motives) and *tatemae* (stated motives).[17] MESC was uncomfortable with the precedent of cooperation between MITI and STA in basic research and so took no action to support the HFSP. Conspicuously absent, however, were steps to undermine the fledgling program. According to Scott Callon, MESC had a standing policy to reduce funding for any university that accepted funds from MITI.[18] While the key scientists involved in developing the HFSP proposal witnessed no such coercion in this case, they suggest there was at least some foot-dragging on the part of MESC—regarding tax provisions for Japanese grant recipients—that made implementing the program needlessly difficult.[19]

MESC regulations prohibited universities and other MESC-affiliated institutes from directly receiving HFSP grants because they qualified as "foreign funds." The Japanese academics who received awards in the first year were forced to accept the money as private individuals and then "donate" it to their university. Under this arrangement, the grants were treated as personal income and thus subject to an income tax of almost 50 percent. MITI and STA officials tried to solve the problem by asking MESC to change university regulations, but they encountered resistance. The more expedient course for MITI and STA officials was to secure special tax-exempt status for HFSP grants from MOF.[20]

The intransigence of MESC should not, however, be overstated. The inertia shown by MESC reflected the closed and inward-looking nature of the entire Japanese science bureaucracy as much as any anti-HFSP agenda. Similar red tape was encountered by researchers at all national labs, including those affiliated with MITI itself. The problem was the lack of any established mechanism for HFSP grants to enter the accounting system of individual national labs that were supported from the same general pool of funds. Any grant entering this general account would lose all identity. In addition, the grant would actually displace other funds. Because of the MOF's rigid limits on growth of the general account, a research organization would only have been able to allow a researcher to accept an HFSP grant by making cuts elsewhere in spending. The confusion generated by this was especially ironic because Japan's budget for the HFSP came from this very same general account.[21]

The problem is illustrated in the case of Kenji Kawano of MITI's Electrotechnical Laboratory (ETL), who was the first researcher from a Japanese national lab to receive an HFSP grant. With the special exemption provided by the MOF, Kawano was able to accept the grant into his personal bank account tax-free. A second set of special regulations drafted by MITI was necessary, however, for Kawano to bring the equipment and supplies purchased with the grant into his lab. ETL researchers were not previously allowed to bring such "personal" items into laboratories. Kawano faced further red tape in the administration of his grant because, even under the revised MITI regulations, he was unable to employ a part-time assistant. Nevertheless, Kawano needed an assistant to feed the monkeys for his experiments on the neural mechanisms of eye movement. On the advice of senior officials at AIST, Kawano was able to skirt the problem by hiring a student under an existing system for "visiting researchers." Kawano simply had to claim that the student hired to feed the monkeys was a qualified researcher whose skills were necessary at ETL.[22]

The bureaucratic obstacles in the administration of the first HFSP grants were, thus, not limited to the inflexibility of MESC. The entire national lab system, including those labs run by MITI, faced a jungle of red tape. Such obstacles are best understood as part of the learning curve of internationalization for the Japanese bureaucracy rather than as symptomatic of MESC playing spoiler in MITI's plans for the HFSP. Nevertheless, MESC displayed more dislike for the HFSP than either the IMS or RWC programs. Unlike the latter programs, which are oriented toward industry, the HFSP is a purely academic program and so represents a direct challenge to MESC's regulatory authority. Although MESC did not attempt to undermine the HFSP, it certainly did nothing to facilitate it.

The third axis of potential conflict among ministries was that between MITI and MOF. At first, MOF was strongly opposed to the HFSP proposal. The ministry worried about the Pandora's box that the program might open. Demands for increased contributions to other international science projects would be far more difficult to manage than budget requests for purely domestic programs.[23] MOF also balked at MITI's apparent attempt to lock it into a major budget commitment by discussing publicly, without any fiscal authorization, a potential HFSP budget of one trillion yen, or roughly $7 billion, over twenty years.

According to Katsuhiko Umehara, the proposal was in a chicken-and-egg situation. MOF was unlikely to provide substantial funds for the program without a major commitment to participate from other nations. At the same time, other nations were unlikely to be impressed by the program without a major financial commitment from Japan. The looming retirement of Nakasone also worried MITI. Without strong political sponsorship, plans for the HFSP might falter, and none of Nakasone's potential successors shared his interest in the life sciences. At least in the short term, however, MITI was in a strong position to bargain for funds. MOF and the Liberal Democratic Party were eager to enact a new consumption tax and MITI's support would be useful in gaining the "understanding" of Japanese business.[24] After this deal, the HFSP became a routine budget item once the program was officially established in 1989.

Easing Foreign Suspicions: Letting Scientists Decide

In September of 1985, AIST organized the Committee on Technology and International Exchange under the leadership of former AIST director Seiichi

Ishizaka. In February 1986, this study group, the so-called Ishizaka kenkyūkai, released a twenty-page report that outlined the basics of a "Human Frontier Program." The report began by discussing the characteristics necessary in future technologies to deal with issues ranging from the graying of industrial societies to the impact of rapid population growth on natural resources and the environment. In response to the "technostress" resulting from man's increased interaction with information technology, the report called for a basic change in the trajectory of technological development. It proposed closer study of biological functions in order to learn from the energy-efficient, self-adjusting mechanisms of living systems.[25]

Although it shared the core values of interdisciplinarity and internationality with later drafts of the HFSP proposal, the Ishizaka report envisioned a more commercially oriented program. It proposed a central HFSP facility with an international staff of engineers and scientists commissioned from both academia and industry. This staff would apply research on the brain and nervous system in such areas as the development of software and intelligent robots, with the results diffused through international symposia.[26] Aware that such a proposal was likely to raise major suspicions in the West, MITI and STA invited an international group of scientists to participate in planning the HFSP. As the HFSP was Japan's first experience in planning such an initiative, the exercise was far from straightforward. There was confusion over what level official would be appropriate to contact and whether these individuals should be approached directly or via foreign diplomats in Tokyo.[27] As an example of this confusion, Japan contacted the private National Academy of Sciences in the United States on the mistaken assumption that it was a federal, policy-making body.[28] Finally, the Ministry of Foreign Affairs asked each G-7 nation to suggest one individual who could nominate scientists to attend a conference in Tokyo during January 1987.

The Tokyo Conference was the first international meeting on what was to become the HFSP. The original AIST proposal had been modified somewhat during a domestic feasibility study in the autumn of 1986. The proposal tabled at the conference still called for a program on higher biological functions that might have applications in the field of information processing, but it left the design of the program open for discussion. Even with this concession, however, the proposal did not diffuse all foreign suspicions about Japanese motives in proposing an international program in the life sciences.

In a confidential memo distributed to U.S. delegates, the Department of State indicated that France was prepared to block consensus on the HFSP if it were not a truly international program that would treat all parties equally.[29] In addition, the United States was concerned by MITI's central role in planning the program, especially because the ministry had no biological research facilities of its own except for a fermentation research center. According to Dr. David Kingsbury, then director of behavioral and biological sciences at the National Science Foundation (NSF), the HFSP "seemed like a clear case of the Japanese trying to get their commercial hooks into international science. It seemed like an unbridled attempt to take over the world pharmaceutical field."[30]

The failure to reach an international consensus at the Tokyo Conference was a serious setback to plans to announce the HFSP at the G-7 Summit in Venice in June 1987. In hopes of still meeting this goal, Japan arranged another meeting of leading scientists at the so-called London Wise Men's Conference of April 1987. This group issued the "London appeal" to the G-7 nations, endorsing a research program in biological functions "expected to contribute to advanced information-processing technologies, and the solution of various problems such as serious diseases, environmental pollution, and depletion of food resources."[31] In reality, the London appeal was no more than a compromise lumping together different Japanese and American ideas on the direction the project should take. MITI and STA still had a great deal of work to do in building an international consensus for their vision of a program clarifying biofunctions in living organisms. This consensus was eventually reached in the meetings of the International Feasibility Study Committee, discussed later in the chapter.

In short, the research themes proposed by Japan raised legitimate concerns in the West about Japanese motivations in proposing the HFSP. Japan was clearly hoping for a program with commercial applications. Nevertheless, its initial proposal at the Tokyo conference left the actual design of the program to an international committee of life sciences specialists. In ceding control to such a group, MITI virtually eliminated any potential for relative gain.

Deflecting Foreign Pressure

Foreign pressure is apparent in every stage of the development of the HFSP from initial planning to the funding of the established program. At the Tokyo conference in January 1987, U.S. delegates attempted to shift the direction of the program toward developing-world issues. Six years later, the U.S. government also tried to link its financial support of the HFSP to increased Japanese funding for the Superconducting Supercollider (SSC). In both instances, however, Japan largely ignored American pressure. Although diplomatic considerations and the lobbying of European governments unquestionably influenced Japanese decisions on the site for the HFSP Organization and the nationality of the first secretary-general, foreign pressure did not always produce the results intended by foreign governments.

In general, the HFSP found a more sympathetic audience in European than American scientists at the Tokyo conference.[32] The Japanese scientists who participated in the meeting acknowledge that the support of their European colleagues was motivated, in part, by the goal of using the HFSP as leverage to increase European Community funding of bioscience research.[33] U.S. delegates at the conference criticized the Japanese plan as too unfocused for the modest level of funding proposed. With the National Institutes of Health (NIH) funding life-science research on a scale over one hundred times greater than that of the HFSP, Japan would do better to fund "non-NIH-style" research. The Japanese reply to this criticism was that NIH programs were neither international nor interdisciplinary.[34] American Nobel laureate Joshua Lederberg argued that the HFSP should apply molecular-level approaches to the study of tropical diseases and other "orphan" problems confronting developing nations. This argument was also rejected by the Japanese, who believed that the United States was trying to push the HFSP research agenda toward developing-world issues in order to limit the possibility of commercial applications.[35]

After agreement was finally reached on the design of the HFSP, the next challenges were deciding the location for the program headquarters and choosing the first secretary-general. Making these choices involved a number of tradeoffs. To emphasize the internationality of the HFSP, STA felt strongly that the headquarters should be located overseas. The first offer to house the HFSP office came from the UK, where the Medical Research Council offered one of its buildings rent-free. STA and MITI were eager to accept this proposal because many academics speak English and a quick decision would have made possible an announcement at the G-7 Summit in Paris during July 1989. Before they could act, France and Italy submitted offers.

France lobbied particularly hard to become home to the HFSP, with President Mitterand personally approaching Nakasone on the matter while in Japan for the funeral of Emperor Hirohito.[36] The city of Strasbourg in France also outbid the English by offering free utilities and the salary of one secretary. The final decision does not seem to have been made, however, simply on the basis of the subsidies offered by the UK and France. It did not escape MITI that firms like Toyota and Nissan had made major investments in the UK. In contrast, France had attracted considerably less Japanese investment, and trade relations with France, as a whole, were more strained.[37] In choosing Strasbourg rather than London as the site for the HFSP headquarters, Japan decided that a Briton should become the first secretary-general of the HFSP. After Britain's first candidate was rejected on the grounds that he was not a biologist, the position was given to Sir James Gowans, an immunologist who had served for ten years as head of Britain's Medical Research Council. The choices of location and secretary-general thus balanced immediate financial considerations with diplomatic sensitivity to the interests of member nations whom it was hoped would become major contributors to the HFSP.

Much to the chagrin of Japan, the United States made no financial contribution to the HFSP during 1989 and 1990 and contributed only $40,000 in 1991 and again in 1992. Indeed, the U.S. government did not make a major contribution to the HFSP until the future of the SSC seemed to rest on a major input of Japanese capital. According to George Brown, then chairman of the House Committee on Science, Space, and Technology, "they have some projects of their own that we've been a little less than forthcoming on. . . . They'll expect a little quid pro quo in terms of support for their human frontiers program."[38]

In his November 1991 visit to Japan, Allen Bromley, director of the White House Office of Science and Technology Policy, announced that the U.S. decision to support the HFSP was in no way connected to Japanese support for the SSC. The United States would continue to support the HFSP even if Japan chose not to support the Supercollider.[39] In closed meetings, however, Washington made a direct linkage between support for the SSC and the HFSP. According to one U.S. official, Bromley essentially told the Japanese, "we'll give you $2 million for the HFSP if you give us $1.5 billion for the SSC."[40] In any case, the United States announced a $3.5 million contribution to the HFSP only three months after this ultimatum without any further commitment from Japan on the SSC. Indeed, Japan never pledged anywhere near the amount hoped by the United States before the SSC project was terminated in 1994. Thus, Japan sidestepped U.S. pressure to link funding for the HFSP to increased Japanese support of the SSC.

Facilitating Interdisciplinary and Intercontinental Collaboration

According to Sir James Gowans, the first secretary-general of the HFSP Organization, the complexity of research on brain functions and other HFSP research themes makes international collaboration a necessity. Unlike traditional grants from national agencies, which tend to place heavy restrictions on the use of funds that can inhibit such collaboration, HFSP grants are much less restrictive and so allow international teams of researchers maximum flexibility in planning and coordinating projects.[41] Designed by scientists for scientists, HFSP grants fund international collaborations among researchers that in the majority of cases would otherwise be impossible.

Yet, the scientific rationale for an international research program in the life sciences was far from clear in early Japanese discussions of what was to become the HFSP. The 1986 report of the Ishizaka kenkyūkai, which first proposed a Human Frontier Program, emphasized the need for Japan to make a greater contribution to international science, but did not present a compelling explanation of the necessity for a collaborative program in the life sciences. The report cites the European Laboratory for Particle Physics (CERN) as a prime example of the trend toward international cooperation in the funding of large-scale projects. Yet, the Ishizaka kenkyūkai's laundry list of research projects to develop robots and improved software shares very little with the huge capital investments necessary in the construction of basic research facilities like particle accelerators. In the Ishizaka report, international cooperation is not simply a means to an end but an end in itself.

The need to bring together complementary scientific capabilities was articulated by an international group of scientists rather than by the Japanese bureaucracy. After the Tokyo conference in January 1987, Japan continued consensus building with the formation of the International Feasibility Study Committee (IFSC), which brought together thirty-four eminent scientists nominated by the G-7 nations and the Commission of the European Communities. The IFSC discussed program activities, research areas, and the most appropriate implementation scheme for the HFSP. To support the discussions of the IFSC, STA commissioned the Nomura Research Institute to survey the main features of life-science research programs at foreign research institutes, and to poll foreign scientists on their suggestions regarding needed improvements in existing research programs. The respondents showed a preference for long-term grants given to international teams that would maximize the opportunity for creativity while minimizing administrative burdens.[42] After meetings in November 1987 and March 1988, the IFSC decided the HFSP would be of most value as a grant program supporting basic research on the biology of living organisms. The basic framework of the HFSP was thus decided by an international group of scientists rather than by Japanese bureaucrats. Although MITI and STA realized their goal of a project focusing on biology, they found the emphasis had shifted from applied to basic research.

First Lessons in Managing International Collaboration

Financial support of the HFSP has been a disappointment for all concerned. Japan's financial commitment has never reached the initial expectations of the other G-7 nations, while the latter have not supported the program to the extent that Japan had hoped. The disappointment of Western nations stems from the high level of funding originally proposed by MITI and the relatively small amount that has actually been budgeted. According to a former STA official, the budget projection of roughly $7 billion over twenty years that was originally released to the press was no more than MITI's "vision." This vision in no way represented the official position of the Japanese government. At that stage in planning, research areas were not specified and program activities had not been defined. When the Japanese government's official HFSP proposal was sent to other G-7 countries in May 1989, the initial Japanese budget appropriation was less than $20 million.[43]

At the outset of the HFSP, Japan seemed optimistic that the budget could be increased to between $60 and $100 million annually, with half the total coming from Japan.[44] Actual budgets have fallen far short of this target. At the HFSP Intergovernmental Conference in 1997, member nations announced the intention of increasing non-Japanese contributions in order to bring the total annual budget to $60 million by 2002. However, HFSP failed to meet even this more modest goal. In 2002, Japan accounted for 64 percent of the $50.7 million contributed by member nations. Over the years 1989 to 2002, total national contributions to HFSP were: Japan ($449.3 million), the United States ($49.6 million), France ($20.2 million), Germany ($16.1 million), the European Union ($13.1 million), the United Kingdom ($8.3 million), Switzerland ($6.1 million), Canada ($5.2 million), and Italy ($3.4 million).[45] As these numbers make clear, the HFSP would not exist without funding from Japan.

Arguing that any nation willing to contribute should be allowed to join the organization, Japan has been eager from the start to increase the budget by expanding membership in the HFSP. The first request for membership from outside the G-7 came from Switzerland immediately after the establishment of the program. Although Japan voted to accept the Swiss offer, other member nations insisted guidelines for the introduction of new members should be established first. Drafted in April 1990, these guidelines require that the scientific capabilities of every potential member nation be assessed by the Council of Scientists, and that the appropriate financial contribution be decided case-by-case by the Board of Trustees. Using these guidelines, the Swiss offer was rejected on the grounds that an annual contribution of $150,000 was insufficient to justify positions on the council and board. Less than a year later, however, Switzerland became the first HFSP member from outside the G-7 with a contribution of roughly $400,000 per year.[46]

The irony in rejection of the initial Swiss offer of $150,000 was that the United States and the UK had not contributed any funds to the HFSP as of that time. The first U.S. funding for the organization came with an in-kind contribution to support any researcher awarded an HFSP fellowship to work at the NIH. With only a handful of researchers likely to work at the NIH, however, the size of the U.S. contribution was expected to be a few hundred thousand dollars at most.[47] The United States did not begin making a more substantial financial contribution to the HFSP until 1993.

A major concern of foreign governments in the early years of the HFSP was that Japan's central role in financing the program might translate into a decisive political influence in program management. In fact, with the possible exception of two early conflicts, Japan avoided any interference in management of the HFSP. One of the early areas of tension in program management was the balance of power between the Council of Scientists and the Board of Trustees. At the outset, the UK questioned the need for two governing bodies. After heated debate, however, all representatives accepted Japan's proposal that there needed to be both: a board to set basic policy and a council of scientists to set research objectives. Central to this compromise was the proviso that the board could not override purely scientific decisions made by the council. However, the distinction between scientific and general policy issues was never clearly defined. This subsequently became a source of conflict.

When the council proposed that the workshop aspect of the program be eliminated and the funds be used to award more fellowships, the idea was rejected by the Japanese members of the Board of Trustees. According to Dr. Joseph Rall of the NIH, who was head of the Council of Scientists during this time, the board's decision was inappropriate for two reasons. First, the council decided on scientific grounds that the workshops did not provide the same degree of benefit as the fellowships; thus, the by-laws of the HFSP would support the council over the board on this issue. Second, the decision was not open to full debate among members of the board. Rather, it was railroaded through the board by its chairman, Hiromichi Miyazaki, in his effort "to control the HFSP."[48] Rall's comments suggest not only a reversal of the intended balance of power between the council and board, but the inappropriate intervention of a Japanese official in management of the HFSP. Again, however, this view rests on the interpretation that eliminating the workshops was a scientific rather than policy issue, a view not shared by the Japanese.

The most potentially divisive conflict came in the so-called Wada-Gowans debate, which provided a second test of Japan's claim to hands-off project management. The debate concerned a disagreement on the meaning of "interdisciplinarity" in the context of HFSP research. In a June 1992 letter to *Nature*, Dr. Akiyoshi Wada, a former dean of natural sciences at Tokyo University and chairman of the IFSC, wrote of his concern that the program was drifting from its original emphasis on innovative, interdisciplinary research.[49] Wada argued the IFSC had selected research areas that intentionally avoided fields with their own journals and professional societies such as developmental biology and immunology. He stated that collaboration with mathematicians and physicists could stimulate the creation of new concepts in biological research. He also suggested that certain individuals involved in the management of HFSP were trying to narrow the focus of the program to conventional themes by claiming that "molecular" fields were too broad and that there were consequently too many research proposals to review.

Wada's letter was seen by many as a criticism of the leadership of Sir James Gowans. Japanese officials were particularly unhappy with what they perceived as Gowans's attempt to change the direction of the HFSP. According to Japanese staff in Strasbourg, he favored a narrower focus for the program and believed interdisciplinarity referred only to the interaction between traditional fields such as cellular and developmental biology. The same Japanese staffers claim to have heard Gowans call Japan's notion of interdisciplinarity "nonsense."[50] The Japanese felt that Gowans did not understand the spirit of the HFSP because he had not been a member of the IFSC. They were vexed that someone who had not taken part in developing the research objectives of the HFSP might be trying to change them.

Gowans and several prominent members of the Council of Scientists counter that he never suggested the HFSP should be narrowed or changed in any way. This group explains that there was never any disagreement between Gowans and Wada at all. The so-called Wada-Gowans debate was based on a misreading of the minutes from meetings of the Council of Scientists during March and May 1991.[51] At the March meeting of the council, a French representative suggested that, in view of the number of excellent research proposals, it might be better to narrow the focus of the molecular-approaches theme in order to reduce the rejection rate for applicants. According to Wada, several members of the council objected to this idea but a report of the meeting drafted by Gowans and later presented to the HFSP Board of Trustees implied that the council had endorsed the change.[52] Gowans argues that the views recorded in the minutes are those of the various council members and not his own. Gowans also points out that the matter was resolved by the council at its May meeting. After taking all arguments into consideration, the members of the council agreed that it was too soon to make changes in the priority areas of HFSP research.

The facts surrounding the tensions between Wada and Gowans are unclear because prominent members of the council sided with each man. According to a council member, the pro-Japan sympathies of John Maddox, then editor of *Nature*, also tended to confuse the situation.[53] Although disagreement remains over the facts of the Wada-Gowans debate, it is clear that any problems were resolved by scientists rather than bureaucrats. A breakdown in project management was averted without Japan resorting to hands-on management of the HFSP.

Contributions to Japanese and International Science

For Japan, the HFSP has value on several levels. To a modest degree, it gave Japan greater credibility as a nation willing to contribute to basic research. Of more tangible benefit, it provided both bureaucrats and scientists important experience in dealing with the international scientific community. Every Japanese scientist and bureaucrat interviewed for this chapter views the HFSP as a significant move up the learning curve of internationalization. Many Japanese researchers were encouraged to apply by the high profile of the HFSP in Japan and so gained much needed experience in writing funding proposals. Japan's national universities were traditionally funded according to a standard input model based on the number of faculty and research chairs. Until the 1990s, and the expansion of MESC's grants-in-aid program, little money was available from other domestic sources to fund research. As a result, many Japanese scientists had no experience in applying to competitive funding programs. Several Japanese proposals in the early years of the HFSP read like a textbook on the history of science rather than a clear exposition of a research project.[54] In providing a new source of funding, the HFSP played a part in freeing researchers from dependence on the rigid *kōza* system in Japanese universities. This system, which places junior faculty members under the control of a senior professor, has been notorious for stifling the creativity of young researchers.[55] As discussed earlier, the HFSP also forced greater flexibility in tax rules and other bureaucratic guidelines governing funding for Japanese researchers.

In addition to bringing Japanese researchers together with their foreign counterparts, the HFSP also gave Japanese bureaucrats their first experience in organizing international scientific collaboration. More than one foreign scientist involved in the early stages of the program characterized the first MITI bureaucrats dispatched to Strasbourg as incompetent and unable to work with the female support staff. According to one scientist, "the universal experience in Strasbourg was that the Japanese who were associated with the program did not know how to conduct themselves in an international setting."[56] The HFSP also made Japanese bureaucrats more aware of the need to improve the domestic infrastructure for foreign researchers. Japanese applicants have faired well in grant and fellowship competitions, but only a handful of foreign researchers have elected to use their awards in Japan. For example, of the 1,015 long-term fellowships awarded to non-Japanese over the years 1989 to 1998, only 11 were used in Japan.[57] While the language barrier remains a problem, Japan simply has fewer world-class university labs than the United States and many European nations. With the Second Basic Plan targeting life science as a priority, and MESC initiating the Centers of Excellence program in 2002, this situation may improve over time. In any event, the reform of the Japanese university system will have to produce dramatic results for the nation to become a more attractive location for significant numbers of Western researchers.

The HFSP is also regarded as a success by the international scientific community. It remains the only substantial source of funding for international collaboration in life-science research in which recipients are not chosen in direct proportion to their government's contribution to the fund. According to Dr. Mary Clutter, former assistant director of biological sciences at the NSF, the value of the research performed with these grants has never been in question.[58] Indeed, five HFSP grant recipients from four countries —working in physics, biology, and medicine—were awarded Nobel Prizes during the 1990s. In 1995 and 2000, the University of Manchester's Policy Research Group on Engineering, Science and Technology—an organization with a strong reputation in auditing scientific institutions—conducted external evaluations of the HFSP. Both evaluations agreed that the HFSP has several unique features among science support programs and succeeds in fostering important research that is intercontinental, interdisciplinary, and usually outstanding in quality. As an illustration of the quality, published articles based on HFSP research have roughly 20 percent higher citation rates than the average for other articles in the same journals. In addition, the HFSP articles also have a slightly higher citation rate than other publications by the same authors.[59]

According to a 2000 survey of HFSP grant recipients, almost 90 percent believed no other program could have funded a similar project in terms of cross-continental collaboration and interdisciplinary research. Almost 50 percent of grantees stated that the research could not have been done at all without the HFSP. Moreover, 70 percent found the program more flexible than domestic grant programs as grantees are able to switch money among salaries, equipment, and supplies as necessary. The grant dimension of the HFSP is more unusual than the fellowship dimension. Almost 75 percent of HFSP long-term fellows believe that they could have obtained a similar research position at their host lab without HFSP support. Nevertheless, 66 percent of this group chose an HFSP fellowship over the alternatives owing to the higher level of funding, the greater flexibility in the use of funds, and the prestige of the award. Thus, although the HFSP fellowship is considered highly desirable, this component of the program is clearly not as novel as the grant component.[60]

Despite the very positive external reviews of the HFSP, the program has not generated the same enthusiasm abroad as it has done in Japan. According to Elizabeth Neufeld, professor of biochemistry at UCLA, the HFSP is the premier program for those wishing to fund international research teams in the life sciences and an excellent source of postdoctoral candidates. She adds, however, that researchers are concerned more with the product—research funds—than with the mechanism that provides those funds. For the most part, the HFSP is simply another possible avenue of funding.[61] Although the contribution of the HFSP to the international community is by no means insignificant, the scale of the program is far too small to impress the world with Japan's commitment to basic research.

—————Chapter 5—————

The Intelligent Manufacturing Systems Initiative

In October 1989, a committee of Japanese academics and corporate executives brought together by MITI proposed an international research program in manufacturing technology called the Intelligent Manufacturing Systems (IMS) Initiative. Under the leadership of Dr. Hiroyuki Yoshikawa of Tokyo University, the so-called Yoshikawa *kondankai*, or roundtable, proposed a leap beyond computer-integrated manufacturing to research on a next-generation production system that would maximize efficiency by integrating the entire range of business activity from order booking through design, manufacture, and distribution.

At first, the IMS proposal received a cold reception from Western governments that perceived the program as an attempt to access Western capabilities in software and systems integration. Washington and Brussels were particularly disturbed by the vague terms of the proposal and the fact that Japan had directly approached foreign firms and universities about their participation. Arguing that Western interests were not sufficiently represented in the evolving framework of the program, both Washington and Brussels asked MITI to place a moratorium on IMS in the spring of 1990. Two years of negotiations followed before the parties agreed to a feasibility study that would develop modalities for international collaboration and then evaluate those modalities in test-case consortia.

The IMS framework evolved significantly over the years from 1990 to 1995. What began as a MITI-sponsored initiative incorporating international participation in planning and evaluation became a fully international program with management and funding responsibilities distributed among Australia, Canada, the European Union, Japan, and the United States. IMS represents a departure from previous international research programs in applying elements of Europe's Framework and EUREKA programs on a global scale.[1] Establishing the basic parameters for the program, the IMS member regions agreed on technical themes, guidelines for protection of intellectual property rights, and the requirement that each consortium must have partners from at least three IMS regions. Working within these broad parameters, firms could develop their own research proposals.

The search for complementary capabilities across regions played a major role in driving the IMS initiative forward during the early 1990s. At each step along the way, American and European pressure played a decisive part in shaping the program. Although the majority of IMS projects are still underway, partners in completed projects report many benefits from participation including improved efficiency and cost reductions in their businesses as well as the creation of common platforms for benchmarking. Nevertheless, they also encountered problems in coordinating funding across regions and ensuring that partners made balanced contributions to projects. Despite its shortcomings, the decentralized management and funding structure developed in IMS seems to provide the most likely model for any global-scale, industrial research collaboration that might be undertaken in the future.

An Umbrella Organization for Industry-Led Consortia

IMS is not simply a departure from earlier MITI research programs but a unique experiment in international R&D collaboration. Firms and universities have the freedom to assemble their own consortia within the broad parameters of the IMS framework, which establishes eligible technical themes, regional membership requirements, and guidelines for protection of intellectual property rights. Developing the IMS framework required overcoming suspicions of Japanese motives in proposing the program, as well as different regional research interests and attitudes regarding government support of industrial research programs.

Building a Framework for Collaboration

The IMS framework was designed by an International Steering Committee (ISC), which met six times between February 1992 and January 1994. The committee was composed of five members each from Australia, Canada, the European Union, the European Free Trade Area, Japan, and the United States. The majority of ISC members were corporate executives, at the vice-presidential level or above, from major firms like ICI, Daimler-Benz, Motorola, Rockwell, Toshiba, and Toyota. Working under the ISC were the International Technical Committee (ITC) and the Intellectual Property Rights Committee. The former recommended technical themes for the feasibility study and developed criteria for selecting and evaluating test-case proposals. The latter developed guidelines for the creation, protection, and equitable dissemination of intellectual property rights.

The third leg of the management structure was formed by five regional secretariats: MITI, the Commission of the European Communities Directorate-

General XIII (later Directorate-General III), the U.S. Department of Commerce, Canada's Department of Industry, and Australia's Department of Industry, Technology, and Regional Development. The secretariats disseminated program information, circulated expressions of interest among potential partners, and organized the various committee meetings. The work of the regional secretariats was supported by private organizations including the IMS Promotion Center in Japan, the Coalition for Intelligent Manufacturing Systems (CIMS) in the United States, the IMS Ad Hoc Group in the European Union, the Industrial Advisory Council in Canada, and the Industrial Research and Development Board in Australia.

The basic modalities of the IMS program were established during the first two meetings of the ISC. The committee agreed that each test case should have partners from at least three of the five regions, and that prospective partners must show how contributions to, and benefits from, each consortium would be equitable and balanced. The ISC further agreed that test-case consortia should have significant industrial participation and that the set of test cases should address as many phases of innovation as possible. The committee stipulated, however, that projects using government funds should involve only precompetitive research. To assist potential applicants in submitting proposals, the ITC identified six general areas as technical themes for the feasibility study: enterprise integration, global manufacturing, system component technologies, clean manufacturing, advanced materials processing, and human and organizational issues. In addition to establishing technical themes, the ITC also developed criteria for the midterm and final assessments of the test cases.

Perhaps the greatest challenge facing IMS planners was devising a framework to manage intellectual property rights (IPR). The IMS program divides IPR into two categories: background rights existing prior to the commencement of an IMS consortium, and foreground rights created during IMS research. With the intent that firms not use their background rights to block partners from using foreground intellectual property generated in an IMS project, IMS guidelines require that background rights be licensed on normal commercial terms when those rights are necessary for the commercial exploitation of foreground intellectual property. The guidelines further propose that foreground intellectual property should be owned by the party or parties generating it and licensed on a royalty-free basis for R&D and commercial exploitation to other partners in the same project.

The IMS rules on IPR represented a departure from those in MITI programs in that the Japanese government acquired no ownership of intellectual property through its provision of funding. The rules also broke new ground on a more general level with mandatory provisions on licensing to third parties and disclosure requirements that aim to eliminate obstacles to participation in IMS.[2] To encourage the diffusion of IMS results, sole owners of intellectual property may license rights to third parties nonexclusively without accounting to other partners. Likewise, a joint owner may also license intellectual property to third parties without the consent of, and without accounting to, co-owners, unless otherwise agreed. To reduce concerns about potential conflicts in enforcing these IPR provisions, IMS requires that all parties provide advance notice to partners of government requirements that might affect their compliance with these provisions. Furthermore, to reduce worries that IPR expressly licensed to one entity may be transferred to an affiliate of that entity, thereby helping a competitor, the IMS rules also require partners to disclose, at the beginning of the project, all relevant affiliates.

After establishing the basic framework for collaboration, IMS planners set about testing the framework in a feasibility study of pilot projects that would shed greater light on the costs and benefits of organizing R&D collaboration on a global scale. After regional evaluations, eleven proposals were submitted for consideration by the ISC. Of the six projects selected as test-case consortia, three disbanded following the feasibility study while the three others went on to become consortia in the full-scale program. Although the test cases that disbanded did so for slightly different reasons, money was a factor in each decision. In the case of the clean manufacturing test case, for example, the Japanese coordinating partner thought potential results too long-term, while the European partner went on to develop a smaller regional project outside the IMS framework. In the rapid product development test case, a lack of government financial support and the costs of supporting academic partners were key factors in the decision of the American coordinating partner to end the project. Three of the test cases decided to submit applications to become consortia in the full-scale IMS program, and subsequently received "fast-track" approval from the ISC.

A survey of all participants in the IMS feasibility study, conducted by the ITC, suggests that the test-case partners were, on the whole, able to identify projects requiring international collaboration and overcome any cultural differences in managing consortia with "equitable and balanced" regional contributions. In the ISC's final report on the feasibility study, Australia, Canada, the European Union, Japan, and the United States agreed that IMS is a "catalytic facilitator for global manufacturing cooperation" that enhances standardization and dissemination of information on developments in manufacturing technology, by bringing together large and small firms, universities, and public authorities in global consortia.[3] Based on the results of the test-case consortia, the ISC concluded that international collaboration through the IMS framework "provided added value which outweighed additional overheads incurred through collaborating on a global scale."[4] Making only minor revisions in the terms of reference that governed the feasibility study, such as a streamlining of the IMS committee structure, the ISC recommended the launch of a ten-year, full-scale IMS program.

The ISC's enthusiastic endorsement of the IMS program must be viewed in context. After spending significant time and energy on the development of the program, the members of the ISC had a vested interest in seeing the feasibility study judged a success. More important, as the ISC itself acknowledges, the survey nature of much of the test-case research did not provide a real test of crucial aspects of research collaboration such as provisions for the protection of intellectual property rights. For example, the IPR provisions dealt with methods of determining substantive rights but not with methods of dispute resolution.[5]

In short, there are limits to what any feasibility study can actually demonstrate. As an executive at one American partner wryly noted, "having a nice honeymoon is no guarantee that your marriage is going to work."[6] Nevertheless, the ISC's recommendation for a full-scale program was by no means a foregone conclusion. This was a consensus rather than majority decision reached by an industry-led committee of thirty representatives from Australia, Canada, Europe, Japan, and the United States. The mere fact that consensus could be reached among a group such as this suggests that industry saw potential in the program. Although some Japanese firms might have considered participation in IMS as a way to reaffirm the "internationalization" of the Japanese economy, the program had no such public-relations value for foreign firms. That several foreign companies have taken part in the full-scale program suggests they consider IMS as a useful supplement to in-house research.

Participation and Funding

After a gestation of five years, a planned ten-year IMS program was launched in April 1995. At the end of 2002, the IMS portfolio included fourteen completed projects, twenty-three ongoing projects, and sixteen proposals awaiting endorsement. With budgets ranging from $1 million to $50 million, the ongoing projects brought together a total of 234 partners. On average, IMS projects have partners representing three regions, with 60 percent of partners drawn from industry and 40 percent from the research community. The average duration of projects is three years. More than half the projects emphasize process and assembling issues, virtual manufacturing, and monitoring and control technologies. Most others deal with flexible and autonomous modules for manufacturing systems.[7]

In view of the relative size and technological level of IMS regions, participation has been fairly well balanced with the share of partners from each region as follows: Australia (6.5 percent), Canada (3.8 percent), Switzerland (8.7 percent), European Union (44.5 percent), Japan (18.5 percent), Korea (3.6 percent), and the United States (14.3 percent).[8] Overall, the participation figures reflect the relative size of the regions and differences in the availability of funding across regions. The figures also illustrate the enthusiastic European response to IMS as well as the more cautious American response. It is noteworthy that European Union participation in IMS has exceeded Japanese participation since the late 1990s. And more important, the European Union has also become the originating region of the majority of project proposals in the review pipeline. Thus, the origins and makeup of IMS consortia increasingly reflect the techno-globalist rhetoric of the program.

In the early 1990s, Yoshikawa and other IMS planners hoped for a program that would commit more than one billion dollars to manufacturing research. As it turned out, plans for the program became more modest over time. At the end of 2001, a total of only $353 million had been committed in ongoing or completed projects.[9] Some regions have dedicated funding for IMS participants while others simply consider IMS-related proposals in their more general grant programs. Whatever the arrangement, movement of funds across regions is not permitted; all funds to support the administrative activities of the regional secretariat and the research activities of participants must come from within a given region.

In Japan, members of the IMS Promotion Center have access to a fund that covers half the total cost of participation in an IMS consortium. The total amount of funds available has hovered around only $11.5 million since 1997—a modest amount for large-scale projects funded by METI.[10] In the United States, $47 million in federal money was set aside for IMS in 1991. However, this budget line disappeared before the start of the full-scale program. Washington took the view that American firms should fund their own participation in IMS because it is an industry-run program. Nonetheless, government funds subsidized U.S. hosting of the Inter-Regional Secretariat during 2002–4. In the European Union, firms can submit an IMS proposal to the Framework Program. During the Fifth Framework Program, both the Competitive and Sustainable Growth and User Friendly Information Society themes accepted IMS proposals. During 1997–98, a total of seventy-two proposals were submitted for evaluation. Of these, sixteen were awarded a total of nearly $34 million. In 2001, the European Union selected thirteen out of thirty-three proposals for a total of roughly $21 million in funding. The only condition is that the European module of the project must be feasible as a self-standing European effort.[11]

Beyond the triad, each of the smaller regions has dedicated funds for IMS in place.[12] Swiss firms apply for funding through the same mechanism as their European Union counterparts. They are able to take part in all European R&D projects but are not allowed to propose or lead projects. Rather than receiving money directly from the European Commission, however, Swiss partners in successful proposals receive support from a Swiss government fund that sets aside roughly $1.4 million per year. Australia has a mix of IMS-specific funds available through the regional secretariat and general R&D support programs. The regional secretariat offers seed funds for consortium formation activities to SMEs and research organizations. In addition, the Department of Industry and Science runs a competitive grant program, with a particular emphasis on SMEs, that offers successful applicants 50 percent support for project costs. Canada offers perhaps the widest range of funding sources for IMS. In addition to the National Research Council and National Sciences and Engineering Council, provincial bodies offer funds for IMS. As in Australia, there is a particular emphasis on funds for SMEs. The Industrial Research Assistance Program offers up to 50 percent support for successful SME applicants taking part in IMS. The bigger challenge for Canada was securing public support for the regional secretariat. As a result, in 1998, IMS Canada became a self-sufficient entity supported by corporate membership fees.

Forces Driving Internationalization

A Project Free of Turf Wars

Bureaucratic politics played no role in motivating or shaping the IMS program. The research proposal for IMS focused on manufacturing technologies that fell squarely within the regulatory domain of MITI's Machine and Information Industries Bureau. Thus, MITI made no effort to expand its bureaucratic turf through IMS. As a result, the IMS program did not generate the conflict with other ministries that is predicted by bureaucratic politics explanations of technology policy. University researchers reported no friction with the MESC because of their participation as fully subsidized partners in IMS consortia. In fact, engineering departments tend to enjoy the closest relationships with industry because of the applied nature of their research.[13] Leading construction firms like Shimizu also reported no opposition from the Ministry of Construction to their participation in IMS. In this case, there was no overlap at all in regulatory domains. Construction machinery and technology had always been regulated by MITI rather than the Ministry of Construction.[14] Thus, there was very little opportunity for bureaucratic conflict in the planning stages of IMS.

Fears of IMS as a Trojan Horse

The IMS proposal was perceived by many in the West as simply the latest Japanese effort to access and indigenize superior Western technologies. Indeed, the polished marketing of IMS led many to see the program as the most sophisticated and, therefore, most insidious implementation of technonational ideology yet. According to a foreign official who attended the initial IMS briefing in January 1990, MITI had clearly learned from the experience of the HFSP. IMS brochures were written in clear English and offered concrete examples of the potential benefits to foreign participants. Also, by avoiding involvement with other ministries that had delayed the launch of the HFSP, MITI would be able to move more swiftly to accomplish its goals.[15]

The IMS proposal was labeled a Trojan horse by those who saw Japan's offer to "share its pre-eminent manufacturing technology" as a thinly guised attempt to access Western capabilities.[16] These suspicions were based on three broad concerns: Japan's decision to contact private organizations as well as government agencies; the terms of collaboration initially proposed by Japan; and the relative national positions of Japan, the United States, and the European Union in key manufacturing technologies.

Government officials in the United States and Europe were angered by the fact that Japan discussed IMS with several private organizations rather than dealing with them alone. George Heaton notes conflicting reports as to which parts of the U.S. government were actually contacted regarding IMS and how they might have responded.[17] According to Dr. Yuji Furukawa, who made the first contacts about IMS, the goal of initial discussions was to gauge the interest in collaboration of American and European engineers who would best be able to understand the goals of the program.[18]

In November 1989, Furukawa visited the National Academy of Sciences and the Society of Manufacturing Engineers in the United States before moving on to Europe where he met with officials from Directorate-General XIII of the Commission of the European Communities, and the UK Department of Trade and Industry, among others. Furukawa explains these meetings as unofficial contacts because IMS was at that time only a draft proposal without any official endorsement or commitment of financial support from MITI. In fact, Furukawa received no travel subsidy from MITI and was forced to arrange funds through the Japan Machine Tool Builders Association.

During this trip, Furukawa proposed that the Society of Manufacturing Engineers (SME) become the point of contact in the United States for any future IMS program. As head of the Japan chapter of SME at the time, Furukawa explains the decision as a natural outgrowth of personal contacts and SME interest rather than as part of a deliberate strategy to marginalize the potential role of the U.S. government. While the academic origins of the IMS program give credence to this interpretation, MITI was not completely absent from the process. According to a MITI official, "we knew that the Department of Commerce was not highly respected by industry so we also approached firms and industry associations directly."[19]

Government officials in both the United States and Europe rejected the notion that the discussions on IMS were informal contacts. Deborah Wince-Smith, then assistant secretary for technology policy at the Department of Commerce, requested that MITI desist from approaching the private sector directly. The U.S. government insisted that any discussion of large-scale collaborative programs take place within the framework of the U.S.–Japan Science and Technology Agreement. MITI countered that IMS was envisioned as a multilateral program and so did not fit within the bilateral framework of that agreement.[20] Meanwhile, Directorate-General XIII argued that any international program involving public funds was de facto a government program and must therefore involve some supervisory role for governments.[21] Both Washington and Brussels asked firms that had already agreed to take part in IMS to withdraw from the program until a more appropriate framework for collaboration had been developed.

Four drafts of the IMS proposal appeared between November 1989 and May 1990. The "Version 1" proposal brought by Professor Furukawa to the United States in November 1989 set out potential research themes but did not lay out a framework for IMS. The "Version 2" proposal, distributed in January 1990 to coincide with meetings that formally introduced the IMS Program to Japanese industry and officials from foreign embassies, was still vague on major aspects of project organization, but stated that the final design of the program should be left to an international committee as had been done earlier with the HFSP. However, the proposal did not specify the location of the main administrative office for the program, raising fears that a central office located in Tokyo would give Japan control over an immense storehouse of knowledge.[22] These fears seemed to be confirmed in April with the establishment of the IMS Promotion Center in Tokyo. Together with a "Version 3" proposal, the IMS center issued an international call for research proposals and scheduled the official launch of the program for September 1990.

These events created the distinct impression among foreign governments that Japan was trying to present the terms of IMS as a fait accompli. As George Heaton notes, "the program seemed to be developing altogether too rapidly, with non-Japanese interests underrepresented, and basic control aspects—overfunding and intellectual property—ill-defined."[23] Based on these concerns, Washington and Brussels asked MITI to place a moratorium on the program until government-level consultations had taken place.

In preparation for a trilateral meeting in Brussels during May, the IMS center distributed "Version 4," which presented a more detailed proposal on project organization and a first draft of guidelines on intellectual property rights. Beginning with the disclaimer that it represented only "a basis for discussion" with the United States and the European Union, Version 4 proposed the creation of a management committee with members drawn from government, industry, and academia, and a technical evaluation committee with members drawn chiefly from academia. Version 4 also proposed that a joint research center, which would serve as the hub of research activities, should be located in the United States or the European Union.[24] This particular proposal was premised on the belief that some part of the research results would be in the form of tacit know-how not easily transferred, and so a greater share of benefits would accrue to the host country than to Japan.[25] Although the European Union pushed to drop the idea of a central research facility in later discussions, Japan's proposal to locate the lab overseas was a clear response to foreign pressure and the criticism that Japan could contribute more to the international stock of scientific and technological knowledge.

In addition to reservations over the organization of the project, there were other foreign concerns regarding funding and protection of intellectual property rights. Both the United States and European Union balked at the notion of Japan providing 60 percent of IMS funding. Although both had been pushing for greater funding of science and technology research by the Japanese government, the idea was more unsettling in practice than theory. Feeling that balanced benefits were most likely to be achieved between partners of equal weight, the European Union called for decentralized consortia with each participant being financed from within its respective region. The United States shared these concerns, arguing that each partner should bring technology and not simply money to the project. In addition to the shared preference for a program of equal partners, both Washington and Brussels worried that pooling of funds would further complicate the challenge of designing intellectual property guidelines for such a large-scale, multicultural collaboration.

The IPR guidelines proposed in Version 4 were a second major source of concern for foreign governments. Suggestive of the academic origins of the IMS proposal and MITI's deliberate low profile, the IPR guidelines were drafted by Professor Furukawa, an engineer, rather than by lawyers. American and European officials were disturbed by the lack of explicit protection mechanisms for both background and foreground information and by terms that encouraged as wide an application as possible of research results. Version 4 proposed, for example, that academic and public research institutions should transfer ownership of intellectual property resulting from IMS research to an international IMS organization in order to maximize potential access to the data.

As IMS had been promoted with the idea of Japanese firms sharing their hardware expertise, these firms were also very concerned by the vagueness of the guidelines. Expressing the fears of Japanese firms, Tetsuya Oishi of Toyo Engineering stated that "our ability to offer production technology is contingent on the establishment of a system to protect IPR. If that occurs, interest in IMS will expand."[26] Another major area of concern for both foreign and Japanese firms was the emphasis placed in Version 4 on Dr. Yoshikawa's ideas about the need for systematization of manufacturing knowledge. Declaring that production technology should be the "common property of mankind," Version 4 called for the integration and systematization of production technology for the shared use of the industrialized world.[27] The concern of American and European officials was that systematization of manufacturing knowledge would simply make foreign technologies easier for Japan to access and indigenize. Yet, it is important to recognize the divergent views within Japan itself regarding systematization. The idea has its roots in academia and has never been widely understood or supported by Japanese industry.

Knowledge systematization lies at the heart of Dr. Yoshikawa's vision of the manufacturing industry of the twenty-first century. The idea is more an academic theory of paradigm change than a pragmatic strategy of technology indigenization. Ascending to the presidency of Tokyo University and later the directorship of AIST, Yoshikawa is one of Japan's most respected academics. Yet, his notion of knowledge systematization received a less than enthusiastic reception among corporate executives. In the words of one Toshiba executive, Yoshikawa's theories have a "dream-like" quality.[28] In short, the fact that knowledge systematization became only a very minor part of the IMS program has less to do with foreign moves to purge technonationalistic elements of the Version 4 proposal than with the lack of corporate interest, among even most Japanese firms, in the systematization of manufacturing knowledge.

On the issue of relative technological position, American and European critics of the IMS proposal did not accept Japanese claims of leadership in computer-integrated manufacturing (CIM). Mark Lieberman, then deputy assistant secretary for technology policy at the Department of Commerce, stated the original IMS proposal would not have produced a "balanced, symmetrical, win-win situation," and that "most of the benefits would have flowed in a direction which our companies are not very comfortable with." Fred Nichols of the National Coalition for Advanced Manufacturing argued that American university research driven by NASA and Department of Defense requirements was more sophisticated than Japanese research in such areas as visual simulation, artificial intelligence, and sensor technology that are crucial to CIM.[29]

One of the earliest and most vocal European critics of the IMS proposal was CECIMO, an association of machine-tool builders, which complained to the European Commission that the program would simply transfer know-how from European firms to their Japanese competitors.[30] One of the major European fears was that Japan would gain access to Western advances in computer-integrated manufacturing and then flood European markets with standardized parts. In July 1990, the European Commission circulated a draft report comparing European and Japanese manufacturing capabilities. The report acknowledged that Japan led in the rapid conversion of designs into manufactured products but attributed this advantage to cultural factors that could not be readily reproduced in the West. The report also suggested that Japanese claims of superiority over Europe in many areas of computer-integrated manufacturing were based on the mistaken belief that European technologies licensed through U.S. distributors were actually American technologies.[31]

In addition to suspicions that IMS was designed to access superior Western technologies, there was concern that IMS was an attempt to impose Japanese factory automation standards on the rest of the world, and so reinforce the dominant market positions held by Japanese makers of machine tools, robots, and programmable controllers.[32] Thus, paradoxically, IMS was viewed as both a stratagem to steal the technologies of Western firms and an attempt to impose more advanced Japanese standards on those same firms. One clearly mistaken fear, in view of the proposed budget for IMS, was that European firms had no choice but to join the program because the amount of money the Japanese were willing to spend would end up wiping out other CIM projects.[33]

In short, the IMS proposal generated several suspicions in the United States and European Union about Japanese motives. Although some of these suspicions appear groundless on close inspection, the proposal itself was vague enough on key issues such as protection of intellectual property rights to raise legitimate concerns. That Japan directly approached firms and universities rather than first working with government officials lends credence to the techno-national ideology interpretation of IMS. Undermining this argument, however, is the fact that the initial proposal also left important details of project organization to be decided by an international committee. In this sense, ambiguity rather than a clear techno-nationalist strategy was the main problem in Japan's IMS proposal.

Foreign Pressure as Catalyst and Constraint

Foreign pressure played an important part in motivating and shaping the IMS program. This is evident in both American diplomatic initiatives to promote collaboration in manufacturing technology and the consistent reference to trade friction and criticisms of "free riding" in official and unofficial Japanese discussions of IMS. The role of foreign pressure is even clearer in shaping the ultimate form of the IMS program. MITI initially hoped for IMS to begin in the autumn of 1990. However, American and European insistence on reshaping the proposal and conducting a feasibility study resulted in protracted negotiations that delayed the launch of the full-scale program until May 1995.

The United States had actively sought to establish linkages with Japan in manufacturing technology prior to IMS. In 1986, the National Science Foundation (NSF) approached the Japan Society for the Promotion of Science (JSPS) about establishing a project to encourage bilateral collaboration in manufacturing research. Teams of academics and corporate executives from both countries met during 1988 and 1990 to discuss themes and management structures for collaboration. At the 1988 meeting, both sides agreed that sensor, control, and computer integration technologies were strong candidates for joint research and decided to develop joint programs in these areas.[34] Thus, the NSF initiative served as a catalyst for bilateral collaboration three years before the IMS proposal.

The second application of foreign pressure to open the Japanese manufacturing industry came during 1988 with negotiations on the revision of the U.S.–Japan Science and Technology Agreement. Manufacturing technology was one of seven fields designated in the agreement as a priority area for development of collaborative projects. However, it was Japan rather than the United States that first tabled the idea of a five-year joint project in manufacturing during these negotiations. Although technological complementarity was a major impetus to Japanese interest in collaboration in manufacturing technology, as discussed next, the weight of foreign pressure in motivating IMS is reflected in all Japanese discussions of the program.

In both official and unofficial Japanese discussions of IMS, the need for Japan to ease trade frictions with the West and make contributions to international science and technology commensurate with its economic strength is consistently emphasized. The final report of the Yoshikawa kondankai, which makes the first official mention of plans for IMS, cites trade frictions and the need for greater international contribution before discussing the technological forces motivating a collaborative research program.[35] The way IMS was presented to the international community also suggests a desire to maximize the public-relations value of the program. Architects of the IMS proposal described the program as a sharing of *tora no ko*, literally translated as "tiger cub," or Japan's most treasured technology.[36] The role of foreign pressure in motivating IMS was also not lost on the Japanese press. In its comprehensive coverage of the early stages of the program, the *Nikkei Sangyō Shimbun* consistently mentions the role of foreign pressure, on one occasion stating that "IMS is more to reduce trade friction than to increase Japan's international contribution."[37] Yet, perhaps, the most cynical testimony to the role of foreign pressure comes from a Hitachi executive, who although maintaining the technological importance of the program to his firm, stated that "MITI cared less about the substance of the program than the fact that it was international."[38]

Both the United States and the European Union played a major role in shaping the ultimate form of the IMS Program.[39] In April 1990, Washington and Brussels each asked MITI to stop making direct contact with firms and industry associations until government officials had agreed to a framework for further discussions. The following month representatives from MITI, the U.S. Department of Commerce, and Directorate-General XIII of the European Commission met in Brussels and agreed to suspend the original MITI proposal. They also agreed that the decision to proceed with IMS could only be made after all three parties reached consensus on modalities for collaboration, research themes, intellectual property rights provisions, and funding arrangements.

A follow-on to the Brussels meeting was scheduled for July 1990 but later postponed as government-industry consultations continued in the United States and Europe. By late summer, the Department of Commerce had drafted a counterproposal based on the results of two IMS workshops organized to canvass the views of industry. In addition to specifying areas of potential collaboration, the counterproposal stated that each party should have equal voting rights and control over the composition of financial and other regional contributions.[40] Soon after, the European Union issued its counterproposal for a Future Generation Manufacturing System. The European Union agreed that consortia should be decentralized, with each participant financed from within its own region. It also called for a feasibility study to work out appropriate modalities for collaboration and provisions for the protection of intellectual property rights.[41]

The American and European counterproposals formed the basis of discussions at a second tripartite meeting held in Tokyo in November 1990, which was also attended by observers from Australia, Canada, and the European Free Trade Association. At this meeting, the American, European, and Japanese delegations agreed to conduct an IMS feasibility study. After a year of further consultations with industry, Australia, Canada, the European Union, Japan, and the United States, adopted Terms of Reference establishing the parameters of the feasibility study.

Western Interest in Complementary Capabilities

Underlying foreign interest in reshaping the IMS program were opportunities to advance manufacturing technology through the pooling of financial resources and the matching of complementary national capabilities. The Version 4 proposal cited six trends that it claimed challenge the foundation of the manufacturing industry in every industrialized society: the diversification of consumer needs, the globalization of manufacturing, the appearance of isolated islands of manufacturing, the hollowing out of industry, the changing labor environment, and the insufficient systematization of existing technology.[42] The first three trends reflect the short-term concerns of firms while the latter three reflect broader societal and academic concerns.

The heart of corporate interest in IMS is responding to the challenges posed by globalization and the diversification of consumer needs. At the management level, firms face new technological challenges as they attempt to coordinate the entire range of corporate activity from research to delivery on a global basis. To date, firms have used information technologies to automate specific processes. IMS envisions connecting such processes in a seamless thread. At the factory level, firms confront the challenge of designing "variable-kind variable-lot" production systems that can respond quickly to custom orders and changing demand. In the long run, IMS sees a shift from present make-to-stock and sell-from-stock practices to manufacturing only the products wanted in only the quantities wanted.

In addition to these corporate concerns, the Version 4 proposal also cited broader societal challenges common to the advanced industrial economies. The first challenge is the hollowing out of local manufacturing capabilities as firms transfer production abroad in search of cheaper labor. Fear about the hollowing out of the Japanese manufacturing sector during the late 1980s was one of the most important factors driving the IMS proposal.[43] The second challenge is bolstering the deteriorating image of the manufacturing sector as students, and even trained engineers, seek employment in sectors offering higher wages. The proposal also cited the need for increased systematization of knowledge reflecting Dr. Yoshikawa's belief that manufacturing knowledge can be systematized in databases to facilitate technology transfer.

Both the United States and European Union agreed the trends identified in the Version 4 proposal represented common challenges to the manufacturing industries of the advanced industrialized nations. As a result, subsequent IMS planning documents drafted by an international committee cite these same trends as well as the additional challenge posed by the need for the manufacturing industry to preserve natural resources and the environment. The idea of using IMS to address the environmental impact of manufacturing was suggested initially by the European Union. Although this idea played an important public-relations role in providing a concise explanation of IMS to those outside the manufacturing community, research on environmental themes did not initially generate significant interest among firms.[44] Nevertheless, following the midterm evaluation in 2000, IMS decided to place greater emphasis on research in clean technologies. In part, this was to keep in step with the European Union, which made sustainable development a more explicit objective of the Framework Programs.[45]

On the whole, there was broad international agreement on the challenges confronting the manufacturing sector but uncertainty in Washington and Brussels as to whether IMS would be an effective means to address those challenges. Version 4 argued that IMS would not only eliminate redundant R&D investment by unifying standardization initiatives, but would also develop better technology by leveraging national strengths through international collaboration. The proposal suggested that IMS could combine Japanese expertise in hardware, such as machine tools and robotics, with American expertise in software and network technology and European expertise in precision machinery.[46] This idea met with cautious reactions from Japanese industry as well as foreign firms and governments uncertain about how to achieve balanced exchange.

The strongest base of support for IMS came from Japanese firms active in the Yoshikawa kondankai during the summer of 1989. Among these were major electrical equipment makers like Hitachi and Toshiba as well as construction firms like Shimizu and Kajima.[47] The IMS proposal was announced to Japan's manufacturing industry at a January 1990 forum attended by over 130 members of the International Robot and Factory Automation Center (IROFA) and the Japan Industrial Robot Association (JIRA).[48] By April 1990, an IMS Promotion Center had been established within IROFA. While the latter is an industry association funded entirely by firms, the former is a *tokushu hōjin*, or special legal entity, funded on a fifty-fifty basis by MITI and membership dues from firms. Within four months, sixty firms joined the IMS center, although many still harbored reservations about the program.

Yutaka Matsumura of Hitachi-Seiki stated that many firms opposed the high membership fee of one million yen or roughly US$7,000 per month. He explained that his firm was taking part in IMS only to gain a better sense of the technological direction being taken by the larger firms in the program.[49] In the same vein, Seiuemon Inaba of Fanuc stated that his company "might provide basic technology in an IMS program but would not release existing know-how."[50]

Despite corporate reservations, the IMS center began a domestic feasibility study in February 1991.[51] Firms organized eighteen test-case consortia, two of which would later become test cases in the international feasibility study. The domestic study was organized to prepare candidate consortia for an international program and to retain momentum until the international IMS program began. Certain firms were dismayed by the delay in beginning the international program and wanted some return on their membership dues in the meantime.[52] MITI reassured the firms that IMS would operate as a national project if the United States and European Union decided to reject the Japanese proposal—another indication that the program was more than a simple response to foreign pressure.

The international response to the Version 4 proposal suggests that despite serious reservations regarding the exact terms of collaboration, both foreign firms and governments saw potential for meaningful technological exchange. Thus, the clearest indications that complementary technological capabilities played an important role in the launching of IMS lay not in Japanese pronouncements, but in the initial interest of foreign firms and the efforts of foreign governments to build on the proposal. In response to the initial call for research proposals in April 1990, the IMS Promotion Center received almost one hundred submissions with sixty-eight coming from Japan, fourteen from the United States, twelve from Europe, and one from Australia. Of these proposals, fifty-six came from firms and thirty-nine from public research institutes.[53] In the United States, United Technologies and Rockwell Automation led the formation of an ad hoc industry group whose members included Digital Equipment Corporation, General Motors, and TRW. The ad hoc group met several times in 1990 to discuss American interests in IMS and dispatched representatives to consult with Japanese firms like Fanuc and Toyo Engineering about potential areas of collaboration.[54] It was also the ad hoc group that asked the U.S. government to take a leadership role in the negotiation of an effective framework for protection of intellectual property rights.

Among the firms that came together in the ad hoc industry group, some have gone on to be active in IMS while others have not. During the feasibility study, executives from both United Technologies and Rockwell served on IMS committees and each firm also acted as the regional coordinator in an IMS test-case project. According to Stan Krueger, former president of United Technologies Japan, "the risks of participation in IMS are quite low so why wouldn't you at least try? The only people who will lose are those who do not play."[55] James Christensen explains that Rockwell joined IMS principally to augment its understanding of emerging standards. "As world leaders in standardization for industrial process and measurement control, we need to understand the types of standards which will be required in the next century.[56]

Although Rockwell went on to take part in two IMS consortia, United Technologies participation in IMS ended after the feasibility study. In addition to absorbing the higher than anticipated management costs in the rapid product-development test case, United Technologies ended up subsidizing the participation of American universities. According to Richard Aubin, who coordinated the clean manufacturing test case, "the involvement of United Technologies was in many respects a giveaway. The firm learned a great deal from the project but also paid a considerable sum for this knowledge. Without a partial subsidy from the U.S. government or a clearer tie-in with the needs of UTC working divisions like Otis and Pratt & Whitney, the firm could not justify further participation in IMS."[57] Although some early proponents became discouraged with IMS, several major American firms including Black & Decker, Caterpillar, Chrysler, Ford, General Motors, and Westinghouse subsequently joined IMS consortia.

Even though many American and European firms recognized the potential for important technological complementarity in the Version 4 proposal, government officials were more concerned about protecting broader national interests and the vitality of national manufacturing industries. As discussed earlier, Washington and Brussels had reservations about specific terms of collaboration, and they were also concerned about how much technology Japanese companies would bring to the program. Although several major firms like Hitachi, Toshiba, and Toyota were charter members of the IMS center, other major manufacturers like Matsushita and Sony were much slower to join.[58] Despite such concerns, however, the United States and European Union worked to reshape the IMS proposal into a framework closer to that of EUREKA. This suggests that reservations about IMS concerned the terms of collaboration rather than a lack of potential for mutually beneficial collaboration.

Although there was no history of Japan–E.U. collaboration in manufacturing technology prior to IMS, serious discussion of U.S.–Japan research collaboration in this area predates the IMS program by four years. In 1986, the NSF and the Japan Society for the Promotion of Science (JSPS) opened talks that produced a 1988 agreement to develop joint programs in product realization and intelligent manufacturing control—two concepts at the core of IMS. With substantial crossover in both technical themes and the personnel involved on the Japanese side, the IMS proposal is in many ways an outgrowth of the NSF-JSPS discussions.

The United States and the European Union were not the only ones to see potential technological benefits in IMS. Although Japan initially proposed IMS as a tripolar collaboration with the United States and European Union, several other nations including Australia, Canada, Korea, and the European Free Trade Association (EFTA) countries expressed interest in joining IMS. For these countries, with their smaller manufacturing industries, the potential benefits of participation in IMS far outweighed the risks. Thus, technological opportunities were clearly the driving force behind their requests to join the program. In the case of Canada, for example, Michael Wilson, then minister for industry, explained that "the question of learning and adopting these techniques is literally one of survival."[59]

Decisions about which countries outside the triad should be allowed to take part in IMS reflect political as well as technological considerations. According to a Japanese source, the United States pushed to broaden membership beyond the triad in order to weaken the voice of Japan in managing the program.[60] The least controversial membership decisions involved Canada and EFTA, which appeared as natural extensions of the United States and European Union, respectively. Indeed, the European Union and EFTA subsequently combined resources to form one regional European secretariat. Much more controversial was the decision in the early 1990s to allow Australia but not South Korea to participate.

Although not regarded as a major manufacturing nation, Australia gained admittance to IMS largely because of its status as a G-7 nation. The initial exclusion of South Korea from IMS was perceived by some Western firms and journalists as Japan's attempt to keep at bay a major regional rival. Kenzo Inagaki, former director of MITI's industrial machinery division, offers another explanation: Korea was not technologically advanced enough to participate in IMS.[61] The IMS Steering Committee concurred that South Korea did not fit the profile of other IMS members. Although Korean *chaebol* (conglomerates) like Hyundai and Samsung had made major strides in exports of automobiles and electronics beginning in the mid-1980s, Korea had yet to become a member of the OECD or the World Intellectual Property Organization (WIPO).

By the late 1990s, South Korea had joined both of these organizations and in 2000 was accepted as a de facto member of IMS pending the European Union's official approval procedures. The timing of this decision was somewhat ironic, however, as the Asian financial crisis had severely weakened the Korean manufacturing sector and sent several *chaebol*, including Daewoo and Kia, into bankruptcy.

Managing Industrial R&D Collaboration on a Global Scale

IMS provides firms, universities, and research institutes with a framework for collaboration on a global scale. Because all IMS proposals require partners from three regions and a coordinating partner from industry, there is a basic assurance that the program will be international in scope and driven by the needs of industry. Proposals must also include a signed consortium cooperation agreement and an intellectual property agreement. Thus, partners have the chance to consider both division-of-labor and legal issues before joining a project. To help facilitate the formation of consortia, IMS offers model cooperation agreements and IPR guidelines, as well as a partner search facility to match interested parties. Ultimately, the proposal must be approved by a panel of experts in each of the participating regions. Thus, IMS also provides some assurance of quality for accepted proposals.

In theory, the structure of IMS should benefit a range of entities. For example, small and medium-sized enterprises have the opportunity to "go global" in a cushioned environment; universities gain exposure to state-of-the-art information for curriculum development; large firms have the chance to develop closer links with a range of corporate and academic partners in an industry-driven environment; and finally, governments have the potential to earn a better return on public funds in projects, addressing environmental and other problems, that are better suited to an international rather than national setting.[62] IMS partners identify several benefits of their participation in IMS, including creating technological complementarity, cost reductions, improved customer-supplier links, and common platforms for benchmarking. In a survey of the twenty-three consortia underway at the end of 2002, for example, six of the lead partners reported cost savings of 20 to 70 percent resulting from their projects while four reported increased sales. In terms of intellectual property generated, partners reported filing thirty-five patent applications and receiving eleven patents. A total of 164 copyrights had also been granted to project partners. Overall, 96 percent of respondents rated their project as successful, while 74 percent were considering a second phase or spin-off from their project.[63] A more complete understanding of the potential of the IMS framework requires a closer look at the experiences of partners in projects of varying degrees of ambition and success.

Early Challenges in GNOSIS and Globeman

With its roots in Yoshikawa's theories of paradigm change in manufacturing, the research agenda of the knowledge systematization or GNOSIS consortium came closest to the original vision for the IMS program. The consortium was nevertheless marked by a disparity between Yoshikawa's vision of long-term change and the shorter-term interests of industrial partners. GNOSIS sought to move the manufacturing industry toward a "post-mass-production paradigm" in which more flexible and reconfigurable "soft factories" produce modular and reconfigurable "soft products" that reduce both resource utilization and waste.[64] In the short term, the post-mass-production paradigm envisions a more environmentally friendly manufacturing industry that also meets the growing demand for more customized products. Theoretically, in the long run, the ultimate goal of soft manufacturing would be to extend the life of each modular component "indefinitely" without breaking the pace of progress in the functions that form the system. Thus, the transition to the post-mass-production paradigm would represent a revolutionary leap beyond small-batch customized production to a manufacturing industry that grows based on the demand for renewal and maintenance.[65]

Although researchers at the University of Tokyo continued to explore the notion of paradigm change over the five years of the project, most corporate partners had little interest in the long-term theories underlying GNOSIS. According to an executive at a Japanese partner, "the idea of an eternal, soft product is stupid."[66] Nevertheless, firms saw merit in some of the short-range goals of the project. Pressed by increasingly restrictive environmental laws, Japanese firms from the electrical machinery and construction industries researched modular design and recycling techniques, while a smaller number of European firms worked on the development of next-generation, reconfigurable manufacturing systems or "virtual factories" able to respond quickly to changing customer preferences. In all, the GNOSIS consortium brought together twenty-two partners from three regions led by Mitsubishi Electric (see Table 5.1).

GNOSIS began as one of the test-case consortia during the feasibility study. In off-the-record comments, several participants suggest that this was actually the most successful phase of the project in terms of international collaboration. All partners were enthusiastic about cross-regional collaboration and funding was available at the same time in each region. Partners in each region issued software tools to partners in other regions to test in their own businesses, and thus generate new data for the refinement of these tools. Ironically, the firms found more opportunities for international collaboration

Table 5.1

Partners in the GNOSIS Consortium

IMS region	Partners
Canada	University of Calgary
Europe	ADEPA, Asea Brown Bovari, IBM France, ILOG, Fraunhofer Institute, Schroff, Swiss Federal Institute of Technology, Tampere University, Tehdasmallit Oy, University of Magdeburg, VTT
Japan	Chiyoda, Mitsubishi Electric, Kajima Construction, National Center for Science and Information Systems, Shimizu Construction, Sumitomo Electric, Tokyo Institute of Technology, Tokyo Metropolitan University, University of Tokyo, Yamatake-Honeywell

Source: GNOSIS Consortium, *Knowledge Systematization: Configuration Systems for Design and Manufacturing*, Final report (March 2000), pp. 19–20.

than they could manage. One of the major lessons of the test case was that it is crucial to consider the costs of technology transfer for both donor and recipient rather than simply the potential for technology transfer itself. With the initial success of the test case, the partners hoped to begin work on a full-scale project within months. However, funding issues and different ratification mechanisms in the different regions created major obstacles. Although the full-scale GNOSIS project officially began in 1996, the European partners were not able to obtain final funding approval from the European Commission, and resume an active role in research, until late 1998—more than halfway through the planned project. The GNOSIS proposal did not fit European Union funding priorities, so the European partners had to significantly revise their proposal to obtain European Union support. In short, regional funding and ratification procedures made the coordination of cross-regional research very difficult.[67] In the words of one partner, "the delays sapped enthusiasm for the project before it could even get off the ground."[68]

Despite the obstacles to international collaboration GNOSIS did achieve some results on a regional basis. Asea Brown Bovari, Europe's leading electrical engineering group, developed a virtual factory demonstrator for a switch-gear factory that reconfigures the production line in response to supply-chain disturbances and changes in customer demand. In Japan, partners from the construction industry expanded work on modular construction and tools to optimize resource allocation in multiple projects in order to increase productivity and reduce environmental impact. Meanwhile, electrical machinery makers developed ecological design-support systems that are now being applied in the development of new products. However, the level of commitment to GNOSIS and the benefits from the project varied widely across regions and partners.

The third largest of Japan's comprehensive electric machinery makers, Mitsubishi Electric (MELCO) was the principal coordinating partner for GNOSIS. Dr. Eiichi Ohno, managing director of headquarters R&D in the early 1990s, was a strong proponent of the IMS program and sat on the ITC during the feasibility study. With his support, MELCO took a leading role in setting up the GNOSIS consortium. As the full-scale program began, however, the lab managing the project became frustrated with the theoretical orientation of the consortium. It soon decided to focus on eco-design research that had real connections to ongoing work in the company while at the same time fitting within the basic GNOSIS framework.[69] Disposal and recycling of electrical appliances is becoming a pressing issue for Japanese firms. During the mid-1990s, environmental legislation was introduced in Japan requiring manufacturers to work with local authorities in finding solutions to disposal problems. Manufacturers anticipate further legislation with take-back ordinances so are now directing increasing resources to disassembly and recycling technologies. However, the task of disassembly is far more complicated than it might at first seem because different models and variations of products must be disassembled using the same machines. As part of its GNOSIS research, MELCO developed a "design-for-environment" tool that uses computer-assisted design data to generate a disassembly sequence for products and provides guidelines for more ecological and economical redesign of the same products.

Other than the design-for-environment tool, MELCO has not realized many concrete results from GNOSIS. In part, this was because there was never a close connection between GNOSIS and MELCO's R&D strategy. From the outset, the firm's attitude was "to keep a hand in and experiment with a new form of collaboration." Unfortunately, however, funding differences between Japan and the European Union undermined this experiment in collaboration. MELCO shared some tools with Chiyoda and Osaka University during the project but feels that the consortium was mostly partners doing their own research and then trying to make it fit within the general framework of the project. In addition, the manpower commitment in Japan and the European Union was very different. Most of the Japanese firms had at least three researchers working full time on the project while ABB and IBM France had only one or two researchers devoting a small share of their time to GNOSIS. As a result of the difficulties in arranging cross-regional collaboration, MELCO gave little thought to extending the project beyond 2000.

Consistently ranking as one of Japan's top construction firms, Shimizu has been active in IMS since the inception of the program. In addition to drafting part of the final report of the Yoshikawa kondankai, Shimizu joined four test cases in the Japanese domestic feasibility study. The firm generally approached participation in IMS as a way to bolster the research of its engineering division on computer-integrated manufacturing and to raise its profile as a global engineering firm.[70] Joining GNOSIS seemed logical because the firm had been working on some of the same environmental themes, though on a much smaller scale. Shimizu expanded its research on modular construction for prefabricated buildings, combining this work with a management system for design documentation that fit nicely with the consortium's emphasis on knowledge systematization. At most points during the project, Shimizu had twelve researchers spending about 25 percent of their time on GNOSIS research. Like MELCO, Shimizu was pleased with the level of international collaboration during the feasibility study, but most of its potential collaborators in Europe left the consortium out of frustrations with delays in funding. Although Shimizu engaged in a limited exchange of researchers with VTT Automation of Finland, most collaboration was with the University of Tokyo. The firm was also frustrated by the two-year lull in research between 1996 and 1998.

Kajima, like Shimizu one of Japan's top construction firms, also joined IMS early on. The firm joined GNOSIS as a way to finance some long-run environmental research.[71] Kajima does not believe it would have participated in IMS without the research subsidy from MITI. A total of three researchers and one manager spent about 30 percent of their time on GNOSIS research over the life of the project. Also like Shimizu, Kajima worked on modular construction research, which it terms a "kit-of-parts factory." Several of the manufacturers in IMS are working on ways to reconfigure production lines. In turn, Kajima anticipates the need to build more flexible factories that can be reconfigured when necessary to accommodate changed production lines. As part of its GNOSIS research, Kajima also developed Emerald, a design-support tool for the kit-of-parts factory. The Emerald software package helps a contractor to procure recycled and reconfigurable "eco-parts" and to generate a construction schedule. It decides the appropriate supplier to contact on the basis of lead time and environmental impact. The system is programmed to prefer recycled parts to new ones and to consider the transport distance of parts to reduce auto emissions. Kajima sees this tool as the most valuable result of its participation in GNOSIS. The firm began marketing an improved version of the product, known as Xemerald, in 2000.

Like GNOSIS, the Global Manufacturing or "Globeman" consortium began as one of the test-case consortia in the feasibility study. The test case consolidated Japanese and European proposals into a project focused on development of technologies for distributed management and product support by global enterprises. Although several partners left the consortium over time, Globeman still stands as one of the largest IMS projects. Indeed, the partners agree that the consortium was initially far too large. The full-scale project began in 1995 with fifty-two partners and ended in 1999 with thirty-seven partners, twenty-one of them companies and sixteen of them research organizations or universities (see Table 5.2). Although the $13.5 million project brought together partners from five regions, the Japanese and European project leaders did much of the work. The regional breakdown of total person-hours committed to the project makes this clear: Australia (17 percent), Canada (9 percent), Europe (28 percent), Japan (44 percent), and the United States (2 percent).[72]

Japan's Toyo Engineering and Finland's Ahlstrom Corporation played central roles in project management and produced some of the more concrete results in the project. While Toyo is a primary contractor for the design and construction of chemical plants and oil refineries and Ahlstrom is major player in the pulp, paper, and fiber industries, both firms share the challenge of distributed management and support for global operations. Initially, Toyo became interested in IMS because of a global slowdown in the construction business during the late 1980s. The program subsequently introduced the firm to the internet and the future importance of IT tools for global management. By the end of the test case, it became clear that Toyo would have to proceed aggressively with the development of IT management tools if it wished to stay competitive. In the words of a Toyo manager, "for firms like us that have no manufacturing facilities, competitiveness boils down to knowledge and skills."[73] Yet, Toyo found that most of the available tools were not mature enough to coordinate international management of multiple contractors for the construction of process plants. Thus Globeman became a way to work with firms in other industries facing similar challenges. In all, a team of eight Toyo managers and researchers worked full time on Globeman for three years. The team agrees that the MITI subsidy was crucial in getting the project off the ground.

The main results of Globeman were fourteen prototype systems for distributed management and support of global operations.[74] In distributed management, Toyo worked with instrument maker Omron and the construction firm Takenaka on Vridge, a desktop system for the design, procurement, and construction of chemical plants and other global engineering projects. Likewise, Ahlstrom worked with two Finnish partners to develop a collaborative management tool for operation of a pulp mill. In distributed support, Ahlstrom developed technologies for remote process monitoring of an Australian process plant from its offices in Finland. Toyo developed similar technologies

Table 5.2

Partners in the Globeman Consortium

IMS region	Partners
Australia	Broken Hill Proprietary, Commonwealth Scientific and Industrial Research Organization, Farley Cutting Systems, Griffith University, Hawker de Havilland
Canada	University of Toronto
Europe	Ahlstrom, BICC, Fraunhofer Institute, Helsinki University of Technology, Intracom, NCR Norway, Norwegian Institute of Technology, Odense Shipyards, Technical University of Berlin, VTT Automation, YIT Corporation
Japan	Daikin Industries, IBM Japan, Institue of Industrial Science, Japan Society for the Promotion of the Machine Industry, Mazda, Mitsui Engineering and Shipbuilding, Nagoya University, Omron, Ricoh, Takenaka, Toyo Engineering, Toyota, University of Tokyo, Yokogawa Electric
United States	Carnegie Mellon, Newport News Shipbuilding, University of Virginia

Source: Brown and Syntera, eds., *Globeman 21, Global Manufacturing in the 21st Century.*

for the remote monitoring of a urea plant in Indonesia. It considers this its most concrete result in Globeman in the short-term but believes Vridge will have a much broader business impact in the long run. The nature of the collaboration in these projects was typical of that throughout Globeman. Toyo performed the actual research with Japanese partners, and Ahlstrom with Finnish partners, but then the companies shared their results and experiences in order to improve their respective processes.

Although most of the Globeman partners were satisfied with the results of the project, they agreed that the consortium was too large to manage international collaboration—and especially the problem of free riding—effectively.[75] To address this concern, the core partners designed a smaller and more focused follow-on to Globeman called the Globemen project. The three-year project developed a generic IT architecture for global distributed management that can be adapted by member firms in different one-of-a-kind engineering and manufacturing industries such as refinery construction or shipbuilding. The learning curve of the managers is also evident in their handling of funding issues for the follow-on project. As in GNOSIS, research in Globeman was initially hamstrung by funding delays in the European Union. However, deeper understanding of regional differences and closer regional coordination made possible funding in both Japan and the E.U. for the entire length of the Globemen project.

Next Generation Manufacturing Systems

The Consortium for Advanced Manufacturing International (CAM-I), based in Arlington, Texas, is the international coordinating partner of the Next Generation Manufacturing Systems (NGMS) project. Founded in 1972 to develop pre-standards in the field of numerical tool control, CAM-I is a member-supported, international consortium of approximately fifty firms conducting research on management and technical themes related to manufacturing. CAM-I became involved in IMS because of the close fit in the research objectives of the two programs and the participation of CAM-I board members from Japan and Europe on IMS planning committees. CAM-I proposed the NGMS-IMS program as a way to allow more firms to participate in CAM-I research without the obligation of becoming a CAM-I member.

NGMS incorporates a bottom-up view of the factory floor with a top-down view of globally distributed collaboration. It focuses on two challenges in next-generation manufacturing: the move from traditional build-and-test methods to more flexible and cheaper digital simulation technologies and the management of global networks of collaborators. These collaborators may be links in the supply chain of one company or several companies working together in a "virtual enterprise." A temporary alliance between firms, a virtual enterprise, merges the core competencies of different members to produce a complex product or system and then dissolves. The ultimate goal of the NGMS consortium is to provide a blueprint for the integration of simulation and distributed management methods that are increasingly necessary in meeting customer needs.[76]

The first phase of the NGMS project ran from 1996 to 2000, during which time NGMS partners spent roughly $46 million and invested a total of 2,900 person-months on the project.[77] Still underway in 2004, the second phase maintains basic continuity in research themes but with a greater financial commitment and a greater degree of international collaboration. The project has brought together twenty corporate partners from three regions representing the aerospace, automotive, electronics, and heavy-equipment industries among others (see Table 5.3). The partners have met at least quarterly and hold an annual three-day technical conference. In the second phase, the regional distribution of partners is Europe (2), the United States (6), and Japan (11).[78]

One of the early management challenges in NGMS involved the differences in funding mechanisms among the three regions. The Japanese

Table 5.3

Partners in the NGMS Consortium

IMS region	Partners
Europe	Aerospatiale Matra Group, Chalmers University, Fraunhofer Institute, IVF, Nokia Research, Renault, SAP AG, VTT Automation
Japan	Fuji Electric, Fujitsu, Furukawa Electric, Honda Engineering, JGC Corporation, Kawasaki Heavy Industries, Kobe University, Kyoto University, Mitsubishi Heavy Industries, NKK, Osaka University, Sony, Tokyo Metropolitan University
United States	Allied-Signal (Honeywell), Caterpillar, General Motors, MEMC, Oak Ridge Labs, Rockwell Collins, Sandia National Labs, University of Illinois, University of Iowa, University of Tennessee, Vanderbilt University

Source: Consortium for Advanced Manufacturing International, *NGMS-IMS Interim Report.*

partners received matching funds from the IMS Promotion Center in Tokyo but no public support was available to American partners. The European partners were also unable to secure public support because of the difficulty in matching the research planned by NGMS to the European Commission's call for IMS proposals. As a result, the research agenda for the first phase of the project was highly regionalized. All partners agreed that this reduced the potential benefits of international collaboration, and thus a concerted effort was made in the second phase to design international collaborations within the financial constraints of the project. Of the thirteen tasks in the second phase of the program, eight are cross-regional, four are being conducted within the United States, and one is being conducted within Japan.[79]

The increased commitment to the second phase of the project reflects a high level of satisfaction with the early research results. In the biological manufacturing systems theme, for example, a team led by Honda Engineering and Fujitsu developed a model of an auto assembly plant without a traditional assembly line. Rather than a conveyor, the system uses biological algorithms to manage teams of mobile robots that dock with guided transports that carry car bodies through the factory. The researchers found that initial facility costs for a "lineless" manufacturing system are roughly the same as for a traditional assembly line but that the operating costs of the lineless system are dramatically lower because of increased productivity from greater welder availability. Running a traditional assembly line that makes

1,000 cars per day costs roughly \$35 million per year; the lineless system would cost only \$4.3 million per year, a savings of almost 90 percent.[80]

In the scalable and flexible manufacturing theme, Rockwell Collins and the University of Illinois collaborated in developing a tool that will help engineers simulate the design and manufacture of printed circuit boards. The small-batch, custom-design nature of Rockwell's circuit board business requires long set-up times for machines. A simulator that identifies design flaws before production is helpful in reducing machine downtime and so boosting the efficiency of the manufacturing line. This collaboration documented a 30 percent savings in the time from design to manufacture of a working circuit board.[81]

One of the cross-regional collaborations in the first phase of NGMS also showed early promise. The Global Algorithms for Logistics Analysis, Execution and Integration (GALAXI) team is developing a software system to minimize the cost of fleet operations by coordinating manufacturing schedules with the movement of materials among factories spread over a wide geographic area. The team divided work across four regions. Researchers at Rockwell Collins and the University of Iowa worked on basic mathematical models while researchers at Fujitsu and Hyundai Motors looked for methods to link these models to real-world conditions. In the final stage, researchers at Karlsruhe University in Germany will attempt to incorporate factors such as human error into the algorithms. According to Rockwell Collins, this project is far too complex for any one company to carry out individually. The number of calculations in the modeling process increases geometrically with each additional variable. Determining the optimal combination of just six variables requires analyzing 720 possible combinations. But when the number of variables is doubled, the number of possible combinations grows to 479 million. Even with very few factories, types of trucks, and materials, the partners in GALAXI are still dealing with numerous variables in their research. Rockwell Collins estimates that every dollar spent on the project yields about four dollars in value. If the project is successful, the industrial partners anticipate reducing the costs of material movement by roughly 30 percent.[82]

Conclusion

Building on the EUREKA model, IMS is the first program to organize large-scale industrial research collaboration on a global basis. The key issue determining the future applicability of the IMS model is whether the program generates sufficient research results that firms and governments can justify the overhead of organizing research collaboration on such a large scale. From the perspective of the booming dot.com economy in the United States during the late 1990s, IMS seemed bureaucratic and distinctly "old economy." Program administration is monitored by governments and the major American players are manufacturers like Caterpillar and Rockwell. An executive at an American participant lamented that "from a U.S. perspective, where everything is fast-food, progress can be agonizingly slow."[83] A midterm evaluation of IMS by a panel of outside experts in 2000 also concluded that the program was too bureaucratic.[84] In response, IMS has since streamlined its committee structures and procedures. At the same time, the results of projects like Globeman and NGMS suggest that the internet age makes IMS research on global management and product support more important than ever before, and that its cross-regional and cross-industry approach makes more business sense than single-company efforts to reinvent the wheel.

The ultimate arbiters of the success of IMS will be the corporations driving the IMS research agenda and the governments subsidizing IMS management. Although the ability of IMS to produce tangible research results remains the real test of success, the program has been carefully structured to reflect the preferences of both of the above constituencies. First, the leadership role played by industry makes IMS less susceptible to the criticism that the program is simply bureaucratic cooperation. Second, the program's focus on manufacturing cuts across numerous sectors, including automobiles, industrial machinery, and consumer electronics. In doing so, IMS deflects the common criticism that industrial technology programs attempt to "pick winners."

Might IMS therefore be a model for future R&D collaboration? If this is to happen, IMS projects must continue to make progress in overcoming two challenges. The first is learning to coordinate collaborations among subgroups of partners while exploiting the global test bed provided by broader consortium membership. The second challenge is overcoming the funding problems encountered by the first IMS projects. The IMS program initially aimed to facilitate precompetitive research that most firms would be unable or unwilling to undertake alone. Yet, only Japan has always had dedicated funding set aside for participation in IMS. American firms have financed their own participation in IMS and European firms have been locked into the funding cycle of European Union grant programs, which initially led to significant coordination difficulties with Japanese partners. Experience has helped to overcome this coordination problem, as in the Globemen project. In any event, IMS has proved most effective when firms, like the American partners in NGMS, are prepared to undertake a project even without a public subsidy.

——Chapter 6——
The Real World Computing Program

The Real World Computing (RWC) program was a $600 million effort to develop fundamental technologies in next-generation computing. It was MITI's largest electronics project during the 1990s, absorbing almost 20 percent of the research budget of the Electronics Policy Division of the Machine and Information Industries Bureau.[1] The RWC program was a departure from earlier computer consortia in allowing international participation and providing flexibility in research objectives and organization. RWC offered three forms of international participation. The first was the possibility of full partnership for foreign firms and research institutes. Four research institutes—one each from Germany, Holland, Singapore, and Sweden—joined the RWC program as full partners. The foreign partners felt the program was fully open to international participation on equitable terms. They also agreed, however, that it failed to leverage the potential benefits of internationalization for both Japanese and foreign members because of the minimal communication among partners.

The second dimension of international participation was the use of university labs in Australia, Austria, Italy, and the UK as paid subcontractors. The third dimension was the Joint Optoelectronics Project (JOP) between the United States and Japan. This was a relatively limited, brokered collaboration, designed to allay the U.S. fear that its participation in the broader RWC framework would disproportionately benefit Japan. The JOP, based on an American prototyping service for VLSI circuits, represented a new mode of international technology collaboration intended to minimize intellectual property concerns and fears of technology leakage.

As mentioned in chapter 3, the opening of the RWC program was basically a token response to the general American pressure for opening of Japanese R&D; there was little direct pressure for MITI to establish an international consortium in the computer field. Although Japan trailed the state of the art in many RWC research themes, MITI did not design the RWC program as an efficient mechanism for accessing and indigenizing foreign technology. Ultimately, the parallel and distributed computing research in the RWC program proved of interest to American firms and research institutes, but the original RWC proposal offered little incentive for them to join.

The RWC program was a departure from earlier, narrowly focused consortia like the FGCP of the 1980s. The RWC program was an umbrella for a loose grouping of research themes such as parallel and distributed computing, optical interconnections, flexible storage and retrieval of multimedia information, and enhancement of the man-machine interface. Japanese firms were happier with the RWC program than its predecessors because they were allowed much greater freedom in choosing research topics. The RWC program also introduced a number of new management principles including more generous intellectual property rights for members, and the participation of Japanese university labs as paid subcontractors, a practice previously prohibited by the MESC. In short, the RWC program differed from earlier consortia on both the domestic and international levels.

An Open National Consortium

The RWC proposal was developed between 1989 and 1992 by a feasibility study committee of Japanese researchers drawn mostly from academia and MITI's Electrotechnical Laboratory (ETL). In July 1992, MITI formally established the Real World Computing Partnership as a *kenkyū kumiai*, or research association, with an administrative office in Tokyo and a central research facility, the Tsukuba Research Center (TRC), in Tsukuba Science City. Over the course of the project, the TRC became the focal point of research on parallel and distributed computing. The staff of the TRC included roughly twenty-five researchers and ten managers, almost all of whom were seconded from the Japanese partners. Complementing the TRC's focus on parallel and distributed computing, eight labs at MITI's ETL served as the focal point for research on the real-world-intelligence theme.

Sixteen Japanese firms, one Japanese industry association, and four foreign research institutes took part in the RWC program. Although the Japan Iron and Steel Federation left the program in 1997, it was replaced by federation member Sumitomo Metals. With the exception of the Japan Iron and Steel Federation, each partner operated at least one "distributed" lab at its own facilities. The majority of these labs had between three and seven researchers devoting most of their time to RWC research. In addition to funding work at the distributed labs, the RWC program also subcontracted research to as many as forty university labs, about 10 percent of which were outside Japan. At the height of the program in 1999, RWC was funding a total of eighty-one research projects conducted by more than 270 researchers at both partner and subcontractor labs.[2] In the first phase of the project, from 1992 to 1996, roughly 50 percent of the RWC budget went to the TRC, 25 percent to the distributed labs, and 25 percent to subcontracted research and overhead expenses. In the second phase of the project, from 1997 to 2001, budget priorities shifted as the allocation to the distributed labs doubled and that to the TRC fell to 25 percent. The first RWC planning documents suggested that up to 15 percent of the total research budget would be allocated to the foreign partners.[3] With the distributed labs sharing no more than 50 percent of the total budget, however, the four foreign partners received a much more modest share of the funding.

Conventional information-processing technologies rely on predefined algorithms. However, the majority of "real-world" information is characterized by a high degree of diversity and ambiguity that makes it impossible to anticipate all possible situations and prepare algorithms in advance. Solving real-world problems requires the capacity to process a variety of diverse information such as images, sounds, and texts. It also requires systems that can deal with ambiguity and learn from experience. The RWC program hoped to make progress in overcoming the limitations of conventional information-processing in these areas. In its first five years, RWC conducted exploratory research on five broad themes: theory, novel functions, massively parallel computing, neural networks, and optical computing.[4] After the midterm evaluation in 1996, however, the program moved to concentrate research resources in two main fields: real-world intelligent processing technologies and parallel and distributed computing technologies. The former combined work in theory with the most promising areas of research from the novel functions theme. The latter shifted the research emphasis from work on technologies for a single massively parallel computer to work on a "seamless" computing architecture for connecting various office computers, usually used independently, to form a parallel computer when needed.[5] The second phase of the RWC program essentially dropped research on neural networks and narrowed the optical computing theme to work on optical interconnections that would support parallel and distributed computing.

The real-world-intelligence field focused on technologies for processing images, speech, and text in an integrated manner, as well as learning and self-organization technologies that enable systems to adapt and evolve through interactions with people and the environment. This research was broken down into the three main themes of autonomous learning functions in intelligent robots; flexible storage and retrieval of multimedia information using self-organizing technologies; and enhancement of the man-machine interface through integration of multimodal information such as words and gestures.[6]

Development of a system powerful enough to support real-world-intelligence capabilities necessitated a second broad area of work on parallel and distributed processing that aims to achieve greater speed and performance by breaking problems into parts and working on each part simultaneously rather than in sequence. In contrast to the diffuse research goals of the real-world-intelligence theme, the parallel and distributed computing field was development intensive and more focused on a clear-cut deliverable—the world's first seamless computing system. A seamless computing system connects various types of PCs located throughout an office or building via a high-speed communication network, yet appears as a single parallel computer to the user; it enables tasks that previously would have required a supercomputer to be performed in small labs and business offices.[7]

Building a seamless system requires overcoming many obstacles. Even in a single workplace, all workers may not use computers with the same architecture. Workers receive upgraded models as their existing computers become outdated. And new hires usually mean an increase in the number of computers in an office. Thus, software for seamless systems must be able to overcome differences in architectures and also adapt to a changing number of machines in the network; the challenge is to build a software architecture that masks the complexity of the heterogeneous environment. This entailed research on programming languages, compilers, operating systems, libraries, applications, and optical interconnections. With their higher information-carrying capacity, optical interconnections address the electrical "wiring limit" confronting designers of parallel and distributed computers. In addition to three of Japan's major computer manufacturers, each of Japan's major optical-fiber firms conducted research on various forms of chip-to-chip or board-to-board optical interconnections. The various research fields pursued by each of the distributed labs, and the manpower commitment to each lab, is summarized in Table 6.1.

According to Dr. Junichi Shimada, research director of the RWC Partnership, the essential research themes were not too different in the first and second phases of the program. The overly ambitious first phase of the program sought the "vertical integration" of novel functions and massively parallel computing technologies to realize flexible information processing. Owing to the difficulty of integrating hardware and software in this vertical manner, the second phase of the program moved toward a "horizontal" approach of more independent research on the same general themes.[8] Unlike Shimada, many of the Japanese partners saw a clear reorientation in the direction of RWC research; some even characterized the first and second phases of the RWC program as entirely different projects. Nevertheless, all believe MITI saw the midterm evaluation as an opportunity to shift to more applied research that would raise the profile of the RWC program.

Table 6.1

Distributed Labs of RWC Partners by Field (2001)

Real World Intelligence	Parallel and Distributed Computing
Multimodal Functions (28) Hitachi (2), KRDL (6), Mitsubishi Electric (7), NTT (5), Sanyo (3), Sharp (5)	Multiprocessor Computing (24) Fujitsu (13), Hitachi (11)
Autonomous Learning Functions (23) Fujitsu (8), Mitsubishi Research Institute (7), SNN (6), SICS (2)	Parallel Applications (16) Hitachi (3), Mitsubishi Electric (4), Mitsubishi Research Institute (3), Sanyo (2), Toshiba (4)
Self-Organizing Information-Base Functions (27) Hitachi (4), KRDL (10), Mitsubishi Electric (6), Toshiba (7)	Seamless Parallel and Distributed Computing (79) a) Systems Fujitsu (7), GMD (3), NEC (26), Sumitomo Metals (7)
Theoretical and Algorithmic Foundations (30) GMD (7), NEC (6), SICS (6), SNN (7), Toshiba (4)	b) Optical Interconnections Fujikura (4), Fujitsu (4), Furukawa (3), Hitachi (6), NEC (6), Nippon Sheet Glass (3), Oki Electric (7), Sumitomo Electric (3)
Real World Adaptive Devices (13) Matsushita (4), NEC (9)	

Source: "RWC Project as Proved by Data," *RWC News*, June 2000, p. 19.
Note: The number of participating researchers for each theme and lab are shown in parentheses.

Forces Driving Internationalization

The bureaucrats and academics who planned the RWC program never defined a clear rationale for why the project necessitated international collaboration. The opening of the RWC program to foreign participation was more of an afterthought than an essential element of project research or organization. As in MITI's other international programs, bureaucratic politics played a negligible role in the opening of the RWC program. In fact, tensions between MITI and the MESC eased considerably after the planning of the FGCP. For the first time, with the RWC program, the MESC allowed university researchers to participate in a consortium that fell squarely within MITI's traditional regulatory jurisdiction. This decision marks one of the MESC's first steps in fostering greater collaboration between universities and firms— a goal that became central to policy by the late 1990s.

Technological complementarity also played a minor role in driving the opening of the RWC program. Although the RWC addressed several themes found in American and European programs, Japan trailed the state of the art in many of these areas. This fact suggests techno-national ideology as an important motivation for MITI's overture to potential foreign partners. Yet, the design of the RWC program did not provide an efficient mechanism for accessing foreign technologies; thus, techno-national ideology is not very useful in explaining internationalization. Finally, the Western lead in computers meant that there was little pressure for MITI to open a program in this area. The opening of the RWC program was mostly a token response to the more general American pressure for the opening of Japan's R&D system.

An Easing of Tensions Between MITI and MESC

Beyond the generic interest of Japanese bureaucrats in cultivating relations with the private sector that maintain the potential for future *amakudari* positions, bureaucratic politics played very little role in motivating or shaping the RWC program. The research agenda of RWC focused on computing technologies that fell squarely within the regulatory domain of MITI's Machine and Information Industries Bureau. Thus, MITI made no effort to expand its bureaucratic turf through RWC. As a result, the RWC program did not generate the conflict with other ministries that is predicted by a bureaucratic politics explanation of technology policy. In the FGCP, academics did not conduct research but only provided advice through working groups. According to Scott Callon, the MESC steadfastly refused MITI requests to allow academics to take an active research role in the FGCP. The ministry made no such objections, however, regarding the RWC program.[9] Over the course of the program, between thirty and forty university researchers worked as paid subcontractors for RWC. The use of academics as subcontractors was a major departure from earlier consortia. This change was not a reflection of any unique quality in the RWC program itself but of a more general evolution in the relationship between MITI and MESC.

Over a decade passed between the planning of the FGCP and the RWC program. Tensions between MITI and MESC during the planning of the FGCP were subsequently reduced by MESC's easing of restrictions on research cooperation between universities and industry. In 1982, shortly after the launch of the FGCP, the MESC began to promote greater connections between industry and universities in order to strengthen the university infrastructure for research. From this perspective, MESC's allowing university researchers to participate in the RWC program is entirely self-interested. The easing of tensions between MITI and MESC illustrates how broader state interests in technological advancement can help overcome bureaucratic rivalries. As discussed in chapter 3, the Japanese government embarked on a range of efforts during the 1990s to increase returns on public investment in science and technology. These initiatives included strengthening the links between university and corporate research through the creation of Technology Licensing Organizations.

More still needs to be done to break down the barriers to greater academic participation in METI research programs. For example, it remains difficult for Japanese academics to take leaves of absence from their universities in order to work outside their campus laboratories. Although the subcontracting of university professors by the RWC Partnership was qualitatively different from academic participation in the FGCP, it was still not true research cooperation. According to Shimada, there was no sincere attempt to integrate university research into work at the TRC. Professors simply received money to write papers on RWC themes, without having any real obligation to the program. More than anything, hiring academics as subcontractors was a quid pro quo for having them serve on evaluation committees.[10] Since 1997, the MESC has made some progress in increasing the mobility of researchers between institutions. Universities and interuniversity research institutes have had the discretion to introduce fixed-term contracts for researchers, although the balance between fixed-term and continuing arrangements varies significantly among institutions.[11] Moreover, this change has only helped mobility in one direction. The university system is more open to corporate researchers but academics still have difficulty joining projects outside their universities.

Distributed Collaboration and the Limits of Techno-National Ideology

The techno-national ideology perspective, as discussed earlier, suggests that Japan uses foreign partners strategically to maximize potential access to foreign technology and so boost its capabilities. The fact that the RWC proposal focused on many research themes where Japan trailed the state of the art would seem to support such an interpretation of the program. The governments of the United States and several European countries discouraged or prohibited participation in the RWC program, despite the interest of individual researchers, on the grounds that Japan would benefit disproportionately from collaboration. However, several important aspects of the program were not consistent with a strategy geared to technology indigenization. The distributed network of RWC labs limited the potential for technology indigenization while intellectual property rules gave equal patent rights to Japanese and foreign partners.

The United Kingdom and the United States proved most doubtful about the RWC proposal. The massively parallel processing theme generated the most skepticism; according to Paul Refenes of University College, London, the United Kingdom was "wary" of collaborating in massively parallel computing, where it felt it was ahead of Japan. Collaboration was only likely to be considered in areas such as neural networks where national capabilities were more in line.[12] The American computer industry had even more reason to be suspicious of Japanese motives in proposing collaboration in massively parallel processing. The U.S. lead in parallel computing was such that, as of early 1993, all sixty of the general purpose parallel computers installed in Japan were made by American firms.[13]

The RWC's decision to use Intel and Thinking Machines parallel-processing computers as development tools also generated suspicions that MITI was using the RWC program to "dissect" the latest American parallel-processing technology. According to an executive of the RWC Partnership, this strategy was indeed used in the FGCP, which analyzed Digital Equipment Corporation's System 20 computer to help Japanese firms catch up on the basic technology of parallel-conjecturing systems.[14] Thus, the RWC purchase of American parallel computers was consistent with a techno-nationalist strategy of accessing superior foreign technology and diffusing that technology among Japanese firms through a national consortium. It should be noted, however, that university and corporate labs in Europe also bought these same parallel computers but were never viewed with the same mistrust.

In addition to concerns about the relative gains likely to accrue to Japan from American participation in the RWC program, the U.S. government was troubled that MITI made direct overtures to American firms and universities rather than proceeding on a purely intergovernmental level. After being approached by ETL officials in 1990 about the possibility of taking part in a follow-on to the FGCP, Bell Labs president Ian Ross contacted the Office of Science and Technology Policy (OSTP) to express his concerns about the Japanese proposal. The OSTP felt it more appropriate that any discussions should proceed on an intergovernmental basis under the framework of the U.S.–Japan Science and Technology Agreement.

According to Dr. Eugene Wong, then associate director for industrial technology at the OSTP, RWC was not a benign basic research program. "It started out being fairly esoteric but became very practical, very commercializable."[15] The official U.S. government position was that U.S.

researchers were free to take part in the RWC program. Yet, at the very least, Washington discouraged participation. In order to make potential participants aware of intellectual property and import-export licensing issues involved in the RWC program, the U.S. government asked MITI to forward any inquiries received from U.S. firms to the Japan Technology Program at the U.S. Department of Commerce.[16] Several American researchers suggest, however, that Washington did even more to restrict participation in the RWC program. According to Michael Arbib, a specialist in neural computing at USC, the OSTP made it clear that he should not think of making any arrangements with the RWC independently. Likewise, Sing Lee, an optical computing expert at the University of California, San Diego, said officials in Washington advised him it would be "very dangerous" to accept money from MITI. Lee feared that taking part in RWC could jeopardize his federal research grants.[17]

According to a U.S. official, the simple question was "what's in it for us?"[18] The consensus in the U.S. government was that RWC research was likely to benefit Japan more than the United States.[19] For Wong, it was only natural that the original Japanese proposal would favor Japan. "This would be a natural assumption, not a surprise, a threat, or any type of impediment to collaboration. American initiatives are intended to benefit the United States to the greatest degree possible."[20] The task for the OSTP was to identify aspects of the RWC program that would be useful to the United States and develop them in a framework that would minimize potential losses from collaboration. In meetings with the OSTP, representatives of industry suggested that the MOSIS model of brokered collaboration, pioneered in the prototyping of VLSI circuits, would provide a transparent mechanism for controlling bilateral flows of technology and so help diffuse suspicions in interfirm collaborations. The specifics of the OSTP's efforts to shape a collaborative project in optoelectronics are examined in the next section as a part of the discussion of foreign pressure.

Although certain research themes seemed to be consistent with a strategy of technology indigenization, the design and management of the RWC were not. As discussed in earlier chapters, first, the foreign partners were allowed to choose the RWC themes in which they wished to participate, and so were not locked into any unwanted collaborations. Second, geographic distance and the distributed structure of the consortium limited interaction and potential information exchange between Japanese and foreign labs. The foreign partners felt that RWC failed to leverage the potential benefits of international collaboration because of the project's distributed structure. They felt isolated because of a lack of contact with other labs rather than threatened by Japanese efforts to access their expertise. Third, the system of brokered collaboration in the U.S.–Japan Joint Optoelectronics Project was designed by the United States and clearly reflected the American preference for "technology access without acquisition." Fourth, intellectual property guidelines, which allowed foreign partners partial, and later full ownership of patents, reduced the opportunity for Japan to reap greater gains from collaboration.

From the outset, the RWC program took advantage of amendments made in March 1991 to the Law Concerning Improvement of the System for R&D in the Field of Industrial Technology.[21] Under the previous law, all patents resulting from publicly financed research projects became the property of the Japanese government. Even the firm that had developed the patent was required to pay a royalty to the government for a license to use that patent. The revised law allowed both Japanese and foreign firms to own up to one half of any patent resulting from an international research project commissioned by MITI or the New Energy and Industrial Technology Development Organization (NEDO). The revised law also allowed MITI and NEDO to license the government-owned portion of the patent at either a reduced rate or free of charge.

The provisions of the revised law were conditional on two requirements: the joint project had to include at least one foreign company or research institute in its membership, and the foreign member had to be from a country in which similar patent rights were available for Japanese companies participating in research projects financed by that government. Although reciprocal opportunities were available to Japanese firms in various countries including France, Germany, Holland, and Sweden, they were not available in the United States, where Japanese firms were barred from participation in the ATP and other projects. Where no analogous rule or practice existed, ownership of intellectual property remained with the Japanese government.

Based on the provisions of the revised law, MITI and the RWC Partnership shared evenly the rights to any patent received by an RWC partner. For any patent received by an RWC subcontractor, rights were shared by MITI (50 percent), the RWC Partnership (25 percent), and the subcontractor (25 percent).[22] The RWC by-laws made two further provisions regarding patent rights. They allowed third parties to use RWC patents without any restriction or charge, provided that the purpose was either testing or scientific research. They also supported dissemination of research results at international and domestic conferences in order to promote their use and application. RWC partners first had to receive approval from MITI, however, for publication of results.

Thus, the initial patent rules for RWC offered foreign partners partial rights to the results of research paid for by the Japanese government and offered

Japanese firms greater patent rights than any previous MITI computer consortium. In October 1999, the Japanese government began waiving its claim to ownership of IPR generated in all government research programs. Japanese law now grants full ownership of patents to registered researchers in government-sponsored projects who create intellectual property as part of those projects. Although the new rules applied to all patent applications during the last two years of RWC, the foreign partners were not in a position to fully exploit expanded ownership rights to intellectual property. As discussed later in this chapter, the foreign partners were not firms with large patent departments but research institutes that lack the staff and resources to actively pursue patents.

A Token Response to Foreign Pressure

Although the United States had been pushing for greater opening of Japan's R&D infrastructure to foreign researchers, there was little direct pressure for the opening of a project like the RWC program. The international community did not hold high expectations for RWC after the limited results produced by the FGCP. Moreover, the RWC failed to generate the same enthusiasm as the HFSP and IMS proposals because Japan trailed the West in several RWC research themes. The lack of foreign pressure in motivating RWC was clear in the indifference of many foreign researchers approached during the planning stages of the program. As discussed earlier, Western governments were more concerned with limiting rather than encouraging participation in the RWC program. Nevertheless, foreign pressure played a key role in shaping one aspect of the program. While rejecting broader participation in the RWC program, the United States developed a proposal for more limited collaboration in the U.S.–Japan JOP. Nonetheless, even though JOP represented an important experiment in bilateral collaboration, the decision to include it within the RWC framework was more a political compromise than a technological necessity.

The task of promoting the RWC program proved challenging for MITI. The ministry contacted science attachés in Tokyo during the summer of 1991 concerning what was then called the New Information Technology Processing Program (NIPT). These briefings were followed over the next eight months by two workshops in Japan at which foreign researchers were invited to contribute their ideas to the program. At both workshops, roughly twenty-five of the one hundred attendees were foreigners. The workshops were followed with visits by researchers from MITI's ETL to Brussels, Bonn, Paris, and London.

The RWC proposal was met with reactions ranging from mild enthusiasm to skepticism. The most enthusiastic reaction came from the German National Research Center for Computer Science, whose involvement in RWC is discussed later in the chapter. ETL researchers remember the French and British as being more unfamiliar with the RWC proposal than the Germans, but still quite positive about the project.[23] Other sources suggest, however, that France and Britain were fairly skeptical. Laurent Kott, deputy director of the French National Institute for Research in Computer Science and Automation (INRIA), believed the exact nature of the scientific opportunities in the RWC program were "vague."[24] INRIA subsequently decided against participation in RWC, reportedly under pressure from other parts of the French government.[25] As with France, no British firm or national institute joined the RWC program as a partner although a lab at the University of Manchester subsequently became a subcontractor.

As can be seen from this skepticism, there was negligible foreign pressure on MITI to open a computer consortium like RWC to foreign participation. As mentioned, the United States did try, however, to pursue collaboration in the area of optoelectronics. However, rather than encouraging American firms to participate in the RWC optoelectronics theme, the U.S. government looked for alternative strategies to engage the Japanese optoelectronics research community. After consultations with U.S. industry, the OSTP proposed an experiment in applying the Metal Oxide Semiconductor Implementation Service (MOSIS) model of brokered collaboration to the prototyping of optoelectronic devices.

The MOSIS began in 1980 as a Department of Defense initiative to establish a prototyping service for defense contractors, government agencies, and universities. MOSIS is seen as an effective way to maintain broad-based design capabilities for custom chips in the face of prohibitive fabrication costs.[26] Operated by the Institute for Information Sciences at the University of Southern California, MOSIS aggregates designs from different sources onto one mask set, allowing designers to order small quantities and to share the cost of fabrication among a number of users. Rather than paying tens of thousands of dollars for a dedicated set of masks and a fabrication run, users can obtain four packaged parts for as low as a few hundred dollars. By drastically reducing the risk, time, and cost of system development for VLSI circuits, MOSIS makes possible frequent prototype iterations that might not previously have been considered.

The JOP applied the MOSIS broker system on an international level by requiring both the United States and Japan to designate a broker with the knowledge to match users and suppliers. The broker served as a facilitator between users, who had novel designs to be fabricated, and suppliers who performed the fabrication. Users had to work through the broker in their own country who in turn worked with the broker in the other country to find suppliers. The system thus provided access to state-of-the-art devices available in the other country without the transfer of any proprietary manufacturing techniques.

As the liaison between users and suppliers, the broker performed a variety of administrative functions such as securing any necessary import or export licenses and providing feedback to both parties concerning design, fabrication, and performance. More importantly, the broker system protected intellectual property, fostered balanced use of supplier capabilities, and contributed to greater standardization.[27] The broker required both users and suppliers to take adequate steps to protect their respective intellectual property by signing agreements on ownership and use of devices. The broker also kept minutes of relevant meetings between users and suppliers that had to be cosigned by both parties. Each broker also had responsibility for promoting JOP in its own country in order to increase the participation of both users and suppliers. Thus, the task of achieving balanced national benefits rested largely with the brokers. The broker system also contributed to standardization. For immature technologies like optoelectronics, standardization of fabrication services would progress more slowly if prototyping were to take place through individual contacts between users and suppliers. Finally, by taking part in negotiations on specifications, the brokers could better monitor standards.

In Japan, the Optoelectronics Industry and Technology Development Association (OITDA) served as broker, and in the United States the Optoelectronics Industry Development Association (OIDA) led a broker team that also included MOSIS, the Microelectronics and Computer Technology Corporation (MCC), and the Consortium for Optical Computing (CO-OP) based at George Mason University. The broker team brought together knowledge of material and component suppliers from OIDA and CO-OP, demonstrated ability in connecting suppliers and users from MOSIS, and detailed knowledge of computing-related R&D in Japan from MCC.

The creation of JOP provides a good example of Washington's exerting pressure to shape a MITI proposal to better fit American preferences. The JOP would not have been established without the United States taking the initiative to propose the program. On an official level, JOP was "an integral part of RWC," rather than a bilateral effort separated from the project.[28] Although JOP certainly focused on accelerating development of optoelectronic devices for computing, many feel the characterization of JOP as integral to RWC served mostly to rationalize MITI's financial subsidy of broker activities in the United States. According to a computer industry analyst, inclusion of JOP within the RWC framework was largely a "face-saving" gesture that allowed MITI to claim U.S. participation in the RWC program.[29] In either case, JOP was only a very small part of the program. Moreover, it concentrated on building research infrastructure and widening access to technology rather than funding actual research on devices. As discussed later, however, the United States was very pleased with the results of the program and is now advocating JOP as a model for cooperation in other areas.

A Search for Complementary Capabilities

The scientific and technological rationale for Japan to initiate an international collaboration like the RWC program is much weaker than in the case of the HFSP and IMS programs. As in the HFSP, sharing of costs and risks was not a compelling motivation for internationalization of the RWC program. Most RWC research was conducted by corporate and university researchers in their own labs and thus the investment in facilities and equipment at the central lab in Tsukuba was quite modest. Even though the RWC budget was only about $60 million per year, RWC subsidies remained an important source of support for several partners. In the case of the Swedish Institute of Computer Science, for example, the RWC subsidy was equivalent to total subsidies received from the European Union Framework Program.

Although each of the foreign partners saw a strong connection between its own research and that of the RWC program, technological complementarity did not provide a convincing rationale for American and European computer firms to join the RWC program. These firms felt they had too much to lose in collaborating with Japan in RWC research. Although Los Alamos National Laboratory began to use RWC research results in the late 1990s, the most compelling part of the initial RWC proposal for the United States was the optoelectronics research theme. Japan has been a leader in optics because of its strong camera industry. In the early 1990s, optical computing became a hot topic in the United States because of research on optical elements being done at both IBM and Bell Labs. President Bush's science advisor, Allen Bromley, contacted IBM's John Armstrong and others for their thoughts on how the United States might engage Japan in collaboration on optoelectronics research. Armstrong was skeptical about the possibility of an "all-optical" computer ever being built but believed optoelectronics for computing was an area with potential that deserved further work.[30]

To learn more about Japanese plans, representatives from the OSTP and NIST attended the first RWC planning workshop, held in Hakone in December 1990. On the domestic front, the OSTP also chaired a series of meetings to canvass the views of industry. The agenda of these meetings was to find an area of precompetitive research where it was possible to build balanced cooperation of benefit to both countries. For American industry, the possibility of securing a MITI research subsidy was not the major incentive for collaboration; "flow of technology was more important than flow of dollars."[31] The main goals of U.S. firms were to emphasize fabrication and collaboration with Japanese firms rather than universities. The OSTP also felt that it was best to test the waters of collaboration in a narrowly defined framework like MOSIS before entering any broader collaborative agreement.

In October 1991, the OSTP proposed the idea of a MOSIS-style collaboration in optoelectronics. At first, there was some hesitation in the Japanese research community as to whether a framework developed for semiconductor devices could be easily applied to optoelectronics.[32] Nevertheless, the proposal enjoyed strong support from MITI. In January 1992, Prime Minister Miyazawa and President Bush issued a joint statement declaring the intention to collaborate in optoelectronics. In December 1992, the general terms of the undertaking were formalized in an exchange of letters between the OSTP and MITI. A joint management committee was set up with five members from each country to oversee the development of the project. After lengthy negotiations, the JOP Implementation Plan was signed in April 1994.

JOP was intended to help meet the increasing demand for speed and throughput in advanced computer systems by addressing the shortage of prototyping facilities for optoelectronic devices. For users, the project could improve the availability of prototype optoelectronic devices, circuits, and modules by providing access to leading-edge fabrication facilities.[33] For suppliers, it could provide an expanded customer base and the opportunity to gain early knowledge of the types of components being incorporated into next-generation systems.[34] The essential task of JOP was to link researchers in two different countries who would otherwise have no easy means of finding one another.

The RWC Program as a Departure from the Fifth Generation Computer Project

RWC researchers delivered a total of 2,689 conference papers during the ten years of the program. Although this number is only slightly higher than the 2,240 papers delivered by FGCP researchers, RWC papers had a broader impact on the computing field as measured by the number of paper citations in the SCISEARCH index, a leading international database.[35] A comparison of the number of patents registered by each program is more problematic because of the 1999 change in intellectual property rules that gave firms full ownership of patents resulting from government-sponsored research.

In 1995, three years after the official end of the program, the FGCP had produced 163 patents. The RWC program had received only 44 patents when it ended in January 2002, although that number was expected to rise significantly in the subsequent years. Thirty-eight patents were registered during the first phase of RWC from 1992 to 1996 and 184 patent applications were submitted during the second phase of the program from 1997 to 2001, mostly in the final year. Yet, only six of these had been approved as of January 2002. Unfortunately, it becomes extremely difficult to track any patent applications and registrations since that time because all rights were transferred to member firms and institutes after the RWC Partnership disbanded. Whereas FGCP patents can be tracked fairly easily by MITI's partial ownership, patents resulting from RWC research lost their "RWC identity" in the patent system following the end of the program.

The results of the JOP are easier to track, however, because it was managed separately from the RWC. Although it did not begin operation until 1995, the JOP enrolled 105 users "who were able to draw on the R&D labs of 14 manufacturers in Japan offering 26 prototype devices, and of 25 manufacturers in the U.S. offering 49 prototypes." In all, the JOP oversaw 85 prototype transactions, which resulted in the publication of 147 academic papers, 27 patent applications, and 7 registered patents as of January 2002.[36]

The story behind publication and patent numbers becomes clearer by contrasting the organization and technological results of RWC with those of the FGCP, which did not include any foreign participation in research or management. The RWC program offered greater flexibility in research objectives and organization than its predecessor and produced more commercially viable results for the central lab in Tsukuba as well as the project participants. Unlike the central lab in the FGCP, the Tsukuba Research Center developed technologies that were quickly put to use by government labs and firms in the United States. Although Japan's major IT firms perceived the value of RWC differently, they agreed that it offered greater flexibility than the FGCP and so provided a better complement to their research interests. The foreign partners felt the program to be fully open to foreign participation on equitable terms yet agreed that RWC failed to maximize the benefits of international collaboration for both Japanese and foreign partners because of its distributed structure.

The RWC program is a departure from earlier MITI computer consortia in terms of MITI's relationship with both firms and the MESC. The program provides an especially marked contrast to MITI's infamous FGCP. Although the FGCP might have enhanced the reputation of Japan within the academic community of artificial intelligence researchers, it was widely regarded as a failure by industry and the mass media, both in Japan and abroad. Leading researchers in artificial intelligence from Stanford, MIT, and NASA concluded that although the FGCP may have had indirect benefits such as attracting higher caliber graduate students to artificial intelligence research, it did not directly accelerate the development of knowledge-based technology in Japan. Instead, it built a relatively closed world by developing a new programming language that could only run on its own experimental hardware—which never entered commercial production. These limitations prevented FGCP "technology from having any impact on, or enrichment from, the practical considerations of the industrial and business worlds."[37]

Scott Callon adds to this negative technical evaluation by discussing the bitter resistance to the FGCP within the government and the private sector. He describes the division within MITI between engineers at the ETL interested in pursuing basic research and career generalists in the Machinery and Information Industries Bureau intent on using the FGCP to catapult the Japanese computer industry ahead of IBM. Callon also documents MESC's refusal to allow academics to take part in the FGCP in anything more than an advisory capacity. Yet, Callon's most dramatic examples of conflict are those between MITI and the private sector. Callon calls the FGCP "the starkest repudiation of assumptions of Japanese government/business harmony."[38] As Callon suggests, firms were reluctant to participate in the FGCP from the outset. MITI employed a divide-and-conquer strategy to enlist the participation of "accommodators" among the major computer firms that felt that they had little choice but to take part in the project. According to a corporate manager, the eventual participation of firms that were hard-line opponents of the FGCP had more to do with the desire to stay in line with the accommodators than with any enthusiasm for the program itself.[39] Even this grudging corporate "support" was not won without major concessions. Most notably, MITI was forced to foot the bill for the entire project without any direct financial contribution from the firms.[40]

Although Callon offers a convincing analysis of the failures of MITI's industrial policy during the 1980s, his argument is much less applicable to the 1990s. The broader focus and flexibility of the RWC program was part of a deliberate strategy to avoid the myopic focus that crippled the FGCP. In addition to the difference in levels of academic participation discussed earlier, the RWC program differed from the FGCP in terms of research objectives, management structure, and the more positive attitude of Japanese firms. These differences reveal that MITI learned from some of the mistakes made in the 1980s. The failure of the FGCP was particularly humiliating. The project came nowhere near meeting its goal of developing a thinking computer and, to make matters worse, it had been launched with more fanfare than any previous MITI project. Learning from this experience, MITI took a much more modest approach to its promotion of the RWC program. Moreover, both MITI and the RWC research partners acknowledged at the outset that only very limited progress could be made in realizing human-like information processing within the scope of a ten-year program.[41]

The RWC program took a more flexible approach to the initial choice of research themes, as well as competition among those themes during the course of the project. In contrast to the monolithic "logic" approach of the FGCP, the primary goal of RWC was not to develop a single computer but to conduct oriented basic research on a range of elemental technologies. The three years of consensus building that preceded the launch of the program led to an eclectic mix of project goals that puzzled many observers. An American journalist described the RWC program as "a loose conglomeration of research rather than a cohesive project in industrial development."[42] According to Takemochi Ishii of Keio University, who chaired the RWC feasibility study committee, "the age when we made development of a single computer the goal of a national project is over."[43] Architects of RWC likened previous MITI projects to climbing Mt. Fuji, but compared their own project to climbing Yatsugatake, a range of eight peaks.[44] Because of this approach, some foreign observers considered the RWC research agenda too unfocused. Commenting on MITI's 1992 RWC proposal, David Kahaner wrote that "there are enough research topics to keep an army of researchers busy for decades."[45]

The first several years of the FGCP were also supposed to be a period of investigating different technologies before choosing areas to focus on for the rest of the project. As Callon notes, however, the major decisions had already been made at the outset by FGCP managers faced with a huge mandate and limited funds.[46] This was not the case, however, in the RWC program, which began with a variety of research themes before narrowing and refocusing research after the midterm evaluation. The change in focus is clearest in the area of parallel computing, where the research emphasis shifted from work on technologies for a single, massively parallel computer to work on PC cluster technology, which allows personal computers to work at the processing level of supercomputers by networking them.

From the outset, RWC was intended to appeal to the interests of firms while still fostering longer-term research than corporate budgets would allow. After the experience of the FGCP, neither Japanese firms nor MITI were eager to have the RWC program dominated by a large central lab. Sending their researchers to such a lab involved not only an immediate opportunity cost for the firms, but also left open the possibility that some researchers might opt for an academic career, rather than returning to their firm, as had happened in the FGCP.[47] However, MITI was split internally on whether to establish a central lab. With no manufacturing capability, a central lab mostly publishes academic papers. Shifting resources to the distributed labs would offer a more direct means of industrial promotion. On the other hand, such an approach would also leave the program without any unifying vision and would make MITI more vulnerable to U.S. criticism of simply handing out subsidies to firms.[48] In the end, MITI opted for a small central lab. Although the Tsukuba Research Center (TRC) received more money than the firms in the first phase of exploratory research, the firms received more than the TRC during the second, more applied phase of the RWC program. The TRC employed only one quarter the number of researchers that had worked in the FGCP's central lab but the two labs ended up receiving roughly equivalent percentages of their respective project budgets. Nevertheless, the TRC achieved far more practical and marketable results with its research subsidy.

Foreign Praise for the Tsukuba Research Center

Dr. Junichi Shimada, research director of the RWC program acknowledges that the program "was pretty much invisible" during its first six years. As research goals became more focused in the second phase of the program, however, the TRC redoubled efforts to make results available worldwide in order to promote the adoption of Japanese ideas and standards. The TRC particularly emphasized making results available while the program was still underway in order to receive feedback from users. As a small research facility that would close in late 2001, the TRC was forced to be far more aggressive in seeking users than RWC's large corporate members, who could apply results in-house. Ironically, with most of Japan's high-tech managers looking toward Silicon Valley for ideas, the TRC was forced to look to the United States for potential users.[49]

The first major achievement of the parallel and distributed computing labs at the TRC was the creation of a seamless computing system with the development in 1998 of RWC PC Cluster II, which connected 64 Intel Pentium Pro 200 MHz processors. The cluster made three major advances. First, a high-performance network used optical interconnections to overcome the communication delay between networked computers. Second, the SCore software system solved the problem posed by heterogeneity among the networked computers. Third, research on programming languages and compilers overcame the problems associated with the transition from sequential to parallel computation.[50] By the end of the RWC project in 2001, the TRC had succeeded in connecting 1,024 personal computers to achieve the eleventh highest computing speed on record.[51] With such growing capabilities, PC clusters are now regularly offered in bids to replace supercomputers in both government and corporate labs. Unlike supercomputers, they offer the advantage of scalability; users can add PCs and high-speed networks as required to increase processing ability. PC clusters also provide a new alternative for users once forced to replace servers with expensive parallel computers.

Unlike the results of the FGCP, which went virtually unnoticed outside of Japan, the results produced by the TRC, in particular the SCore software system, were highly praised and quickly utilized internationally. In what Shimada describes as a happy coincidence, the first big break for RWC came with the decision by Los Alamos National Laboratory to use the SCore system as part of its own cluster research in the Accelerated Strategic Computing Initiative. According to Peter Beckman, senior scientist in the Advanced Computing Lab at Los Alamos, "the SCore system provides us a way to organize a cluster in a coherent way. Without that system we would be at a loss for how to schedule, and get all jobs running at the same time." The SCore system was also well received by the university community in the United States and Europe. Dennis Gannon, head of the Extreme Computing Laboratory at Indiana University, described RWC's PC Cluster II as "the best PC cluster architecture in the world," and the University of Bonn adopted SCore as the middleware for Parnass2, Europe's fastest Linux cluster.[52]

The SCore system also entered industrial use—even before the end of the RWC program. In Japan, Mitsubishi Electric began using SCore in 1999 for real-time computer simulation and testing of control devices in power systems and Alta Technology, a leading American supplier of parallel computer technologies, adopted SCore in its own PC clusters.[53] In 2001, Fujitsu tested successfully an SCore-based Linux cluster that connected thousands of distributed server systems.[54] Since the end of the RWC program, development of SCore software has continued under the banner of the PC Cluster Consortium. Members of this open-source consortium include AMD Japan, Dell Computer K.K., Hewlett-Packard Japan, IBM Japan, Intel K.K., and SGI Japan.

To hasten the adoption of cluster systems, the TRC also developed applications for parallel and distributed computing including the parallel protein information analysis system (PAPIA). PAPIA makes possible high-speed analysis of protein structure and sequence information via the World Wide Web. For example, a multiple sequence alignment of sixty-four kinase enzyme sequences would take seventy-nine minutes on a single-processor computer but only eighty-nine seconds on a PC Cluster II.[55] According to Constantine Polychronopolous, director of the Center for Supercomputer R&D at the University of Illinois, there is no question that PAPIA "is a very important application especially for the biomedical industry, pharmaceutical industry, and the research community."[56]

The major contributions of the real-world-intelligence labs at the TRC came with the development of information retrieval technologies with immediate commercial applications as well as progress on more fundamental human-interface technologies. One of the first advances during the second phase of the RWC program was development of a technology for speech retrieval that would help summarize important information scattered throughout recordings of long business meetings. To eliminate the problem of postprocessing such long recordings, the TRC developed a way of "browsing" recorded speech that patches together relevant portions of a recording into shorter summaries of major topics.[57]

By 2000, the TRC had also licensed Media Drive Corporation to begin commercialization of its system for real-time retrieval of multimedia information. Media Drive's CrossMediator for Video 1.0 released in 2000 was the first product in the world to allow video search by voice on a personal computer. Built for Mac OSX, Version 2.0 allows users to search video, sound, and text data using either voice or keyboard. For example, users can locate a song in a database by humming the tune or can find a particular scene in a video with a keyword search input via the voice recognition system.[58] In addition to the above work on information retrieval, the TRC also developed software for a very basic prototype of a multimodal, interactive personal computer (MMPC-net) that could be operated by a combination of human gestures and speech in real time. Although the first version of the software recognized fewer than fifty words and associated gestures, it used less than 10 percent of the power resources of a laptop computer.[59]

More Flexibility for Japanese Firms

MITI faced three challenges in making the RWC program attractive to Japanese firms.[60] The first was rooted in the structure of the Japanese information technology industry and the decreased relevance of MITI in corporate research planning. In Japan, there are several major firms in each field of information technology with basically the same level of skills and resources. With all the major players trying to propose standards, it is hard to create a de facto standard. In view of the dominant position of firms like Microsoft and Intel, Japanese firms now look to the United States for standards rather than to MITI consortia, which once helped provide coordination in this area. The second challenge arose from corporate disappointment with the results of the FGCP. As discussed earlier, MITI's response was to make RWC broader in scope and more flexible than its previous research consortia. Yet, this approach produced a third challenge. Initially, the RWC research agenda covered three very different subjects: optoelectronics, platforms, and applications. However, the corporate liaison with MITI would represent only one of these groups within the firm; he could not represent or take responsibility for the interests of the other two groups. This obstacle initially reduced the profile of the RWC program within the corporate research community.

Shimada believes that ultimately corporate perceptions of RWC, and other MITI programs, are shaped by the roles of individuals within each company. Top management approaches programs like RWC as useful sources of "free money" to support long-range research. Middle managers, who must deal with government red tape daily, see the programs as annoying responsibilities. And junior-level researchers are largely indifferent. Although participation in MITI projects may afford them the opportunity to do slightly more long-range research than otherwise, their day-to-day activities remain largely the same.

The Japanese members of the RWC Partnership fell into three groups. The first consisted of the main players in Japan's computer and industrial electronics industries: Fujitsu, Hitachi, Mitsubishi Electric, NEC, Oki, Sanyo, and Toshiba. Although their enthusiasm for the RWC program varied, most took part in more than one research theme. The firms showed greatest interest in research on man-machine interfaces, parallel computing applications, and optical interconnections. This group was rounded out by Matsushita and Sharp, two firms better known for consumer electronics, which ventured into the field of computing in the 1990s. The second group consisted of Japan's major optical-fiber firms: Sumitomo Electric, Furukawa Electric, Fujikura, and Nippon Sheet Glass. The role of these firms in the RWC was much narrower than that of the microelectronics firms. Each of them approached MITI about joining RWC after the official launch of the program; none was involved in the initial planning of RWC. In addition, the four firms took part only in research on optical interconnections.

Along with the microelectronics and optical-fiber firms, three other firms also took part in RWC: Mitsubishi Research Institute, NTT, and Sumitomo Metals. With very different interests than the firms in the first two groups, these outliers played a relatively minor role in the RWC program. Although it is a wholly owned subsidiary of Mitsubishi Electric, Mitsubishi Research Institute (MRI) joined the RWC independently of its parent company. MRI is a consulting firm that derives roughly half its income from contract research for the Japanese government. Unlike other firms in the RWC program, MRI is not a manufacturer and so had a different perspective on the program than other firms. Participation in the RWC program was essentially a way to make money and to bolster the skills of MRI's research staff.[61] Nippon Telephone and Telegraph (NTT) was even more of an outlier than MRI. NTT, Japan's leading telecommunications company, was also a member of the FGCP before joining the RWC. Five researchers from NTT's Basic Research Laboratories used high-resolution electromagnetic sensors to study attention mechanisms in the human brain. One of the few research themes that continued on the same trajectory throughout the ten years of the program, this was the most basic research conducted in RWC.[62] Finally, Sumitomo Metals played the smallest role in the program. It joined the RWC program in 1998, taking the place of the Japan Iron and Steel Federation (JISF), which withdrew from the partnership in 1997. JISF's role as a founding member of the RWC Partnership reflects the interests in the early 1990s of major steel firms like Nippon Steel and NKK in diversifying into the computer field. As this interest waned and the direction of RWC shifted following the midterm evaluation, the program became less relevant to JISF members. Only Sumitomo Metals chose to remain part of the program.

Although a total of fifteen Japanese firms took part in the RWC program, this chapter focuses on the experiences of the major computer and industrial electronics makers in the first group. These firms have a long history of participation in MITI computer consortia and were the most active members of the RWC Partnership. For these reasons, their experiences provide the sharpest contrast between RWC and earlier consortia such as the FGCP. The motivations for joining the RWC program, and the perceived value of participation, varied across the major electronics firms. Some of the more established computer makers saw the RWC program as a useful supplement to R&D funding during the recession of the 1990s while others viewed participation in the RWC, like that in other MITI programs, as part of standard operating procedure and a way to keep an eye on competitors. Although individual firms approached the program somewhat differently, there was common agreement on four main points. First, those firms that also took part in the FGCP considered the RWC program as more flexible and a better complement to their own research interests. Second, the firms agreed that RWC research themes such as man-machine interfaces and optical interconnections will become increasingly important over time. Third, they agreed that RWC research became much more applied during the second phase of the program. And finally, all believed that the benefits of internationalization were minimal in the RWC program. With much of RWC's research being done independently at company labs, the Japanese firms had very limited interaction with the foreign partners.

NEC and Fujitsu, Japan's two main computer makers, say they would have done research very similar to that in the RWC program, although perhaps on a smaller scale, even without the MITI subsidy. According to Norio Tsubouchi of NEC's R&D Group, "NEC received money for research that it wanted to do. There was no reason not to take part in the program."[63] A MITI subsidy is not a free ride, however. The "subsidy covers only researcher sala-ries, about 65 percent of costs. The company pays all overhead and other costs." NEC made the largest manpower commitment to the program with forty-seven researchers, more than half of them working full time on RWC, spread across four research themes. Out of the four themes, the most impor-tant was parallel and distributed computing, which fit nicely with NEC's strength in supercomputers and its new emphasis on internet applications. Refocusing its research in this area in 1997, NEC developed a programming tool for seamless computing systems that operates with a graphical user in-terface. It also designed a new chemical screening system for the pharma-ceutical industry.[64] In the real-world-intelligence field, NEC developed adaptive chips that can improve performance by reconfiguring their archi-tecture to the structure of target problems. Even before the end of the RWC program, prototypes of these chips were being tested in the printing industry, and in the prosthetics industry for use in artificial hands. Although pleased with the RWC program overall, NEC would have liked it to have been more focused, with more limited membership and larger budgets for top firms.

Fujitsu made the second-largest manpower commitment to the RWC pro-gram with a total of thirty-three researchers working at distributed labs and two researchers assigned to the TRC.[65] Fujitsu's interest in the RWC changed during the course of the program. Initially, Fujitsu regarded its research on autonomous learning functions in mobile robots as its most important work in the RWC program. With the growing importance of the Internet during the late 1990s and the midterm redirection of RWC, however, Fujitsu began to put more emphasis on parallel and distributed computing. The most com-mercial aspect of this research was the Comet network processor, which was first used to broadcast Ryuichi Sakamoto's opera *Life* in September 1999. The main application of the technology is facilitating remote collaborations via the Internet.

In addition to computer makers, Japan's largest electrical machinery manu-facturers also took part in RWC. Hitachi management likened the explor-atory research during the first half of the RWC program to *asobi* or "play" for researchers.[66] Nevertheless, the firm's RWC research projects were not designed solely for the program. In multimodal functions and optical inter-connections, in particular, Hitachi was already planning similar research on a smaller scale; according to Atsushi Otomo of the Corporate R&D Promo-tion Office, "there was a natural coming together of Hitachi and RWC re-search objectives in these two areas." At the height of its manpower commitment in 2000, Hitachi had twenty-six researchers working in five RWC research areas.

Beginning in the second half of the RWC program, eleven of these researchers worked on compiler technology to extract higher performance from multiprocessor systems. Research on this theme continued after the end of the RWC program in METI's Advanced Parallel Compiler Project. Although the results of this research were the closest to market for Hitachi, the multimodal and optical interconnection labs also succeeded in developing actual systems. Hitachi's multimodal lab created a prototype system for translating spoken Japanese into Japanese sign language, a system of signing unique to Japan. The system translates gestures, input from a sensor glove worn by a hearing-impaired person, into synthesized voice and text. In turn, spoken Japanese is translated into a three-dimensional animation of Japanese sign language for the hearing-impaired. A prototype of this system was tested successfully in the offices of the Nagasaki prefectural government before the end of the RWC program. Since then, the technology has been adapted for applications including automatic teller machines.[67] Although the market for welfare systems is small, Hitachi believes the potential applications of the underlying technology are much broader.

The second largest of Japan's electrical machinery makers, Toshiba, initially was less active in the RWC program than some of its competitors. The first half of the RWC program emphasized massively parallel computing, which was not a priority area for Toshiba at the time. The firm joined the RWC program to keep up with developments in the field and monitor the work of competitors. According to a manager at Toshiba, participation in the first half of the RWC program was *hoken* or insurance.[68] By the end of the project, Toshiba had twelve researchers in three labs spending roughly 70 percent of their time on RWC research. The work at two of these labs would not have taken place without the RWC subsidy because it was too far removed from short-term business needs. However, the work of the parallel applications lab on "data-mining" was considered very practical. This lab worked on algorithms that help identify "hidden" patterns or relationships in massive databases. Management anticipated the integration of research results into Toshiba products within two years of the end of the RWC program.

The third largest of Japan's electrical machinery manufacturers, Mitsubishi Electric (MELCO), was primarily interested in taking part in the RWC program for the research subsidy.[69] Although MELCO would have pursued some research themes without the MITI subsidy, it would not have undertaken others. The RWC allowed MELCO to follow long-standing interests such as computer vision while exploring new applications for seamless computing. A total of seventeen researchers working in three labs devoted most of their time to RWC research. MELCO received its largest share of RWC funding for work on an artificial retina chip. The firm began research on optical neurocomputing in 1986 and completed a prototype of the world's first optical neurochip in 1990. MELCO continued this basic line of research within the RWC program. The chip has a broad range of possible applications in areas such as security sensors and facial recognition systems. Part of MELCO's broader semiconductor business strategy, this research would have been undertaken even without the RWC subsidy.

MELCO labs also worked on two other themes in the area of real-world intelligence. The information-base lab worked on interactive query expansion for more focused database searches while the parallel applications lab worked on new ways to process large amounts of sequence data such as amino acid sequences. Both of these projects were more basic than work on the retina chip. MELCO believes work on database management would have been far more modest without the MITI subsidy and the parallel applications research probably would not have been undertaken at all. Although generally pleased with the research opportunities in all three themes, the firm would have liked more funding for the distributed labs. Nevertheless, MELCO made good use of results from the central lab in Tsukuba. The Industrial Electronics and Systems Lab at MELCO developed a real-time power simulator system on a PC cluster using the TRC's SCore software. Until the 1990s, firms needed to build miniature power systems with real generators in order to test new control devices. Today, digital simulation is the main form of testing. Because of the size and complexity of power systems, however, one CPU is insufficient for real-time simulation. MELCO believes that parallel processing with SCore opened up a range of new opportunities for real-time simulations in power systems and numerous other applications.

Although long-established in the information technology field, Oki Electric is a good example of the optical-fiber firms that were active in the RWC program.[70] Oki focuses on network hardware and services rather than stand-alone computer research. Like the optical-fiber firms, Oki worked only on optical interconnections. And since there was no optical interconnection lab at the TRC, opportunity for collaboration or discussion with other RWC members was severely limited. A total of seven researchers at two labs devoted roughly half of their time to RWC. For the entire ten years of the project, one lab researched wafer bonding technology for the integration of optical interconnections mounted on a single semiconductor chip. This was long-range research that Oki would only have undertaken as part of a national project. Oki plans for the results of this research to be applied in high-performance servers by 2005.

With the refocusing of the RWC program on seamless computing, a second Oki team began work on parallel fiber, optical interconnections. This research reached commercial application even before the end of the RWC program, producing a more compact and inexpensive interconnection than the conventional alternatives. With numerous applications for this technology in Oki's core businesses of network exchanges and switching, the firm would have undertaken this research even without the MITI subsidy. In addition to accelerating the progress of Oki's research, the RWC program also brought together Oki researchers from the optoelectronic and computer fields. Management doubts this would have happened as easily without the RWC.

Overall, the computer and electrical machinery firms would have preferred a smaller and more focused RWC program with a separate project on optical interconnections. They also agree that ten years is far too long for a national project in information technology because the field moves so quickly. Today, firms are directing substantial resources to development of mobile computing and household appliances with Internet interfaces—areas not even under consideration when the RWC began. Both managers and researchers agree that five years or less is a more realistic time frame for IT-related projects, but recognize that projects with short time horizons can be difficult for bureaucrats to organize because of the conflicting business plans of firms. In view of the troubled Japanese economy, however, the government has moved decisively toward such shorter-term projects. With the launch of the Focus 21 initiative in 2003, all ministries are now emphasizing R&D projects with high commercial feasibility that are expected to create new markets within three years.[71]

Equal but Limited Opportunities for Foreign Partners

A fundamental test of the value of MITI's internationalization of research programs is the evaluation of those programs by foreign participants. Though they differ in size and budget, the four foreign partners in RWC are all research institutes that conduct both basic and applied research. Two of them work explicitly to seed innovative start-up firms; none is involved in manufacturing. As research institutes, the foreign partners also tend to lack the staff and resources to apply for patents; they share a preference for publication of results in the open literature. The motivations for joining the RWC program and the general experience in participation were the same for each of the foreign partners. All believed there was a close fit between their own interests and the research plans of RWC, but they also shared disappointment with some aspects of the program's structure and administration.

The foreign partners agree the RWC program provided needed funds for important research without any discrimination against non-Japanese participants. They also agree, however, that the lack of communication among distributed labs limited the potential benefits of collaboration for all members. Owing to lack of funding for travel to other RWC sites, the foreign partners felt isolated. They also complain of the administrative burdens imposed by Japanese accounting rules. The evaluation of RWC is, thus, mixed. The foreign partners applaud RWC as an open program that supported interesting and important research; nevertheless, they feel the program failed to realize the potential benefits of internationalization for both Japanese and foreign partners because of its distributed structure.

The German National Research Center for Computer Science (GMD), established in 1968, became part of the Fraunhofer Institute in 1999. Roughly 70 percent of GMD's $120 million annual budget comes from the government with the remaining 30 percent from external sources including German industry, the European Union Framework Program, and other collaborations. The staff of 1,200 includes over 700 researchers working in systems design, telecommunications, intelligent multimedia systems, and scientific computing.[72] Of the four foreign partners in the RWC program, GMD has the strongest ties with Japan. In 1977, it established a liaison office in Tokyo to monitor Japanese research in computer science, and beginning in the late 1980s, to organize joint research projects with Japanese partners. The first fruit was cooperation with NEC in parallel computing that led to the establishment of NEC's first European research laboratory in GMD's Techno-Park in 1994. In addition to collaborating with Hitachi and Fujitsu, GMD joined with the city of Kitakyushu in 1998 to open a new research lab specializing in telecommunications and underwater robotics. Yet, the major collaboration to date is GMD participation in the RWC program.

The initial German reaction to the RWC program was mixed. In December 1991, MITI organized a workshop in Germany to introduce the RWC proposal to over fifty representatives of German industry and academia. Although researchers in German firms were interested in the program, managers decided against participation. They believed that Germany led Japan in several areas of RWC research. In addition, they thought the projected overhead was too high to justify participation when programs like ESPRIT offered greater funding and more potential for interaction. Neither the German government nor German industry objected, however, to GMD participation in the RWC program. Depending on funding in a given year, GMD had between five and ten researchers working full time both in the theory and algorithms field and in parallel and distributed computing. After 1994, GMD also had one researcher working at the TRC. The main motivation for participation in the RWC program was the close fit with GMD's research interests. GMD would have been working in these areas even without RWC funding. The decision to join the parallel and distributed computing field was particularly easy as Japan had become the world leader in this area. With GMD helping to design compiler software for the SCore operating system, the collaboration between GMD and the TRC in distributed computing was the strongest of that with any foreign partner.

Overall, GMD was happy with the quality of research in the RWC and eager to participate in any follow-on projects. Yet, it also saw "definite room for improvement" in accounting procedures, communication between distributed labs, and the ability to exploit research results with German industry. Communication between most RWC partners was limited to meetings at an annual conference. Moreover, Japanese intellectual property laws posed a significant obstacle to using results, particularly in the first half of the program. Because fifty percent of all results belonged to the Japanese government until 1999, reports could not be distributed without clearance. Consequently, bureaucratic rigmarole was involved in any request to publish results or exploit those results with German industry. Although the 1999 revision of intellectual property laws covering government-funded R&D solved this problem, GMD believed the results should have been more open and more actively distributed from the outset.

The Swedish Institute of Computer Science (SICS) is a nonprofit research foundation sponsored by the Swedish government's National Board for Technical and Industrial Development, and an association of seven major firms including IBM Sweden and Sun Microsystems. The main purpose of SICS is to contribute to the competitive strength of Swedish industry by bridging the gap between academic and industrial research in computer science.[73] SICS has a staff of eighty-five researchers, over thirty with doctorates, conducting research in real-time computer architectures as well as software and man-machine interaction for distributed systems. More than two-thirds of its budget comes from the Swedish government, industrial sponsors, and research commissioned by Swedish and foreign firms. The remaining third comes from participation in collaborative research programs, with roughly 10 percent of annual funding during the 1990s coming from RWC.

Before joining the RWC program, SICS had undertaken a number of more informal and unsubsidized collaborations with Japanese researchers. Although SICS did not participate in any of the RWC planning workshops, it kept abreast of emerging plans and contacted the RWC Partnership about membership in the autumn of 1992. The basic motivation for applying to RWC was researcher interest; SICS would have tried to undertake the same general research without the MITI subsidy. While six researchers worked full time on very basic research in stochastic pattern computing, two researchers worked closely with MITI's ETL on autonomous robots that learn from their environment.

The Swedish government and SICS's industrial sponsors encouraged participation in the RWC program. The Swedish government was interested in promoting greater research cooperation with Japan through grant and exchange programs and, in the case of RWC, worked energetically to establish contacts between SICS and MITI. According to Janusz Launberg, information and planning manager at SICS, the enthusiasm of the Swedish government for RWC arose, in part, from the desire "to not put all its eggs in the European basket." Swedish firms also encouraged the participation of SICS in the RWC program as a way to learn more about research activity in Japan and to gain some insight into collaboration with Japanese partners. Participation in the RWC program opened fewer opportunities for collaboration than initially hoped, however, because Swedish firms thought cultural barriers were still daunting.

SICS was enthusiastic about the research agenda of RWC but had some reservations about the organization and administration of the program. RWC funding allowed SICS to do research it could not otherwise have afforded to undertake. But, in many respects, the administrative burden of the RWC program compared unfavorably with the European Union Framework Programs. According to a SICS researcher, RWC funding was "relatively generous," but the administrative burden was "overwhelming." RWC grants had to be renewed annually whereas European projects require much less paperwork once a program has been established. Furthermore, the "payment culture" during the first half of the RWC program had some disadvantages relative to the Framework Programs. Although the timing of payments was more predictable and reliable in RWC, exchange-rate fluctuations made planning very difficult. On the grounds that no institution, including banks, should make a profit on MITI research grants, the ministry did not allow the foreign partners to insure exchange rates. As a result, foreign partners did not know in advance how much funding would actually be available in the local currency. To remedy this problem, in the second phase of the program the RWC Partnership provided supplemental funds to foreign members in order to make up for any budget shortfalls arising from exchange-rate fluctuations. The greatest disappointment for SICS was the lack of communication and information exchange in RWC compared to "very lively" collaboration in European Union programs. With the exception of the annual RWC conference, the only real lines of communication were those between SICS and researchers at the TRC and ETL.

The Foundation for Neural Networks (SNN), the third of the European partners in the RWC program, was established in 1990 as part of the Dutch Ministry of Economics' Informatics Stimulation Program. SNN, a nonprofit consortium of university institutes that researches computer algorithms modeled on information processing in the brain, has collaborated with a diverse group of firms to find neural solutions for specific industrial problems. Recent collaborations include work with Korg and Yamaha on music transcription, with Philips on medical diagnostics, and with Shell on gas-leak protection. SNN is also active in the European neural network research community. It was a partner in the ESPRIT Stimulation Initiative for European Neural Applications and serves as a managing node in NeuroNet, a network of excellence set up by the ESPRIT Division for Basic Research in 1994.[74]

SNN took part in two RWC research themes that were central to its own mission. A team of eight researchers, who devoted roughly three quarters of their time to the RWC program, worked on the design of algorithms to enable learning and reasoning up to the order of 1,000 variables, an order of magnitude larger than the state of the art. The main application of this research is a medical diagnostic system developed in collaboration with the Utrecht University Hospital. A second team, consisting of five researchers, worked on algorithms for robot navigation using data supplied by the TRC. Although the medical diagnostics system still required substantial development at the end of the RWC program, the robot navigation research had already attracted significant interest from several Dutch firms planning spin-offs in the area of surveillance technologies.

As with the other European partners, SNN was generally pleased with the RWC program. The physical and cultural distance of SNN from Japan made collaboration difficult, but not impossible. SNN researchers made several visits to both the TRC and ETL that aided RWC research and facilitated contacts with other labs in Japan. Dr. Bert Kappen, program manager for SNN, feels the quality of research performed by many Japanese industrial partners could have been stronger, but that the quality of research by all academic partners was very good to excellent. He believes a lack of leadership was the main shortcoming of the RWC program. "The project would have benefited from a brilliant scientist who could define a coherent research direction. The lack of leadership meant that each research theme had to act more or less on its own." Kappen also believes that at the start of the RWC program MITI should have established an international advisory board to assess the merit of research proposals.[75] Despite these shortcomings, SNN considered RWC a valuable project that addressed important issues and would be eager to participate in any follow-on program.

The only foreign partner from outside Europe was the Institute of Systems Science (ISS) at the National University of Singapore, which merged with another research institute in 1998 to become Kent Ridge Digital Labs (KRDL). One of the most dynamic software labs in Asia, KRDL had created more than ten spin-off companies by 2001. KRDL specializes in applied research in neural networks and multimedia, with an emphasis on language and image processing. The majority of funding to support the staff of 250 researchers comes from the Singaporean government. Additional funds have come from collaborations with Apple, Ericsson, Hewlett Packard, Johns Hopkins, and Microsoft.[76]

The ISS decided to join the RWC program after a 1991 visit to Singapore by researchers from the FGCP. The RWC research of the ISS, and later KRDL, dealt with real-world intelligence. Roughly ten researchers worked full time throughout the program on multimedia indexing technologies. The object of this research was to extract and describe the contents of image databases at a semantic level, such as *tree* or *sky*, rather than by simple visual features such as color or shape. In the final year of the RWC program, KRDL began negotiations to commercialize some of this technology in an online photograph business. A second area of research on face-recognition technologies began in the second phase of the RWC program. A team of six researchers succeeded in developing the world's most advanced face-recognition technology in terms of invariance to changes in hairstyle and facial hair.

KRDL found participation in the RWC a positive experience and hopes to participate in future Japanese government projects. The RWC program provided an international forum for exchange of ideas and results, a steady stream of funding, and introductions to several potential new partners in Japan. KRDL also found the more applied focus in the last five years of RWC a better fit with its own more market-driven mission. Like GMD, however, KRDL had some concerns about lack of interaction between distributed labs and administrative red tape. Although the planning workshops were very interactive and provided a good opportunity for international input, communication was limited during the first phase of the program. Despite advances in electronic communication, KRDL thinks that distance and language barriers limit potential collaboration with Japanese partners.

Conclusion

Bureaucratic politics played no role at all in motivating MITI's decision to open the RWC program. Techno-national ideology, however, may at first seem relevant to this decision because Japan trailed the state of the art in many of the areas first targeted by the RWC program. Nevertheless, the design of the RWC did not provide an efficient mechanism for accessing foreign technologies; thus the role of techno-national ideology was actually quite limited. Differences in relative national capabilities also limit the explanatory power of technological complementarity. The RWC proposal may have offered important research opportunities to smaller research institutes in Asia and Europe, but useful opportunities for the United States were initially limited to the JOP. As a result of the differences in national capabilities, there was no pressure for MITI to establish an international consortium in the computing field. Thus, the opening of the RWC program was largely a token response to the general American pressure for opening of Japanese R&D.

The RWC program was unlike earlier consortia in research objectives and organization as well as in MITI's relationship with MESC. Unlike the FGCP, the RWC program ultimately succeeded in producing commercially viable results of interest to American firms and government research labs. The RWC program provided only modest subsidies to conduct research beyond the horizon of most corporate budgets, but these subsidies became especially important during the 1990s as firms were forced to cut research budgets and streamline their R&D operations. Japanese firms that also took part in the FGCP agree that RWC was a more flexible program that better complemented their research interests. Nonetheless, both Japanese and foreign partners believe that the RWC program did not realize the potential benefits of internationalization because of its distributed structure and the lack of communication between labs.

——Chapter 7——

A Broader View of Japan's Techno-Globalism

With fully international management structures, the HFSP and IMS stand apart from other research programs initiated by MITI. As an open, national program, RWC is typical of the approach followed in organizing many other projects including the Hypersonic Transport Propulsion System project (HYPR), the High-Performance for Severe Environments project, and the Micromachine project. These projects have tended to have smaller budgets and more limited foreign participation than the RWC but foreign partners have been pleased with intellectual property rules and levels of information exchange. Although semiconductor projects established by MITI since the mid-1990s demonstrate important limits to techno-globalism in certain technologies, they have been drawn into more significant international collaboration than is widely acknowledged.

Like MITI, MESC and STA both began to place new emphasis on international collaboration in the late 1980s. Each expanded international fellowship programs and established "centers of excellence" that might attract more foreign researchers. As part of the administrative reform of government in 2001, MESC absorbed the STA and became the Ministry of Education, Culture, Sports, Science and Technology (MEXT), known in Japanese as the Monbukagakushō. The implications of this change for international collaboration will become clearer over time as the two bureaucratic cultures are forced to adapt and bureaucratic structures are reorganized. As of early 2004, MEXT has consolidated activities in some areas such as space research but not in others such as fellowships for foreign researchers. One of MEXT's major responsibilities will be coordinating Japanese participation in megascience projects such as the International Space Station and the International Thermonuclear Experimental Reactor (ITER). Even in the world of basic science, however, the cost-saving rationale for international collaboration is far from inexorable. During the 1990s, Japan pursued independent projects, with no commercial potential, in astronomy and high-energy physics rather than choosing to collaborate with the United States.

International Collaboration in Aerospace, Micromachines, and Semiconductors

As three controversial and very different responses to the forces driving internationalization of research, the HFSP, IMS, and RWC programs provide important insights into MITI's techno-globalism. Yet, the HFSP and IMS stand today as one-of-a-kind programs. Despite their respective merits, neither has turned out to be typical of the path MITI followed in opening its research programs to foreign participation. Like the RWC, most other MITI programs that have involved foreign firms are best characterized as open, national consortia. These projects tend to have smaller budgets and, with the exception of perhaps the hypersonic engine project, more limited foreign participation than the RWC program. The size of the foreign partners also varies greatly, from major firms like Intel, General Electric, Motorola, and BASF to nonprofit research organizations like SRI International and start-ups like IS Robotics. Although foreign firms usually play no role in the initial planning of these projects, they are generally satisfied with the degree of information exchange among partners and the disposition of intellectual property rights.

Aerospace

The HYPR provides an important reference point for two reasons. To begin, HYPR was one of the first cases of MITI incorporating the idea of a central research role for foreign firms into plans for one of its industrial projects. The international negotiations on HYPR also resulted in the revision of MITI rules on intellectual property rights in large-scale research projects with foreign participation. Launched in 1989 by MITI's Agency for Industrial Science and Technology, HYPR ran for ten years with a total budget of roughly $250 million, a sum that absorbed more than one third of MITI's annual aerospace budget.[1] The project was intended to lay the groundwork for development of a hypersonic engine rather than to achieve the much-longer-range goal of building a fully functional engine. HYPR succeeded in developing a subscale prototype for a combined-cycle engine that would enable flight at Mach 5. The prototype integrated a turbojet engine that functions from subsonic speeds to Mach 3, and a ramjet engine that operates from Mach 3 to Mach 5. The prototype has only one-tenth the thrust believed necessary for a four-engine hypersonic transport and does not meet the temperature requirements of hypersonic flight. MITI developed a Mach 5 engine because U.S. and European programs were focusing on Mach 2.5 transports and Mach 25 spaceplanes. At the outset, MITI officials acknowledged that a hypersonic commercial aircraft might never actually be developed, but believed it possible that such a vehicle could be in service by 2025.[2]

HYPR was organized around three Japanese and four foreign firms working under contract with MITI's New Energy and Industrial Technology Organization (NEDO). The Japanese partners were the country's three leading manufacturers of aircraft engines, the so-called heavies: Ishikawajima-Harima Heavy Industries (IHI), Kawasaki Heavy Industries (KHI), and Mitsubishi Heavy Industries (MHI). The foreign partners were General Electric (GE) and Pratt & Whitney of the United States, Rolls Royce of the United Kingdom, and SNECMA of France. Although less advanced in overall design capabilities than their foreign counterparts, the Japanese partners took the lead in design and development of the prototype hypersonic engine. Nonetheless, the foreign firms played more than a token role in the project.

Initially, all partners collaborated in selecting a target engine configuration. Over the course of the project, GE worked on design of the turbo-shaft's main bearing and lubrication system and tested the subscale turbofan in its high-altitude test facility. Pratt and Whitney helped to design and test the ramburner and provided assistance in developing specifications for methane fuel. On the European side, Rolls Royce worked on turbofan engine emissions and noise while SNECMA worked on exhaust nozzle design, noise suppression, and ramjet emissions.[3] Each of the foreign companies assigned five to ten engineers to the project; the Japanese partners had roughly five hundred engineers charging at least part time to the project. The distribution of research funds from MITI reflected this overall division of labor. Roughly 65 percent of the annual budget for HYPR was allocated to the three Japanese partners, 25 percent to the foreign partners, and the remaining 10 percent to four Japanese national laboratories that played a supporting role in research.[4]

HYPR allowed the foreign partners to conduct Mach 5 research, which was not heavily funded in either the United States or Europe, and to learn more about the strengths and weaknesses of their Japanese partners.[5] Both GE and Pratt & Whitney were satisfied with the research results in HYPR and the flow of information between partners. Both firms took part in HYPR in the belief that even limited participation was preferable to a major research program going forward without any American involvement. With Japan as a major terminus for any high-speed aircraft, the American firms also thought Japanese involvement in the development of a high-speed transport was inevitable. In addition, the foreign partners had the financial incentive provided by the MITI subsidy and the opportunity to gain increased insight into the design capabilities of the major Japanese engine makers.[6]

Nevertheless, the initial negotiations on their participation in HYPR were long and complex. The formal agreement between NEDO and the foreign companies was not signed until early 1991, over a year after the official launch of the project. The major stumbling block in these negotiations was the treatment of intellectual property rights. As pointed out in chapter 6, before 1991 MITI owned any intellectual property (IPR) generated in its large-scale projects and effectively controlled the disposition of that IPR. Wanting to avoid restrictions on the use of any IPR that might be generated in the project, the four foreign firms joined together to press MITI for more liberal terms. As a result, MITI decided to grant both domestic and foreign participants 50 percent ownership of any IPR generated in an international project, as well as the right to license the government-owned portion of that IPR at minimal or no charge. Firms could use the IPR freely in their own research and needed to negotiate with MITI over fees only if they were con-templating an outward license.[7] The ministry considered addressing IPR is-sues on a case-by-case basis but thought it better to change the regulations themselves because it anticipated similar complaints in the future.[8]

Although HYPR achieved its goal of advancing hypersonic engine de-sign, the utility of the project has been called into question because MITI never planned a parallel project to develop a plane sufficiently sophisticated to use such an engine. As the Japanese economy worsened in the 1990s, MITI was forced to scale back plans for hypersonic research and began to characterize HYPR as a way to establish the credentials for participation in any future international collaboration on a supersonic transport. At the end of the HYPR project, MITI began a four-year collaboration with the same firms on the design of a more quiet and fuel-efficient turbofan engine in-tended to fly at speeds between Mach 2 and Mach 3. According to a MITI official, "the limitations of the national budget forced us to reconsider the strategy of the ramjet, and focus more on short-term, lower risk technology which could be applied to a Concorde successor."[9]

Supporting the work of HYPR, the High-Performance Materials for Se-vere Environments Project (1989–97) conducted research on carbon compos-ites, intermetallic compounds, and fiber-reinforced intermetallic compounds suitable for supersonic and hypersonic engines. Starting at a very modest level of only $2.3 million in 1989, annual funding flattened out at roughly $18.5 million by 1994.[10] Participants in the project included nine companies, a pe-troleum industry organization, four universities, and six government labs. In contrast to HYPR, there was little foreign involvement in the project. The only foreign member was Crucible Materials Corporation of the United States, which conducted research on production and evaluation of niobium aluminide powders.

Crucible Materials was approached by MITI, which had a particular interest in the company's knowledge of powders and the ceramic mold process. Crucible was eager to join the project, feeling it was a good match with the company's broader research strategy.[11] The company's main criticism of the project is that its goals were too ambitious. Although the basic design of the project was set before Crucible joined, the firm had freedom in the design and execution of its research proposal. Eight to ten Crucible engineers charged about one third of their time to the project. In general, the manpower commitment increased during the course of the project as the subsidy received from MITI grew from $20,000 to more than $250,000 per year. Crucible found participation in the project to be very rewarding. The company had no concerns about IPR, feeling the consortium's rules to be more generous than those in U.S. government research programs. Despite problems caused by distance and language, Crucible rated the level of cooperation in the project at eight out of ten. Reflecting this general satisfaction, the company submitted a proposal to MITI for follow-on research.

Micromachines

After RWC and HYPR, the Micromachine Project (1991–2001) was one of the open national consortia with the highest profiles during the 1990s. Consisting of very small yet highly sophisticated functional elements, micromachines are designed to perform highly precise tasks in applications such as microsurgery and inspection systems for difficult-to-access areas such as underground pipes. Participants included twenty-two Japanese firms, an American start-up, an American research organization, and an Australian university (see Table 7.1). Like HYPR, the Micromachine Project had no central research facility. MITI established the Micromachine Center in 1991 to administer a distributed research project with an estimated budget of $250 million over ten years. Disappointed with the progress of research, however, MITI eventually reduced the budget to $184 million, or an annual average of about $750,000 per firm—even though some firms, such as Denso, received more than twice as much as others.[12]

As with RWC, the opening of the project was largely a token response to foreign pressure with opportunities to exploit technological complementarities at the margin. Facing criticism for free-riding on basic research conducted in the West, MITI planners sought a research theme with minimal potential for short-run commercialization that would also build on traditional Japanese strength. The field of micromachines made sense because it took advantage of Japan's comparative advantage in robotics and was not receiving significant funding in the West. In the United States, research concentrated on what

Table 7.1

Partners in the Micromachine Project

Japanese Partners	Aisin Cosmos, Denso, Fanuc, Fuji Electric, Fujikura, Hitachi, Kawasaki Heavy Industries, Matsushita Research Institute, Mitsubishi Cable Industries, Mitsubishi Electric, Mitsubishi Heavy Industries, Murata Manufacturing, Olympus Optical, Omron, Sanyo, Seiko Instruments, Sumitomo Electric Industries, Terumo Corporation, Toshiba, Yaskawa Electric, Yokogawa Electric
Foreign Partners	IS Robotics (USA), SRI International (USA), Royal Melbourne Institute of Technology (Australia)

Source: Micromachine Center, *Micromachine Technology National R&D Project*, Pamphlet. Tokyo: Micromachine Center, 1994.

has become the field of microelectronic-mechanical systems (MEMS). Rooted in semiconductor process technology, MEMS refers to small sensors and actuators built on planar silicon substrates. Compatible with batch fabrication, these devices have applications such as air bag sensors and inkjet printer-heads.[13] In contrast, Japanese research was attempting to integrate a broader range of semiconductor and mechanical process technologies in applications such as micromotors, pumps, and robots. Because of their inherent complexity, these devices are more suited to customized rather than mass production.[14]

Although the Micromachine Project opened research in an area of relative Japanese strength, the difference in research emphases in the United States and Japan limited the potential to exploit complementary capabilities. In addition, the small potential market for micromachines may also have dissuaded some American firms from joining the project. Even still, the scale and focus of MITI's project initially worried some American scientists. Micromachines were pioneered in the United States at Bell Laboratories and MIT, but it was the Japanese government that was making the first real commitment to micromachine research. In 1990, as MITI planned the micromachine project, the NSF was allocating only $2 million per year to support research in this field.[15] Despite the opportunity to receive a MITI subsidy, however, American universities stayed away from the project. The likelihood of hostile treatment by the American press left many universities, especially publicly funded ones, reluctant to take part.[16]

Once underway, the project focused on developing fundamental micromachine technologies for three basic applications: maintenance of power plants, microfactories, and medical procedures. The first theme envisioned development of microrobots that could perform sophisticated inspection and repair functions in highly confined spaces such as inside the tubes in a power plant. The microfactory theme aimed to develop a desktop system that integrates materials preparation, assembly, and inspection of precision parts such as those in watches and cameras. In the medical applications theme, researchers pursued several projects including diagnostic and therapeutic systems for cerebral blood vessels and sensing technologies for monitoring contact pressure during catheter and balloon operations.

Only one research organization (SRI International) and one start-up (IS Robotics) from the United States ultimately joined the project. SRI International is an independent, nonprofit corporation that performs a broad spectrum of research under contract to government, business, and industry. Research is SRI's only product; it does not compete with industry in the manufacturing of devices or systems. Almost all of SRI's staff of 1,400 researchers are based at the firm's headquarters in Menlo Park, California. The firm has conducted a variety of research and consulting for Japanese firms since the establishment of its Tokyo office in 1961.[17] SRI worked with MITI on some minor projects during the 1960s and 1970s, but the scale and scope of its activity increased dramatically in the late 1980s with MITI's push toward R&D internationalization.

Dr. Ronald Pelrine, chief SRI researcher in the Micromachine Project, decided to submit a research proposal to MITI after being informed of the program by SRI's Tokyo office. Pelrine considered the Micromachine Project important, but was not worried that it would give Japan any decisive advantage over other nations in this technology. He believed it very unlikely that any single project, no matter how successful, could change relative national capabilities. The field was already large, with much of the significant work being done commercially without any government involvement. Pelrine proposed work on artificial muscles, an ongoing interest in SRI's advanced automation lab, which appeared to fit well with the goals of the project. By the end of the project in 2001, research had reached an application stage, but SRI planned to continue refining the technology. In the last two years of the project alone, SRI researchers succeeded in increasing the strain, pressure, and response time parameters of the muscles by five to thirty times.[18] The technology has a range of applications from micropumps to insect-like legs for inspection robots that would be more effective than wheels in overcoming obstacles like the rivets and welds found in industrial piping.

Although the Micromachine Project was distributed in structure like the RWC program, SRI seemed to enjoy a higher level of interaction with Japanese firms than some of the foreign partners in the RWC. Dr. Pelrine held regular technical discussions with a number of project members and visited

several Japanese laboratories. One of the more significant benefits of participation, according to Pelrine, was the commitment to a long-term goal rather
than a short-term payoff. This approach enabled his team to do fairly basic
engineering research with potentially important long-term applications. Of
course, on a purely business level, such long-term contracts also hold a strong
appeal for SRI's management.

Initially, SRI had some concerns over the IPR rules in MITI programs,
but, in Pelrine's words, found MITI "helpful in changing problem areas."
SRI executives were also able to satisfy Department of Commerce concerns over IPR rules because the results of much of their contract research
would be in the public domain. SRI was also impressed with MITI's quick
turnaround time in approving public presentation of research results—in
some cases taking less than twenty-four hours. As with the foreign partners
in the RWC program, SRI was most frustrated with MITI's accounting procedures. On the whole, however, it was happy with the project. Taking part
in METI research programs has become a standard component of SRI's
contract research.

The second American partner, IS Robotics, is a small firm founded in
1990 by researchers from MIT's Artificial Intelligence Laboratory and NASA's
Jet Propulsion Laboratory. Now the research arm of iRobot, IS Robotics works
mostly for the Defense Advanced Research Projects Agency and the Office
of Naval Research. IS Robotics became involved in the Micromachine Project
through personal contacts made at a trade show. The firm believed its core
competence in behavior-based technologies scaled down well to the
micromachine level and fit well with the research theme on pipe inspection
technologies.[19] Before joining, the firm checked with the U.S. government
about its participation but found the Department of Commerce less concerned
about potential problems than the firm was itself. In the first half of the project,
IS Robotics had seven of its ten researchers devoting roughly 15 percent of
their time to the project.

IS Robotics had minimal interaction with other partners in the first half
of the project, but felt that the flow of information at conferences was satis-
factory and evenhanded. As with SRI, IS Robotics' major disappointment
with the project was MITI's accounting system, which required that firms
be reimbursed for their research expenses rather than receiving the research
subsidy up front. To circumvent this system, IS Robotics arranged to become a subcontractor to MHI in the second half of the program. Although
concerned that this represented a "loss of status" for IS Robotics and for the
international profile of the project, MITI agreed reluctantly to the change.
The contract work for MHI produced the 2PHLM Robot for inspection of
ships and nuclear power plants. The robot has four modular tentacles that

allow it to alter its shape and gait to perform a given task. Able to move in unfamiliar environments using its tactile sensing capabilities, the robot has a squirming gait suitable for crawling through pipes and an inching gait for negotiating obstacles.

The Japanese partners cite mostly generic benefits from participation in the project. Firms such as Denso and Yokogawa mention the guarantee of long-run financial support from the government as the most important benefit because it allowed them to buy equipment that would have otherwise been beyond their budgets. Others mention the importance of the second phase of the project in bringing together researchers from companies in different businesses. For example, Olympus worked with Omron and Murata on development of an industrial catheter. Finally, all the Japanese partners acknowledged the role of the Micromachine Center in minimizing the transaction costs of information collection and dissemination.[20] In addition to several fundamental technologies developed by the respective participants, the project succeeded in developing two main prototype systems, one close to market and one that served more as a showcase for its component technologies.

For plant maintenance, a team consisting of Sumitomo Electric, Matsushita, and Mitsubishi Electric developed an experimental chain-type micromachine less than one centimeter in length. The robot can inspect the pipework in power plants without any disassembly of the pipe system. Moving at 7.2 m per hour, the microrobot detects cracks by noting increased resistance when it passes an electric current through the pipe.[21] In addition, seven firms collaborated in the design and construction of a prototype microfactory, less than one square meter in size, that can manufacture gear boxes less than one centimeter across. Far too slow for mass production, the prototype is most noteworthy for its component technologies. For example, the microfactory has no moving conveyor belts; Fuji Electric developed an electromagnetic transport system that moves the microparts along individually programmed paths. The microfactory also has no furnaces; Seiko Instruments developed an electrochemical process for forming the metal gears used in the gear box. Although this technique is slow, it represents an important alternative to drilling and grinding because it does not produce any dust, one of the major causes of malfunctions in microgears.[22] Altogether, the Micromachine Project produced 1,421 papers, 600 patent applications, and more than 150 registered patents. Although the project did not set out to develop finished products, a few did reach market even before the project ended. These included an ultrasonic probe for medical diagnosis and a system of shape-memory coils for use as actuators in fiber scopes and catheters.[23]

In evaluating the Micromachine Project, an outside committee of academics and industry experts concluded that the project advanced precision mechanical machining technology, but criticized that the demonstration platforms, particularly the microrobots for power plant inspections, did not address mainstream industrial needs. The committee recommended that subsequent research projects pursue silicon-based MEMS technology more aggressively and focus on applications in information and communications technology as well as medicine.[24] In choosing the theme of micromachines for partly political reasons, MITI seemed to have bet on the wrong technology. While the micromachine business remained limited, the MEMS market developed rapidly in the late 1990s, eliciting greater government funding for this field in both the United States and Japan.

Semiconductors

Although MITI may have opened a range of projects to foreign participation, the renewed promotion of the semiconductor industry that began in the mid-1990s seems more consistent with techno-nationalism. Kenneth Flamm describes the consortia of this time as part of a dense network of government-industry collaboration closed to any meaningful foreign participation. Flamm is correct that these projects could have been more open. The behavior of MITI and Japanese chipmakers clearly shows the limits of techno-globalism in the high-stakes world of semiconductors. MITI had the opportunity to involve foreign firms more fully in its projects, and private consortia had the chance to work more closely with their European and American counterparts. Yet, they chose a more nationalist approach to research because of the importance of the semiconductor industry to the Japanese economy and the increasingly intense pressures of international competition. Nevertheless, the techno-nationalist characterization of these programs has to be qualified in two important ways. First, Japanese and foreign research projects have not always been identical in organization or approach; therefore, differing research priorities can sometimes help explain the decision to establish a national project rather than join a foreign one. Second, and more important, techno-nationalism has been tempered by the need for at least some projects based in each leg of the triad to increase collaboration with one another in order to deal with the costly transition to next-generation technologies.

As in Japan, firms in Europe are pursuing both open and closed approaches to chip development. Although the Inter-University Microelectronics Center (IMEC) collaborates with both American and Japanese counterparts, the Microelectronics Development for European Applications-Plus (MEDEA+) project brings together over 220 partners from only European countries. Established in 2001, MEDEA+ is an industry-led initiative that will run until

2008 under the banner of the EUREKA program. It channels private and public funding into a range of projects involving chipmakers and their suppliers, design houses, and research institutes. Members have budgeted almost $2 billion for thirty-six projects over the first four years of the program.[25]

As these numbers suggest, the manufacture of semiconductors is costly. Fabrication costs continue to rise while rapid advances in technology continue to shorten the useful life of investments. The stakes have grown even higher as the industry has moved toward new wafer sizes and lithography (etching) technologies. Planning for the transition from 200 mm to 300 mm wafers during the mid-1990s, for example, brought the industry to a crossroads. The high costs of conversion forced firms to come together and develop uniform standards in advance of the transition. Unlike in previous transitions, no single firm was prepared to take the lead. To begin, the shift to 300 mm wafers required a massive overhaul of manufacturing tools and a fundamental change in the design of fabrication facilities. In contrast to the $1 billion spent on development of 200 mm tools in the 1980s, the development costs of 300 mm wafers, according to experts, would exceed $10 billion. In addition, Intel and IBM had both found that the costs of leading previous transitions outweighed the benefits of first access to new capabilities.[26] Collaboration was a necessity for even the strongest firms in the industry. The question was what firms would come together to collaborate and how international those collaborations might be.

Beyond the challenge of converting to 300 mm wafers that faced semiconductor firms everywhere, two further challenges confronted Japanese bureaucrats and industry leaders. First, by the mid-1990s, Japanese chipmakers were encountering more intense international competition than a decade earlier. Korean and Taiwanese firms had emerged as leaders in "commodity" DRAM chips, and Intel and a handful of other American firms continued to dominate the higher-end microprocessor market.[27] Japanese producers were being squeezed from both sides. Second, the semiconductor industry had become increasingly important to the sluggish Japanese economy. While Japan's total manufactured exports increased by only 15 percent during the 1990s, semiconductor exports grew by 114 percent. And from 1992 to 1997, while employment in the manufacturing sector declined by 800,000, the semiconductor industry added 50,000 jobs.[28] Gripped by a sense of crisis, MITI and Japan's leading chipmakers embarked on a series of projects to revitalize the Japanese semiconductor industry.

This undertaking began in 1994 with the founding of the Semiconductor Industry Research Institute of Japan (SIRIJ) by the nation's ten largest chipmakers: Fujitsu, Hitachi, Matsushita, Mitsubishi Electric, NEC, Oki, Sanyo, Sharp, Sony, and Toshiba. In 1995, SIRIJ approached MITI for funding of collaborative research in several semiconductor technologies. MITI agreed to fund nine research themes as part of a new consortium to be called the Association of Super-Advanced Electronics Technologies (ASET) program. With a budget of roughly $300 million over five years, ASET emphasized lithography and other semiconductor process technologies but included two projects on disk drives and one on liquid-crystal displays. The Japanese subsidiaries of IBM, Merck, and Texas Instruments, as well as the members of SIRIJ, joined ASET. At the same time, SIRIJ members established the privately funded Semiconductor Leading Edge Technologies (SELETE) consortium to undertake evaluation and development of 300 mm wafer technology. The way ASET came together provides further evidence of the changing nature of MITI's innovation policy during the 1990s. Rather than being reluctant participants in a top-down industrial policy, semiconductor firms played a "guiding role in orchestrating the publicly funded ASET project."[29] Nevertheless, some analysts criticized ASET as inconsistent with the rhetoric of techno-globalism.

Kenneth Flamm argues that ASET and SELETE should be considered as parts of a single government-industry initiative essentially closed to foreign participation rather than as two distinct programs—a publicly subsidized program open to foreign firms and a private program closed to foreign firms. In the first place, the two programs shared the same Japanese members and their research agendas were closely intertwined. For example, the results from ASET would be transferred to the more applied SELETE consortium at the development stage, and ASET's most important research project on ArF lithography would be physically located at SELETE's facilities. Furthermore, ASET was not nearly as international as MITI contended. The five core projects in semiconductor process technology included only Japanese participants, with foreign firms "relegated to marginal areas of the ASET research agenda" not designated for priority funding. According to Flamm, opening ASET to limited foreign participation enabled MITI to deflect charges of techno-nationalism. Similarly, splitting semiconductor research between "public" and "private" programs allowed Japan to stay within 1993 GATT guidelines permitting government subsidies of no more than 50 percent of the cost of any precompetitive development activity.[30]

There is no question that both ASET and SELETE could have been more open to foreign participation. ASET could have integrated foreign members more fully into its activities, and SELETE could have collaborated more closely with Sematech on the evaluation of 300 mm wafers. In 1995, Sematech established the International 300 mm Initiative (I300I), which included six U.S. and seven foreign members. SELETE declined the invitation to join I300I, citing language barriers, the distance between Japan and Austin, Texas, and differences in philosophies of manufacturing, in particular, the belief of some Japanese chipmakers that unique production equipment was necessary to differentiate their products.[31] However, the reasoning behind this decision may have reflected more than simply techno-nationalism.

First, SELETE and I300I were not identical programs. Although they shared the same fundamental goals, SELETE was more ambitious and more heavily funded. I300I focused only on the evaluation of 300 mm tools at individual suppliers' facilities, but SELETE worked on evaluation and development at a central facility. In addition, members contributed roughly $280 million over the five years of the SELETE project—giving it an annual budget nearly twice that of I300I in absolute terms, and nearly three times larger on a per member basis.[32] Second, like I300I, SELETE included an important dimension of openness with its policy of testing tools from suppliers worldwide. By 1998, only 50 percent of the tools evaluated by I300I were made by U.S. firms while only 60 percent of tools evaluated by SELETE were made by Japanese firms. According to Rose Marie Ham, both SELETE and I300I demonstrate "an unprecedented level of cooperation within and across national borders . . . without parallel in the history of this and other capital intensive, politically charged industries such as automobiles and aerospace."[33]

Since the late 1990s, the web of collaborative arrangements between semiconductor consortia has grown dramatically but there are still pronounced limits on collaboration—especially between consortia based in Japan and the United States. In 1998, Sematech allowed three European and two Asian firms—Philips Semiconductors, STMicroelectronics, Infineon (formerly Siemens Semiconductor Group), Hyundai Electronics, and the Taiwan Semiconductor Manufacturing Company—to join a new subsidiary called International Sematech. Japanese firms, however, were not invited to join. Politically, such an invitation would have been difficult because Sematech was originally conceived to improve U.S. competitiveness relative to Japan. In addition, the European and Asian firms that were invited to join tended to buy more American-made tools than their Japanese counterparts.[34] Although International Sematech did not invite Japanese membership, its parent organization went on to initiate several collaborations with Japanese firms. In 1998, I300I entered into a joint equipment evaluation and demonstration agreement with SELETE to facilitate tool demonstrations and the sharing of results from 300 mm equipment evaluations. Then in 1999, as Sematech dissolved the International Sematech subsidiary and made foreign firms full-fledged members, the consortium announced an agreement with Hitachi to work on semiconductor manufacturing equipment.[35] It also made another overture to SELETE. Sematech CEO Mark Melliar-Smith visited Japan and expressed a desire to move from information sharing to actual research collaboration. "With collaboration, we can save 50 cents on the dollar, rather than the 3 cents saved with cooperation, which tends to be at the back-end and much of which is window dressing."[36]

Although most of the collaboration between SELETE and the now renamed International Sematech continues to focus on information sharing and standard setting rather than research, the number of collaborative projects has increased. In July 2000, the two consortia announced a joint project to support implementation of standard software requirements for 300 mm equipment.[37] One year later, they announced a collaboration in equipment engineering capability that represented a "major step toward standardized worldwide e-manufacturing guidelines." The addition of SELETE to the initiative brought almost 90 percent of the world's chipmakers into alignment.[38] Like SELETE, the ASET program also set about expanding its ties outside Japan. In May 2001, ASET entered into talks with the Intel-backed Extreme Ultraviolet Limited Liability Company (EUV LLC) following public statements by Intel CEO Craig Barret, among others, that the development of EUV lithography is so costly and difficult that Japanese input and know-how is crucial to precompetitive research.[39]

This move toward increased collaboration in EUV lithography occurred as METI and Japan's chipmakers began a second campaign to strengthen the position of the semiconductor industry. This began with the launch of three projects in 2001 (see Figure 7.1). First, Japanese firms launched the Advanced Semiconductors through Collaborative Achievement (ASUKA) project. With an estimated budget of roughly $690 million over five years, ASUKA plans to develop system-on-chip technologies on the scale of 90 to 65 nanometers, or billionths of a meter. The project draws on the resources of both SELETE and the Semiconductor Technology Academic Research Center (STARC). As its 300 mm wafer evaluation project ended in 2000, SELETE geared up to develop semiconductor production equipment as part of ASUKA. Meanwhile, STARC moved beyond its role of strengthening ties between industry and academia to become a developer of design software for ASUKA. Although METI subsidized the construction of a clean room in Tsukuba, the vast majority of funding comes from industry.

Some firms openly questioned plans for the project. Yukio Sakamoto, president of Nippon Foundry, worried that it would be very difficult to make ASUKA a success in view of the large number of participants.[40] Yet, all eleven equity investors in SELETE eventually signed on to the project. Although ASUKA claimed to be "open to any firm interested in participating," such opening has been modest at best.[41] Samsung Electronics joined the project, but as a contractor rather than a full-fledged member. Collaboration with foreign-based consortia has also been limited but in 2002 ASUKA began

Figure 7.1   **Major Japanese Semiconductor Consortia** (2003)

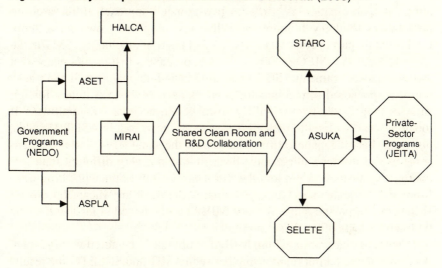

working with Europe's IMEC. After a first phase of experimentation with each other's design assets, the two began an "equal partnership" for the development of new "system-on-chip" design technologies.[42]

As Japan's chipmakers formed ASUKA, the government launched two complementary programs, both with more modest budgets. The High-Performance and Agilent Cleanroom Association (HALCA) set out to make existing production tools more efficient for low-volume runs of specialized chips. Budgeted at $54 million, the three-year project received only $33 million from government.[43] Organized by ASET and METI's National Institute for Industrial Science and Technology (AIST), the Millennium Research for Advanced Information Technology (MIRAI) project is a more ambitious seven-year venture to develop insulation materials necessary to improve the processing speed and power consumption of circuits in the 45–65 nm range. With government support of 25.2 billion yen ($215 million), MIRAI mobilizes more than seventy researchers from the twenty-four member firms and twenty-nine researchers from AIST. Reflecting METI's promotion of industry-university collaboration, two of the five research groups are led by university researchers.[44]

Initially, some foreign observers criticized METI for establishing MIRAI rather than joining a collaboration between IMEC and ISMT on gate-stack technologies for circuits smaller than 100 nm. MIRAI, however, has a broader focus than the latter project. In addition, work on gate-stack technologies in MIRAI is led by university researchers and so results are more likely to be published in the open literature. Nevertheless, foreign participation in the project is limited. Only Intel and Samsung have joined MIRAI. Intel characterizes its participation as part of a two-pronged approach to research on photomasks for EUV lithography. While investing in its own mask shop, Intel is taking part in consortia in each leg of the triad, including ISMT in the United States and IMEC in Europe.[45] The company's first experience with a Japanese project came in ASET. According to an Intel manager, Japan's government-sponsored semiconductor projects have been open to any foreign firm, as long as the firm is willing to make the necessary commitment. It took one year for Intel to pass all the necessary tests to join ASET. He adds, however, that all Japanese firms had to pass the same tests. And as burdensome as the red tape might have been, it was not very different than that confronting firms wanting join the European Union. Framework Programs. More than bureaucracy, language remains the most significant hurdle for U.S. firms; all business in ASET and MIRAI is conducted in Japanese, so the transaction costs of participation remain very high.[46]

In short, collaboration within MIRAI is obviously centered within Japan. And, as with the earlier relationship between ASET and SELETE, the results of the government-funded MIRAI will be delivered to the privately funded ASUKA for implementation. In 2003, MIRAI and ASUKA also began cooperation in three areas of chip development including ion injection into silicon wafers. This was the first formal collaboration announced between the two projects that share the same lab in Tsukuba. Although intended to reduce redundancy, this collaboration produced complaints about overlap between the two projects and inefficiency.[47]

These complaints have been drowned out, however, by discussion of the controversial government project undertaken by the Advanced System-on-Chip Platform Corporation (ASPLA). With a subsidy of 31.5 billion yen ($250 million), eleven Japanese firms are working on the design of semiconductor devices at the 90 nm node. Although Intel is monitoring the progress of the project, it had no interest in taking part in this effort that is focused on short-term goals. Launched in 2002, ASPLA aims to have a model pilot line running by 2004. This time frame reflects the reorientation of METI R&D programs toward more commercial results as well as METI's increasing ambition to shape the business strategies of Japan's chipmakers. METI wants to steer Japan's integrated-device manufacturers toward a new foundry strategy. According to Hidetaka Fukuda, director of the IT Industry Division of METI's Commerce and Information Policy Bureau, "the differences in production technology among the major chipmakers are not so significant. . . . There is no need for every company to invest so much in the same precompetitive areas."[48] ASPLA's mission is to standardize a system-on-chip technology base on which each firm can build its own business. In addition, the project aims to accelerate the progress of ASUKA and MIRAI by using their 65 nm processes on its pilot line. And, as part of its plan to establish an open system-on-chip platform, ASPLA also intends to verify designs developed by overseas companies and research institutions.[49]

The more intrusive ASPLA program, with its focus on a shared foundry, has engendered considerable debate among firms. Although some see it as an important way to revitalize the industry, others suggest it may be gambling on the wrong technology, or, in its reliance on a common technological base, simply suffering from the risk aversion of bureaucrats and the lack of vision that burdens already struggling Japanese chipmakers.[50] There is even broader concern about the pressures for restructuring that have accompanied METI's recent increase in support for the semiconductor industry. As consortia came together, Toshiba and Fujitsu established a new partnership in chipmaking and Hitachi and Mitsubishi Electric integrated their chip operations. Some industry publications have questioned whether these agreements are simply consolidating similar operations rather than bringing together complementary capabilities. They have speculated that the firms will end up wasting considerable time and resources just trying to establish a working relationship, much as happened to the banks that merged to form the Mizuho Financial Group, and will run into serious difficulties as a result.[51]

Both the private and government-subsidized consortia have produced noteworthy results. In 2003, for example, SELETE overcame a major hurdle in the development of electron beam photolithography for circuit patterns of less than 90 nm. In the same year, ASET made progress in the fabrication of high-performance masks for EUV lithography and developed a light-bending optical connector that will help shrink the size of servers by over 90 percent.[52] Yet, it is unclear if these kinds of results will be enough to revitalize Japan's semiconductor industry. Even though they feel compelled to organize collaborative projects, METI bureaucrats have not been terribly confident of success. Nonetheless, subsidies are an easy sell to companies in difficult financial positions that continue to join these programs.[53] Ironically, some blame the industry's continued problems on a failure to apply the results of recent semiconductor projects rather than the failure of these projects to produce results. According to an industry insider, SELETE did an excellent job of developing 300 mm tools, but it was Taiwanese firms that came up with more competitive strategies for applying the technology.[54] In view of the technological challenges on the horizon, both private and government-subsidized projects are likely to remain a feature of the Japanese semiconductor industry for some time. If METI chooses to emphasize more short-term and near-market projects like ASPLA, however, promotion of the industry is likely to take on a more closed, nationalist character.

The Ministry of Education and International Collaboration in Basic Science

Mired in an economic slump for more than a decade, Japan appears as a shadow of its former self. Every year, the International Institute for Management Development in Switzerland—one of Europe's most respected non-profit research organizations—ranks the major industrialized countries in eight areas. Since the early 1990s, Japan's ranking has declined markedly in areas such as quality of financial system, corporate management, and human resources. Overall, the nation dropped from first place in 1993 to thirtieth in 2002. According to the 2002 survey, Japan remained near the top in only one area. With its high R&D expenditures and large number of researchers, it ranked second in science infrastructure.[55] Yet, this commonly held view of Japan as number two in science behind the United States has been challenged on the basis of both quantity and quality of scientific research.

According to Yoshiyuki Ohtawa, figures for Japanese R&D expenditures, especially for university research, are vastly overestimated. Unlike in the United States, for example, Japanese R&D data are gathered not only from universities but from junior colleges as well and, until recently, grouped funding for the natural sciences with that for the humanities and social sciences. In addition, data on R&D spending also cover labor expenditures, including the salaries of teachers. Thus, according to Ohtawa, international comparisons of R&D spending, based even on data collected by the OECD, can be highly misleading. Such comparisons became even more skewed in the late 1990s with the budget cuts forced on all Japanese ministries. As the labor costs that account for almost 80 percent of the Ministry of Education's expenses were driven up by wage increases, the ministry was left with less money to support actual research and with virtually nothing for the improvement of facilities and equipment.[56]

Japan's method of calculating R&D expenditures may help explain why seemingly large research budgets have not produced proportionate results. In 1999, spending on scientific research in Japan totaled $133 billion, compared with $233 billion in the United States, $54 billion in Germany, and $28 billion in the UK. In that same year, Japan ranked second behind the United States in the number of papers published in major academic journals worldwide. However, despite spending more than twice as much as Germany and almost five times as much as the UK on research, Japan ranked behind these nations in terms of the influence of its papers, as judged by the number of secondary references in other journals. In addition to blaming differences in accounting practices and the language barrier for this shortcoming, many Japanese researchers point to the lack of flexibility in the management and funding of scientific research.[57] They fault the rigid division of labor within the postwar Japanese science bureaucracy for this inflexibility.

Taken together, the Ministry of Education, STA, and MITI accounted for approximately 85 percent of the Japanese government's annual science and technology budget throughout the 1990s. With its regulatory authority encompassing machinery and information technologies, MITI had the highest participation by industry in its research programs. But its programs totaled only about 13 percent of Japanese government expenditures on science and technology. The STA received almost double that share, with roughly 25 percent of the annual budget, and the Ministry of Education even more, with approximately 47 percent of the government's annual science and technology budget, including research salaries. Although cooperation between MESC and MITI increased in the 1980s and 1990s, as discussed in earlier chapters, there was very little cooperation, or even coordination, between MESC and STA.

The Ministry of Education oversees research at Japanese universities and at several interuniversity research institutes. The latter, which includes world-renowned facilities such as the National Laboratory for High Energy Physics (KEK), provides the major venue for university researchers to interact with foreign scientists. The ostensible duties of STA included the planning and implementation of basic science and technology policy as well as overall coordination of the budget and administration for all science and technology activities. However, because STA had only agency status and lacked MITI's regulatory authority over industry or MESC's authority over the university system, its actual powers were quite limited. Nevertheless, STA carved a niche in the coordination of Japanese participation in megascience projects and the initiation of basic research projects that helped it break down traditional barriers between industry, universities, and national research institutes. During the 1990s, approximately 25 percent of STA's annual budget was set aside for the promotion of international programs, including environmental research, large-scale collaborative research projects, and international exchange programs. As part of the government's administrative reorganization, STA was closed in 2001 and most of its responsibilities were absorbed by an expanded the Ministry of Education.

Administrative Reform and the Science Bureaucracy

Japan's most recent push for administrative reform began in November 1996 with the formation of the Administrative Reform Council (ARC) under Prime Minister Ryutaro Hashimoto. The creation of the ARC set off a year of political wrangling among ministries fighting to protect their turf and, in some cases, their very existence. A year later, the ARC produced a plan to reduce the number of central government ministries and agencies from twenty-three to twelve beginning in January 2001. In addition to streamlining the government, the reforms also called for a substantial reduction in the ranks of government employees through a cutback in new hiring, a reduction in the number of public corporations attached to ministries, and the conversion of many publicly funded institutions such as national labs and hospitals into independent entities. The reforms also aimed to strengthen the policy-making powers of the prime minister through the creation of a Cabinet Office that assumes the authority of the former Economic Planning Agency, oversees the Defense Agency, and establishes four new advisory councils to devise and coordinate national strategies in areas that include science and technology policy.[58]

Many remain skeptical that the administrative reform will produce meaningful change. Edward J. Lincoln dismisses the reforms as "nothing more than a rearrangement of the organizational diagram for government."[59] Still, he acknowledges that even such reshuffling might improve the efficiency of government by reducing the number of contested domains among rival ministries. Lincoln is quick to point out, however, that such a result could actually give bureaucrats a larger role in policy making; the fewer the conflicts between ministries, the fewer the opportunities for politicians to influence policy by mediating disputes between bureaucrats. Several organizations have been merged as part of the administrative reform of the science bureaucracy, and this has already reduced substantially the number of potential interministry and interagency conflicts. Somewhat counterbalancing this reduced opportunity for political mediation may be the new authority given to the Cabinet Office. As part of the reform, a revamped Council for Science and Technology Policy (CSTP) assumed at least nominal responsibility for Japan's science and technology planning, including setting priorities for resource allocation and evaluating relevant institutions and programs. The CSTP has the prime minister as its official head, but its day-to-day management lies with the Minister of Science and Technology, a newly established position located in the Cabinet Office. Other members include ministers with research-related responsibilities, the president of the Science Council of Japan, five academics, and two industry representatives. The secretariat of roughly 100 staff members is drawn mostly from the bureaucracy.[60]

Although the CSTP is only an advisory body, it was designed to be a "control tower" for science and technology policy that could stand above the various ministries. Regardless, its reliance on a staff of mostly bureaucrats means that its secretariat may become simply a new venue for settling rivalries among the reduced number of ministries. Even with this limitation, however, the CSTP has for the first time brought a new coherence to science and technology planning on a government-wide basis. For example, it played a significant role in designing the Second Basic Plan (2001–6), particularly the setting of government research priorities. The CSTP defined four primary research themes that have guided research funding across all government ministries: life sciences; information and telecommunications; environmental sciences; and nanotechnology and materials. Ministries submit their R&D budget requests to MOF, which forwards them to the CSTP, which in turn ranks them against the priorities of the Second Basic Plan.[61]

Despite its new influence in policy coordination, the CSTP is far from an instrument of control for politicians. Countering the Koizumi government's efforts to reduce the number of public corporations, the CSTP has objected to abolishing or privatizing any public corporations involved in R&D; it argues that remaining competitive with the United States and the European Union requires preserving such government-supported bodies. In addition, the council has objected to changing the existing system of budgetary appropriations for capital investments in such public corporations that allows complete discretion in the way funds are used.[62] In this case, both bureaucrats and scientists have been anxious to see the system remain unchanged, the former to preserve postretirement jobs and the latter to maintain access to research funding.

When the interests of bureaucrats and scientists are divided, however, the influence of the CSTP is greatly weakened. The CSTP also pushed for reform of the Science Council of Japan (SCJ), a national organization of elite academics, affiliated with the Ministry of Public Management, that has advised the government on scientific and ethical issues such as brain death. The CSTP contended that the SCJ was too slow in preparing reports on issues such as global warming and human cloning. It recommended that the SCJ be restructured and even converted into an independent administrative institution. This proposal met with harsh criticism from the SCJ, which argued that its legitimacy would be lost if it became a corporate body. With high-profile appeals from some of Japan's top scientists, the SCJ was able to divide the members of the CSTP and defeat or at least forestall the proposed reform.[63] Thus, the CSTP may play an important role in coordinating science and technology planning, but it is by no means a "control tower" dictating policy.

Although the Ministry of Education may have less formal authority than the CSTP in setting the basic direction of science policy, it still commands more than 70 percent of Japan's R&D budget and is widely regarded as a "winner" in the administrative reform process. The secretariat of the newly expanded MEXT, which was officially established on January 1, 2001, oversees seven bureaus, including three that deal with education, three with science and technology, and one with sports and youth. The Science and Technology Bureau has policy and planning divisions, as well as a division of international affairs. The Research and Development Promotion Bureau oversees support for small and medium-sized research programs and cooperation with industry, and the Research and Development Bureau has responsibility for large-scale research programs formerly administered by STA, including ocean and earth sciences and space research and development.[64] The hope is that reducing duplication of effort will increase efficiency in policy making. However, the differing organizational cultures of MESC and STA make that a difficult task. Less than 20 percent of MESC's budget was devoted to science and virtually none of the ministry's staff had science or engineering backgrounds. In contrast, STA focused on science and technology and almost all of its staff were trained as engineers or scientists.[65]

STA bureaucrats were devastated by the announcement that the agency would be absorbed by the Ministry of Education. Viewing themselves as the vanguard in the reform of the Japanese R&D system, STA officials considered MESC paralyzed by the conservative professors' union and too slow to embrace necessary reforms.[66] Despite the likelihood that STA would be swallowed by the much larger MESC, the agency still petitioned for full ministerial status, arguing that its focus on large-scale international science collaborations did not fit well with MESC's focus on the university research system. This appeal was doomed from the start. During the deliberations of the ARC, Prime Minister Hashimoto repeatedly criticized the "sloppy performance" of STA in managing Japan's nuclear research program, especially the Power Reactor and Nuclear Fuel Development Corporation (PNC)—an STA public corporation.[67] A string of PNC technical failures and scandals resulted in months of negative headlines that embarrassed the Hashimoto government. In December 1995, PNC attempted to cover up a sodium leak at the Monju fast breeder reactor. Then, in March 1997, an explosion at PNC's Tokai reprocessing facility led to a low-level contamination of the immediate environment. Only months later, STA officials discovered that PNC had failed to report that many barrels stored at its facilities had been leaking low-level radioactive waste for more than twenty years.[68] These failures sealed the fate of STA.

International Collaboration under MEXT

The ultimate effect of administrative reform on international collaboration will not be clear for some years to come. MEXT is still working out the kinks of reorganization and consolidation. In some areas, the consolidation is well underway. In October 2003, MEXT merged its three aeronautical and space agencies to form the Japan Aerospace Exploration Agency (JAXA). On the one hand, this may be a simple instance of redrawing the organizational chart of the space science bureaucracy. On the other hand, this change may have important consequences for policy. For example, researchers from the former Institute of Space and Astronautical Science (ISAS) worry that the merger will put their basic scientific research in the shadow of the more commercial research carried out by the former National Space Development Agency (NASDA).[69] In either case, NASA and the European Space Agency will have the advantage of dealing with only one Japanese agency.

In other areas, MEXT seems prepared to tolerate at least some duplication. One of the major challenges confronting the ministry has been reconciling the activities of the Japan Society for the Promotion of Science (JSPS), which oversaw international fellowship programs at MESC, and the Japan Science and Technology Corporation (JST), which managed basic research programs and international exchanges at STA. Transformed into independent administrative bodies in 2003, the two organizations take slightly different approaches to project funding. The JSPS uses a "bottom-up" approach to fund research across a broad range of disciplines from the humanities to the natural sciences, and the JST takes a more "top-down" approach to funding research that might sow the seeds for new industries. Despite these different approaches, they often end up funding research in similar fields. MEXT has taken steps to reduce the overlap between the JSPS and the JST by transferring or adapting a few specific funding programs. At present, however, it seems content to differentiate the JSPS and the JST primarily by program approach rather than research field.[70]

Placed under MESC jurisdiction in 1967 as a *tokushu hōjin* or special legal entity, the JSPS oversees the ministry's domestic grants-in-aid program and several international fellowship programs. Its budget for Japan's fiscal year (JFY) 2002 totaled 173.8 billion yen or roughly $1.5 billion. Of this amount, 74 percent went to university research through the grants-in-aid program, 19.7 percent to fellowships for young researchers—including postdoctoral fellows from overseas—and 3.6 percent to international programs.[71] The oldest of the international programs is the Invitation Fellowship for Research in Japan, which was established in 1960. In JFY 2002, the JSPS awarded 489 short-term fellowships to researchers from Asia (152), Oceania (15), Africa (4), Europe (162), Russia and the NIS (23), North America (129), and South America (4). It also made 161 long-term awards to fellows from Asia (77), Oceania (9), Africa (7), Europe (41), Russia and the NIS (12), North America (14), and South America (1).[72] Although this program has grown and become more competitive over the years, the statistics suggest that scientists from the West, particularly from the United States, are most interested in short-term visits to Japan. The majority of invited fellows come from East and South Asia. A major drawback of this program is that it focuses on nurturing already existing relationships between scientists rather than creating new ones. Rather than allowing foreign researchers to apply to the program directly or through diplomatic channels, it requires that they be nominated by Japanese scientists interested in hosting them.

Along with increasing the number of Invitation Fellowships for Research in Japan, the JSPS introduced the Postdoctoral Fellowship Program for Foreign Researchers in 1988 to attract younger scientists. This program has grown rapidly in recent years. In JFY 2000, the JSPS awarded 1,225 fellowships. By JFY 2002, it awarded 1,711 fellowships to researchers from Asia (1,142), Oceania (50), Africa (76), Europe (297), Russia and the NIS (56), North America (74), and South America (16).[73] Unlike the Invitation Fellowships Program, however, applicants for a postdoctoral fellowship may be nominated by their respective governments. In addition to managing these fellowship programs, the JSPS established the International Cooperative Program for Advanced Research in 1992. This program supports small-scale, joint-research programs with counterpart foreign academic institutions like the U.S. National Science Foundation (NSF), the French National Research Center for Science, and the British Royal Society.

The JST was established in 1996 through the merger of the Research Development Corporation of Japan (JRDC) and the Japan Information Center for Science and Technology (JICST). In the early 1980s, the JRDC became STA's primary instrument for promoting basic research and international collaboration. Between 1989 and 2000, the JRDC and then the JST administered the STA Fellowship Program. During these years, the program awarded 3,168 short- and long-term fellowships to foreign scientists for conducting research at national laboratories and public corporations not affiliated with the university system. Although responsibility for the STA Fellowship Program was shifted to the JSPS in 2001, the JST continues its concentration on the "individual" in basic research programs. Most notably, the JST manages the Exploratory Research for Advanced Technology (ERATO) Program and the International Cooperative Research Program (ICORP).

ERATO was established in 1981 as a way to break down institutional barriers to innovative basic research in Japan. Drawing on surveys of junior researchers, the JST selects general research themes and senior scientists to direct projects funded at roughly $16 million over five years. Each project

director has complete discretion in recruiting a team of roughly twenty researchers from industry, academia, and government research institutes. Although intended to be a domestic program, ERATO has evolved to include
some international participation. Several projects have one research team
located overseas. And of the forty projects initiated since 1993, three have
directors based in the United States—although each of the three comes originally from Japan. Pleased with the results of ERATO, STA established the
ICORP in 1989.

ICORP is essentially an international version of ERATO. The JST and a
counterpart foreign research agency select a general research area and project
directors to lead complementary local research groups of roughly ten members each. A project runs for five years, with funding of approximately $30
million shared equally by the JST and its counterpart. Since the mid-1990s,
two or three new projects have been launched each year (see Table 7.2). In
1995, elements of ERATO and ICORP were combined in the Core Research
for Evolutionary Science and Technology (CREST) Program. CREST offers
five-year grants worth up to $10 million in one of seven strategic areas. Re-
flecting the emphasis that began in the mid-1990s on maximizing the returns
from government-sponsored research, CREST is a more strategic version of
ERATO intended to facilitate greater university-industry collaboration and
provide a stronger technological base for the nation's economy.[74] Although
most project teams are made up of only Japanese researchers, project directors are free to recruit team members from abroad.

Megascience Projects

In addition to funding the fellowships and basic research programs administered by the JSPS and the JST, the new MEXT oversees the large-scale programs formerly managed by STA. These include Japanese participation in
international megascience collaborations such as the International Space Station (ISS) and the ITER, as well as the operation of major domestic research
facilities such as the Spring-8 synchrotron radiation facility.

The ISS is the largest and most complex international science collaboration in history, bringing together the United States, Canada, the European Union, and Japan as well as the Russian Federation and Brazil. With
an estimated final cost of between $60 billion and $100 billion, the ISS
will consist of six experimental modules and one habitation module.[75]
Japan's experimental module, *Kibo*, arrived at the Kennedy Space Center
for prelaunch processing in June 2003. Controlled from the Tsukuba Space
Center, the module will allow four astronauts to perform experiments on
board or in an experimental facility exposed to outer space. Japan spent over

Table 7.2

Projects Supported by the International Cooperative Research Program
(1990–2002)

Research term	Research area	Primary international partner
2002–2007	Dynamic nanomachine	Yale University
2002–2007	Entropy control	Pohang University (South Korea)
2001–2006	Calcium oscillation	Karolinska Institute (Sweden)
2000–2005	Photon craft	Shanghai Institute of Optics
2000–2005	Cell mechanosensing	SUNY Buffalo
1999–2004	Biorecycle	Kasetsart University (Thailand)
1999–2004	Quantum entanglement	Ecole Normale Supérieure, CNRS (France)
1998–2003	HIV-1 sSubtype-E vaccine	Ministry of Public Health (Thailand)
1998–2003	Nanotubulites	CNRS
1998–2003	Single molecule processes	University of Naples
1997–2002	Cold trapped ions	University of Oxford
1997–2002	Chemotransformation	University of Twente (Netherlands)
1996–2001	Neuro genes	University of Ottawa
1996–2001	Mind articulation	MIT
1995–2000	Ceramics superplasticity	Max Planck Institute
1994–1999	Quantum transition	U.C. Santa Barbara, University of Notre Dame
1993–1998	Subfemtomole biorecognition	Uppsala University (Sweden)
1992–1997	Supermolecules	Louis Pasteur University
1991–1996	Microbial evolution	Michigan State University
1990–1995	Atom arrangement-design and control for new materials	Cambridge University, University of London

Source: Compiled from data at www.jst.go.jp (July 2003).

$3 billion for the development of *Kibo*, a sum that absorbed approximately 20 percent of the annual budget of the former National Space Development Agency.

Japan is also making one of the larger physical contributions to the project. It is providing 25 percent of the pressurized volume of the space station, a contribution that NASA characterizes as "amazing for a country which has never done manned space flight before."[76] NASA had hoped to launch *Kibo* in 2006 and complete assembly of the ISS by 2007, but the loss of the space shuttle *Columbia* in February 2003 may delay this schedule. Nevertheless, the Japanese government is already hoping to cut the cost of operating *Kibo* by outsourcing a portion of management and funding responsibilities to the private sector. MEXT will ask pharmaceutical and electrical-machinery firms to form a consortium to help share the funding burden because Japan's experiments are expected to focus on protein crystals with likely applications in medicine and new materials.[77]

After the space station, the ITER is the largest research endeavor among nations in the triad. With completion of its planned experimental fusion reactor by 2015, the ITER program will take a major step in the development of nuclear fusion as a viable energy source. The project began in 1992 with an engineering and design agreement signed by Canada, the European Union, Japan, the Russian Federation, and the United States. ITER ran into trouble in 1998 when the United States withdrew from the project, citing failure to agree on a final design plan and budget estimates approaching $12 billion.[78] The departure of the United States left Japan and the European Union as de facto project leaders and slowed progress even more. Japan was cautious about further committing to the project because of the restructuring of its science bureaucracy and continued budget pressures arising from the weakness of its economy. By late 2002, the members of ITER had agreed to a scaled-down reactor that would cost only $5 billion. Yet, Japan and the European Union had still not decided how to share costs. Tokyo proposed that it shoulder 22 percent of the construction cost and that Brussels bear 44 percent; Brussels countered that each should contribute 33 percent.[79] This deadlock was broken in January 2003 when the United States decided to rejoin ITER. The project gained even more momentum when China and South Korea joined over the subsequent months. After more than a decade of planning, the members of ITER set early 2004 as the target date for deciding the financial contributions of each partner, dividing the contract work, and making the largely political decision of where to build the reactor. The United States had missed its chance to bid for the project when it withdrew from the program. Canada, the European Union, and Japan all put forward candidate sites in the hope of becoming the global center for fusion research.

Decisions Against International Collaboration

As with MITI's more nationalistic approach in semiconductors, sometimes the Ministry of Education has chosen to pursue an independent course rather than take part in parallel research programs in the United States or Europe. In high-energy physics, for example, both Japan and the United States opted to build parallel facilities to produce B-mesons rather than collaborate on the construction of a collider. And in astronomy, each country decided to build an optical telescope eight meters in diameter on the same Hawaiian mountain-top. Both Japanese and American scientists defend the decision to invest in separate colliders as justified on scientific and financial grounds. In the case of the telescope, Japanese astronomers were able to convince the government that their need for more viewing time could only be met by having a Japanese facility. Although the construction of a national telescope does not provide Japan with any commercial benefits, it strengthens Japanese basic science. The B-factory and telescope cases illustrate that even in large-scale, basic science the logic of collaboration is by no means inexorable for any country.

In view of the high costs of building particle accelerators and the lack of short-term commercial returns from research, high-energy physics is attractive for international collaboration. Indeed, the experimental verification of the top quark in 1995 illustrated well the international character of much research in this field. Over eight hundred scientists from countries including Brazil, Canada, France, India, Italy, Japan, Korea, Russia, and the United States worked on the two colliding beam experiments at Fermilab in Chicago that verified the existence of the top quark. Moreover, the Japanese and Italian governments covered roughly one-third of the equipment costs for one of these two experiments.[80] Despite this background of international collaboration, Japan's National Laboratory for High-Energy Physics (KEK) and the Stanford Linear Accelerator Center (SLAC) decided to build separate B-factories rather than collaborate on the construction of a single accelerator.

According to Professor Yoshitaka Kimura, vice-director of KEK, it made both scientific and financial sense for Japan to pursue its own B-factory.[81] The goal of both the KEK and SLAC B-factory programs is to further understanding of the fundamental differences between matter and antimatter through study of the charge-parity violation phenomenon. Kimura explains that Japan has a strong interest in this phenomenon because a large part of the theory builds on the earlier work of two of Japan's most prominent scientists. In addition to this sentimental reason for building the B-factory, Kimura explains that parallelism in Japanese and American facilities is a boon to science. The existence of two facilities means not only increased access for physicists, but results of greater statistical significance. Although the goal in building each facility is the same, the KEK accelerator draws on different technologies that provide better beam conditions. Kimura also explains that the B-factory could be built within existing facilities for roughly $350 million as opposed to the billions of dollars needed to build, for example, a next-generation linear collider. Thus, the B-factory keeps KEK facilities at the cutting edge while still leaving funds for collaboration in larger international projects.[82] To the delight of MEXT, Japan's parallelism paid off. In

June 2001, the B-factory achieved the world record for the highest luminosity ever produced at a collider beam facility.[83]

As in the field of high-energy physics, Japan has taken part in several international collaborations in astronomy. In x-ray astronomy, Japan worked with the United States and United Kingdom on the *Ginga* probe launched in 1987. MESC's Institute of Space and Aeronautical Science (ISAS) also worked with NASA on development of the *Geotail* satellite launched in 1992 to study the earth's magnetospheric tail. Each country contributed roughly $80 million to the project, with Japan assuming primary responsibility for development of the satellite and NASA for its launch.[84] In contrast to this collaboration in space-based systems, however, as mentioned above Japan has taken a more independent approach in land-based telescopes. In 1991, Japan began construction on Hawaii's Mount Kea of an eight-meter optical telescope named "Subaru" rather than joining the Gemini project led by the United States, which was building a similar telescope on the very same mountain. Although the Subaru and Gemini telescopes draw on slightly different technologies, they provide essentially the same capabilities. Initially, Japanese astronomers planned to build a much more modest telescope than American or European astronomers. Japan first proposed development of a 3.5 meter telescope in the 1970s, when America and Europe were proposing far more ambitious 15 meter telescopes. The rationale for collaboration should have become stronger, however, during the 1980s as the technical target of all three projects converged on construction of a telescope roughly 8 meters in diameter. Making collaboration even more compelling, the U.S. Congress capped spending on the Gemini project at $88 million in 1991. With the future of the project thus in jeopardy, the NSF recruited the United Kingdom, Canada, Chile, Argentina, and Brazil as partners.[85]

Rather than joining Gemini, however, the Japanese continued work on Subaru. By this time the next stage of the Subaru project was funded and the construction date already set. However, according to Professor Keiichi Kodaira, director general of the National Astronomical Observatory of Japan, work on Subaru would have continued even without these commitments. Kodaira believes that the duplication in the Subaru and Gemini projects is actually positive because it allows astronomers greater viewing time for what is a relatively low premium in the world of big science. He explains that Japanese astronomers, who have no optical telescope in Japan because of poor visibility conditions, deserve to have their own telescope. In short, "Japanese astronomers want to play their own violin."[86] As this case illustrates, national governments will sometimes fund national projects in basic science with no commercial payoffs even when international collaboration offers a cheaper alternative.

The Case Studies in Context

In evaluating the HFSP, IMS, and RWC programs in the context of other industrial technology consortia organized by MITI, as well as international programs in basic science managed by the Ministry of Education, four main lessons emerge. First, the HFSP and IMS programs are unique in terms of their international funding and management structures. The majority of MITI's international programs are variations on the open, national project model found in the RWC. Nevertheless, the experience of foreign partners in the HYPR, Micromachine, and High-Performance Materials projects suggests that they can still benefit from open national programs, even when those programs have smaller budgets than the RWC. The American partners in these programs, which range from large firms like GE to start-ups like IS Robotics, have been satisfied with the quantity and quality of information exchanged with Japanese partners as well as the rules on intellectual property.

Second, there are clearly limits to Japan's techno-globalism as seen in semiconductor consortia during the 1990s. Both MITI and Japanese firms had the option to collaborate more fully with consortia in the United States and Europe, but chose a more nationalistic research strategy because of the importance of the semiconductor industry to the Japanese economy and the intense pressures of international competition in both the commodity chip and microprocessor markets. Despite these choices, however, both MITI and Japanese chipmakers have been forced to increase international collaboration in view of the expense and complexity of the transition to next-generation wafer and lithography technologies.

Third, the Ministry of Education oversees several international fellowship programs, but there is still a significant imbalance in researcher exchange with the advanced industrial countries. Despite efforts to make Japan a more attractive destination for foreign scientists, most applicants for long-term fellowships come from East and South Asia.

Fourth, the B-factory and optical telescope cases demonstrate the limits of the cost-sharing rationale for international collaboration, even when the research has no commercial application. Both Japan and the United States chose to pursue parallel programs in very basic science when collaboration offered a cheaper alternative. However, the Ministry of Education's ability to pursue independent projects has decreased since the end of the 1990s. Budget constraints have compelled the ministry to move toward increasing financial contributions to international collaborations rather than initiating large-scale projects at home.

—Chapter 8—
METI and the Future of Techno-Globalism

Globalization can help Japan return to higher growth. An increase in competing imports would drive up productivity and the entry of new players into the market through foreign direct investment would help undermine the cartel arrangements that bind so many Japanese firms together.[1] Of course, vested interests in every corner of Japan's political economy oppose any sweeping change. The Japanese economy remains the most closed among the advanced industrial nations. Yet, Japan has not retreated from globalization entirely. All major nations are pursuing a strategy of managed globalization that attempts to balance the political costs and economic benefits of opening. While the exact balance will not be the same for all nations, there are certain areas that should lend themselves relatively easily to opening. For Japan, government-subsidized R&D programs in industrial technology should be one such area. With no adjustment costs for voters or politicians, and no threat to the power of bureaucrats, the barriers to opening should be quite low. Moreover, most Japanese firms likely to take part in such programs have already initiated their own R&D collaborations with foreign firms or research institutes. Although there may be some hesitation to open projects in highly competitive sectors like semiconductors, there should be less concern about collaboration in areas of frontier research more removed from the market.

The case studies analyzed in this book suggest that foreign pressure and complementary capabilities have played a more important role in internationalization than either bureaucratic politics or techno-national ideology. They also suggest that the increased flexibility of research programs in the 1990s provided a better complement to the interests of Japanese firms than the consortia of the 1980s. Although Japan's long history of techno-nationalism has made many scholars suspicious of MITI's motives, the ministry's programs have offered foreign firms nondiscriminatory terms for participation and sharing of results, and depending on the technologies involved, meaningful opportunities for collaboration. Nonetheless, MITI has never adopted formal guidelines on foreign access to its programs. And, the benefits of international collaboration for both domestic and foreign participants have been limited by the distributed structure of most projects. Despite these limitations, the administrative reform of Japanese government may offer some new hope for increased international collaboration. Under the now METI, the AIST has been transformed into a quasi-independent institution that will have to attract private funding. As part of its mission to build closer links with industry, the new AIST has already held symposia to promote joint research with foreign firms and begun to recruit foreigners to lead R&D projects.

The Origins of MITI's Techno-Globalism

The HFSP, the IMS, and the RWC program were distinct responses to the challenges of leading-edge research in the diverse fields of life science, manufacturing, and information technology. The history of these programs demonstrates that bureaucratic politics and techno-national ideology have been far less important in driving internationalization than advocates of these approaches would contend. Foreign pressure played a key role in encouraging MITI to open its research programs, but there is no simple relationship between the application of foreign pressure and opening. In some cases, MITI ignored foreign preferences or simply made the token gesture of opening projects of little interest to foreign firms or governments. In other cases, the ministry responded enthusiastically to foreign requests to match complementary capabilities in areas such as manufacturing, aerospace, and energy technology. In these cases, MITI's techno-globalism can be understood as a response to the same forces driving internationalization of corporate R&D and government-subsidized research programs throughout the triad.

The Reasons for Opening

Bureaucratic politics played only a very limited role in the opening of the case-study projects. The RWC and IMS programs fell squarely within the regulatory domain of MITI's Machine and Information Industries Bureau. Only the HFSP, with its emphasis on basic research in the life sciences, fell outside MITI's traditional jurisdiction. As a pet project of Prime Minister Nakasone, however, the HFSP enjoyed a particularly high profile, which insulated it from bureaucratic conflict. Although MESC did not actively support the HFSP, it allowed Japanese academics to play a leading role in the design of the program.

The absence of bureaucratic friction in these programs is the result of more than the intervention of the prime minister or a simple lack of conflict between regulatory domains. Relations between MITI and MESC evolved in the 1980s as industrial technology programs began to draw on more basic research. Until 1982, researchers at national universities were prohibited from undertaking joint projects with corporate researchers. To strengthen academic research, MESC began to encourage greater collaboration with industry by allowing the assignment of corporate researchers to university labs, corporate endowment of university chairs, and greater academic participation in MITI research programs. MESC regulations no longer limit university researchers to participation on advisory committees as was the case in the FGCP. University labs participated as paid subcontractors in the RWC program and as full partners in IMS.

As Japan's economic downturn deepened during the 1990s, bureaucrats in search of a model looked to the United States where start-ups established by academic entrepreneurs had become industry leaders. Piecemeal policies to bolster university research soon evolved into a more systematic campaign to increase research collaboration between firms and universities. The Basic Law for Science and Technology (1995) gave university researchers greater freedom to work with industry and the Technology Transfer Law (1998) encouraged the formation of licensing organizations at universities to promote the commercialization of patents held by professors. These changes in MESC policy were not simply the result of defeat in a bureaucratic struggle with MITI, but representative of the policies of governments everywhere to maximize the returns on publicly subsidized research. The same concerns are evident in the European Union's new focus on technology diffusion and America's use of Cooperative Research and Development Agreements (CRADAs) to promote the commercialization of technologies developed at national labs.

If techno-national ideology is to provide a convincing explanation of MITI's decision to open its research programs to foreign participation, the initial proposals for these programs should reflect a systematic attempt to access and indigenize of foreign technologies in areas where Japan trails the state of the art. The case-study projects, however, do not reflect a clear and consistent strategy of technology indigenization. Although MITI's HFSP proposal envisioned a central research facility with an international staff applying research on the human brain to the development of industrial technologies, the ministry left the actual design of the program to an international group of scientists. What emerged from their discussions is a basic research program that uses peer review to select proposals submitted by international teams of researchers. With MITI making no claim to any intellectual property that emerges from research, there has been no distinct channel for technology indigenization in the HFSP.

The IMS proposal generated much interest among American and European firms and so brought the most cautious reaction from their national governments. As was noted in earlier chapters, government officials in the United States and Europe were particularly troubled by the fact that Japan recruited foreign firms and universities directly, rather than first going through official channels. As with the HFSP proposal, however, Japan left responsibility for project design and management to international committees with representatives from government, industry, and academia. As a result, IMS evolved from a MITI project into a fully international program with a decentralized management and funding structure. Nevertheless, the initial proposal failed to confront key issues such as the protection of intellectual property rights and so raised concern within Western governments.

As an open, national project with research objectives and organization decided by Japan, the RWC program is more representative of internationalization than the HFSP or IMS. With Japan setting the terms of collaboration, it should also be a more likely expression of techno-national ideology. The RWC appeared especially suspicious because it focused initially on several technologies in which Japan trailed the state of the art. Yet, key aspects of program design made RWC a less than efficient mechanism for accessing and indigenizing foreign technology. First, foreign partners could select the themes in which they wished to participate and so were not forced into unwanted collaborations. Second, the foreign partners agreed that the distributed structure of the consortium limited interaction between all members and so sharply curtailed the potential benefits of internationalization. Thus, techno-national ideology played a minimal role in the opening of the RWC program.

The signing of the revised U.S.–Japan Science and Technology Agreement in June 1988 followed by MITI's move toward techno-globalism less than a year later suggests a strong causal relationship between foreign pressure and the opening of these programs. Yet, the link between foreign pressure and opening is much less straightforward than might at first appear. Although beginning in the mid-1980s the United States urged Japan to contribute more to basic research in the life sciences, this pressure did not always succeed. The United States hoped that by threatening to cut off Japan's access to data from the Human Genome Project the Japanese government would increase its financial support for that program. Rather than increasing funding for the Human Genome Project as the United States expected, MITI continued to place priority on funding for the HFSP. Furthermore, Japan resisted later American pressure to focus the HFSP on tropical diseases and other problems confronting the developing world.

In contrast to the pressure on Japan to contribute more to life-science research, there was much less foreign interest in collaboration in information technology. The FGCP was widely regarded as a failure, and Japanese firms continued to trail the West in most computing technologies. Although the RWC program attracted the interest of research institutes in Europe and Singapore, it seemed a token response to American requests to gain increased access to Japan's national system of innovation. Nevertheless, the U.S. government was successful in inducing MITI to initiate the U.S.–Japan JOP as part of the RWC program. An experiment in bilateral technology collaboration, JOP allowed mutual access to prototype optoelectronic devices through a broker system that minimized American concerns about technology leakage.

Foreign pressure was most effective in the opening of the IMS program. This is evident in American initiatives to promote collaboration in manufacturing technology prior to IMS. The U.S. government first approached Japan about establishing a bilateral project in manufacturing in 1986, and then expressed interest in further collaboration during the revision of the Science and Technology Agreement. Japanese awareness of this pressure is clear in consistent mention during the early discussions of IMS of the need to respond to criticisms of "free-riding." The effectiveness of pressure is evident in the protracted negotiations over the program. MITI initially hoped for IMS to begin in 1990, but American and European insistence on reshaping the proposal and conducting a feasibility study delayed the launch of the full-scale program until May 1995.

The opportunity to match complementary scientific or technological capabilities is not equally present in each of the projects discussed in this book. Yet, even for semiconductor consortia, this opportunity provides a stronger rationale for opening than sharing of costs. This is because MITI has paid 100 percent of direct costs in all programs except the HFSP and IMS, which became multilateral programs. Not surprisingly, the role of complementary capabilities is strongest in these two programs, which attracted the most interest in the United States and Europe. Technological complementarity was much weaker in the proposal for the RWC program.

Bringing together the complementary scientific capabilities of scientists from across the world is fundamental to the mission of the HFSP. Sir James Gowans, the first secretary-general of the HFSP Organization, has contended that the growing complexity of research in the life sciences is driving greater collaboration among researchers around the globe. Yet, traditional grants from national agencies restrict the use of funds and so can inhibit meaningful international collaboration. Much less restrictive HFSP grants allow international teams of researchers the flexibility to plan and coordinate research projects more efficiently. Thus, HFSP grants institutionalize, at least temporarily, the informal international collaborations among researchers in the life sciences. The HFSP awarded nearly 600 multiyear research grants to international teams of researchers between 1990 and 2003, with the average size of the award rising from $600,000 to more than $1 million during this time. During the first decade of the program, roughly three quarters of the grants involved labs on at least two continents; almost a third brought together labs on three or more continents.[2] No other grant program in the natural sciences promotes this degree of global collaboration.

Complementary technological capabilities also played a decisive role in motivating the IMS program. The initial IMS proposal suggested the program would eliminate redundant R&D investment and raise the quality of R&D by bringing together complementary national strengths. The proposal argued that the IMS program could combine Japanese expertise in hardware with American expertise in software and systems integration and European expertise in precision machinery. The best evidence of the importance of complementary capabilities in launching IMS lies in the initial interest elicited from foreign firms and in foreign governments' eagerness to capitalize on the proposal instead of rejecting it as no more than a ploy to gain access to Western technologies. Foreign pressure would not have been so strong without the existence of complementary strengths in manufacturing. The IMS program has brought together many firms, especially from Japan and the European Union: Its twenty-three consortia underway at the end of 2002 involved 234 partners—roughly 60 percent of them firms. Only nine of the projects were led by Japanese enterprises.[3]

Unlike in the HFSP and IMS programs, technological complementarity played a minimal role in the internationalization of RWC. Because RWC was an open national program, it was less responsive to foreign interests than either the HFSP or IMS. Although national research institutes from Singapore and three European countries joined the RWC program as full partners, American and European computer firms felt they would have more to lose than to gain through participation in RWC. At first, the only compelling part of the RWC proposal for the United States was the optoelectronics research theme, and this was simply because of the strength of Japan's optics industry. As noted in chapter 6, Washington responded to the RWC proposal with plans for only limited cooperation in prototyping of optoelectronic devices. Yet, technological complementarity increased over the course of the program as RWC emerged as a leader in parallel and distributed computing. Both Los Alamos National Laboratory and Alta Technology, a leading American supplier of parallel computing technologies, began using RWC software for PC clusters in the late 1990s. Following the end of the RWC program in 2001, development of this software continued in the open-source PC Cluster Consortium, whose members include the Japanese subsidiaries of AMD, Hewlett-Packard, IBM, and Intel.

Adapting to a New Era

Assessments of the effectiveness of MITI research programs have come in three major waves. With each successive wave, analysts have become more skeptical of the value of these programs. The first wave began in the early 1980s, based on the widely perceived success of MITI's VLSI Project (1976–80), after which Japanese firms dominated the world market for then state-of-the-art 64K RAM microchips. The perceived success of the VLSI Project generated a great deal of interest in the "Japanese model" of research cooperation. The positive evaluation of MITI programs during this time is, perhaps, best illustrated by the trepidation in the United States and Europe following MITI's 1982 announcement of its FGCP. The launch of this program spurred Europeans and Americans to begin their own collaborative research programs including ESPRIT and the Microelectronics and Computer Technology Corporation.

A second wave of more sober assessments began in the late 1980s as it became clear that the FGCP would come nowhere near reaching its initial goals. Analysts like Martin Fransman and Gerald Hane believe that MITI consortia raise the technological level of Japanese firms, but that these consortia fail to produce revolutionary technological breakthroughs. Other analysts, such as Daniel Okimoto, Sully Taylor, and Kozo Yamamura, argue that the benefits of MITI programs were in secondary areas such as researcher training and compensating for the lack of researcher mobility in the Japanese labor market. A third and more critical view that emerged in the 1990s depicted MITI programs during the preceding decade as examples of anachronistic industrial policy pushed upon reluctant firms. Much of this criticism came in newspaper and magazine articles by individuals, with little Japan experience, whose objective was to warn of the risks in the Clinton administration's activist technology policy.[4] Yet, this wave also included Scott Callon's rich empirical account of the interministry and interfirm conflicts that led to the unraveling of MITI computer consortia in the 1980s.

Callon argues that the increased size and competitiveness of Japanese firms, Japan's movement to the technology frontier, and the tensions resulting from Japan's trade surplus crippled MITI's industrial policy during the 1980s. Although he is highly skeptical of the value of research consortia, Callon concedes that competitive pressures make them almost inevitable. The Japanese experience, he contends, suggests four basic lessons for governments that fund R&D consortia: the promotion of competition rather than cooperation; shared funding and decision making with the private sector; pluralism and diversity in funding profiles; and funding cycles of no more than four years.[5]

Callon argues persuasively about the problems of MITI computer consortia during the 1980s, but his analysis is limited in scope and time. In its design of consortia during the 1990s, MITI began adapting to its decreased leverage over firms and the difficulty of picking winners in the era of frontier research. Indeed, MITI had already implemented at least two of the changes that Callon recommends before his book appeared in print. Increased pluralism and diversity in funding profiles mark the clearest departure from past MITI programs. Consortia during the 1980s provide several examples of highly focused technology bets that failed to pay off, including nonsilicon devices in the Supercomputer Project and symbolic logic programming in the FGCP. Although MITI attempted to put the best possible spin on the disappointments of the 1980s, it also took steps to make subsequent programs much more flexible. Within the multilateral framework of IMS, firms have complete discretion in putting together their own consortia. And in more typical, open national projects like RWC and ASET, firms have had freedom to choose their own research topics. MITI was no longer attempting to force firms into collaboration at the development end of the innovation process.

As the 1990s ended, however, MITI programs were still out of step with their Western counterparts in funding arrangements and duration. Unlike American and European programs, MITI programs did not require firms to share in the direct costs of research. The programs also tended to run significantly longer than comparable foreign ones. The RWC and other programs launched in the early 1990s were planned to run ten years. By the latter half of the 1990s, new projects averaged between four and six years, but this was still longer than projects in both America's ATP and the European Union's Framework Program, which have averaged two to four years. Because some projects like RWC are more basic in orientation than American or European projects, a longer duration may be appropriate. In any case, the rapid changes in communication and information technologies during the 1990s, which led to the reorientation of the RWC program after 1996, seemed to have driven home the lesson that shorter is often better in high-tech R&D projects.[6]

Although Callon argues that governments should promote competition rather than cooperation in research programs, the choice is often more nuanced than a simple dichotomy between competition and cooperation permits. The relative importance of each varies according to the structure of the program and the industries concerned. Like EUREKA in Europe, IMS is a decentralized program in which firms assemble their own consortia to collaborate on common objectives. Often coming from different industries, participants in IMS projects have been frustrated not by forced marriages, but by problems such as policing deadwood partners. However, collaboration was a less realistic approach in the RWC program where most members were competitors in either the computer or optical-fiber industries. Rather than choosing to force cooperation or promote competition among the RWC participants, MITI allowed them to pursue a wide range of largely independent projects. The integration of research done in isolation by different firms can be an effective means of combining the strengths of competitors. Although this approach did not work well in the Supercomputer Project, the black-box division of labor has been successful in precompetitive aerospace projects such as HYPR and the International Aero Engines V2500 Project.

Finally, in some instances, a government's decision to promote cooperation simply follows the lead of the private sector. For example, facing the enormous costs and technological challenges of the transition to larger wafers and new lithography technologies, semiconductor firms have joined together in private and public consortia in all three legs of the triad. The collaborative approach of the Japanese government's ASET project reflects the willingness of firms to collaborate in the private-sector SELETE consortium. In SELETE, the nation's ten leading chipmakers are working on the preliminary development of advanced device processes in nine areas. As part of the ASUKA project, SELETE members are also collaborating on more focused goals such as developing 65-nm-ready system-on-chip technologies, including transistor and interconnection modules. In short, the choice between cooperation and competition in government programs should depend on the technological challenges and firms involved.

MITI's R&D programs launched since the early 1980s have played a much smaller role in the research strategies of firms than those during the era of catch-up industrialization. In the 1990s, these programs also began to serve a very different purpose. Research objectives became broader and more flexible in order to cope with the accelerating pace of innovation and better accommodate the needs of more independent firms. Research subsidies also became more important for firms forced to cut back on long-term research during tougher economic times. Of course, the emphasis and design of programs will continue to change as policy makers face new demands and learn new lessons.

With Japan's protracted economic slump, the nation's commitment to bolstering basic research may be fading. The government's draft budget for FY 2003 boosted spending on science and technology by 3.9 percent, but the bulk of funds are allocated to short-term, applied projects.[7] As part of this government-wide policy, METI announced a 40 percent cut in the budget for existing R&D programs through the termination or scaling down of projects considered unlikely to produce commercial results.[8] At the same time, it planned to spend $359 million on forty-two new projects as part of the Focus 21 initiative that aims to create new markets within three years.[9] Unlike research programs during the 1990s, the Focus 21 projects will also involve some cost sharing with the private sector.

Gijutsu Rikkoku in an Era of Globalization

Although the Japanese economy has become more open to trade and foreign investment, the persistence of barriers during the 1990s has been thoroughly documented across a range of sectors.[10] For this reason, it is easy to be skeptical about the opening of MITI research programs. Discussion of MITI's techno-globalism is further complicated by the fact that translation of Japanese terms is often colored by preexisting beliefs about Japan's technology and economic policies. A prime example is the term *gijutsu rikkoku*, which is formed by the Chinese characters for "technology" and "rebuilding a country." *Gijutsu rikkoku* has been translated as both "nation-building through technological development" and "techno-nationalism."[11] The nuance is, of course, very different. The former is essentially neutral; the latter suggests the image of a closed, mercantilistic nation.

The problem is not simply with translation. The terms "techno-nationalism" and "techno-globalism" themselves can be a source of confusion. For example, both suggest that collaborators in research programs are self-interested, seeking the best possible return on their participation. In distinguishing between techno-nationalism and techno-globalism in MITI's programs, this book has challenged each of the three major variations of the techno-nationalist argument: the programs reflect a systematic attempt to access foreign technologies; the programs are simply a tactical maneuver in a broader techno-nationalist strategy; and the programs are token gestures that offer little or no opportunity for balanced technological exchange. Each of these arguments has serious weaknesses.

The first variation—that MITI's international programs have been intended to access and indigenize foreign technologies—ignores the fact that the programs have not been particularly effective mechanisms for accomplishing this objective. For example, in the HFSP and IMS, MITI left the final design of the programs to multinational committees, thus eliminating all concerns about asymmetrical access. In the more representative open, national projects, the basic goals and organization are decided in Japan, and then the projects are opened to foreign participants. Nonetheless, the distributed structure of such projects—including RWC, HYPR, and the Micromachine Consortium—greatly limits the potential for accessing foreign technology.

The second variation of the argument—that MITI's techno-globalism is simply a tactical maneuver in a broader techno-nationalist strategy—suggests that MITI allowed genuine opening in select areas of fairly basic research in order to disarm its critics. Yet, even this degree of opening poses a challenge to Richard Samuels's notion of continuity in Japan's techno-national ideology. Subsidizing foreign partners and sharing research results with them in order to gain access to foreign technology represents more than a tactical shift in Japanese policy. The test of techno-national ideology is not simply the existence of programs to develop national capabilities. Such programs are common in every advanced industrialized country. Japan's move to the technology frontier, the subsequent changes in MITI's ability to promote R&D, and the pressure for Japan to contribute more to the international community have sufficiently changed the means available to access and indigenize foreign technology that even the initial proposals for MITI's open research programs cannot be described as part of a strategy of technology indigenization. In short, the goal and not simply the means of accessing foreign technology has been sufficiently compromised by new circumstances to represent a major discontinuity with the techno-national ideology of earlier eras.

The third variant of the techno-nationalist view—that the opening of MITI programs offered no opportunity for meaningful foreign participation—dismisses the ministry's research programs as of little importance to even Japanese participants. As discussed in the previous section, however, MITI's more flexible approach to consortia in the 1990s provided a better complement to the needs and interests of Japanese firms. The value of these programs for foreign partners depends on both the mode of collaboration and particular technologies involved. The aim of any government technology program is to advance the national interest. In some MITI projects, the research agenda or subsidy have been of sufficient interest to justify the transaction costs of participation for foreign firms or institutes. Although projects like IMS, HYPR, and ASET attracted the interest of leading Western firms, RWC did not.

In short, the three variations of the techno-nationalist argument fail to capture the nuances in MITI programs during the 1990s, which covered a wide range of technologies and forms of collaboration. The evidence also fails to support the image of MITI's techno-globalism as exceptional. The move toward more open industrial policies began with Europe's techno-regionalism in the early 1980s. Today, domiciled foreign firms participate as equals in the Framework Programs and nondomiciled foreign firms from most advanced industrial countries can also take part, though without any subsidy from Brussels. In the United States, concerns about national security and economic competitiveness have been major obstacles to the opening of industrial R&D programs. Nevertheless, the ATP among others has been conditionally opened to domiciled subsidiaries of foreign firms. In response to foreign pressure and opportunities to take advantage of complementary foreign capabilities, governments throughout the triad began opening research programs during the 1990s.

In the context of this global movement toward more open forms of technology promotion, MITI's experiments in the internationalization of research programs appear much less cynical than the ministry's critics suggest. The basic fact of opening is explained by the same forces that have driven greater opening throughout the triad. The fact that MITI opened research programs earlier and on more liberal terms than the United States and the European Union can be explained by the greater foreign pressure on Japan to contribute more to the international community and the greater insulation of Japanese bureaucrats from political pressures. American bureaucrats face difficult domestic battles justifying any kind of industrial promotion programs, let alone those that might subsidize foreign firms. And bureaucrats in the European Union must answer to all member governments. MITI faced no such battles at home.

Toward the Future

From MITI to METI

As Japan struggled to deal with slow growth and a deeply troubled banking system during the 1990s, confidence also began to erode in the nation's position as a leader in science and technology. Despite the progress made with the First Science and Technology Basic Plan, a great deal was yet to be done. As Japanese policy makers looked across the Pacific, they saw the U.S. economy growing and American firms playing a leading role in the Internet revolution. At the end of the decade, MITI made a stark assessment of the shortcomings in the nation's industrial technology system. It noted that Japan develops very few technologies that have a strong impact in the global market, seldom plays a major role in determining international standards, and lacks the venture-capital market and linkages between academia and industry that help nurture innovative start-up companies. These concerns reinforced MITI's resolve to increase the flexibility and dynamism of its own research institutes and to promote closer ties between government, industry, and academic researchers.[12]

Although the bursting of the dot.com bubble in the United States initially calmed fears in Japan about falling too far behind Silicon Valley, the resulting slowdown in the American economy cut deeply into the sales of Japan's major high-tech firms. This led to a round of major job cuts that proved to be another serious blow to Japan's confidence in its credentials as a high-tech leader. Amid this increasing insecurity about national capabilities in science and technology, Japan was embarking on a government-wide administrative reform program intended to make government leaner and more efficient. The near crisis mentality concerning technological capabilities provided the motivation for change; the administrative reform provided a genuine opportunity for change.

Passed in 1998, the Basic Bill for Administrative Reform of Central Government called for a reorganization and streamlining of the structure of government by January 2001. It required a reduction in the number of ministries and agencies, a reduction in the number of advisory bodies attached to ministries, and the conversion of many publicly funded institutions such as national labs and hospitals into independent administrative agencies.[13] The decision to move ahead with administrative reform put ministries on the defensive against a range of reform proposals. Under a proposal floated by the Liberal Democratic Party's Administrative Reform Promotion Headquarters, MITI's responsibilities would be divided among an economic ministry, a service industry ministry, and a production and distribution ministry.[14] Another proposal would have had MITI's responsibility for setting external trade policy integrated within the Foreign Ministry's function of setting overall diplomatic policy.[15] Faring much better than several other ministries, MITI managed to fend off these attacks. The Ministry of Post and Telecommunications was folded into the new Ministry of Public Management, MOF was stripped of its regulatory bureaus, and the Ministries of Transportation and Construction were forced to merge. Not only did it retain the powers and jurisdiction of its predecessor, but the new METI also assumed some functions of the former STA and Economic Planning Agency.[16]

Vested interests have resisted many parts of the reform program. Bureaucrats, hoping to maintain opportunities for postretirement employment, have consistently tried to thwart the efforts of politicians to reduce the number of public corporations affiliated with ministries. Many aspects of the reform process also seem cosmetic, especially the reduction in the number of ministries. For example, the Ministry of Education simply absorbed the former STA. This has created a massive bureaucracy that oversees roughly 70 percent of the nation's science and technology budget. Although the centralization of policy making should reduce the overlap and conflict that existed between MESC and STA, the day-to-day administration of basic science has not been radically altered by the reorganization. Nevertheless, the administrative reform has had important implications for both METI's place in Japan's science and technology system and the way the ministry conducts research and development.

With STA being absorbed by the Ministry of Education, METI became a smaller player in science and technology policy. Prior to the reorganization, MITI had significant influence on science policy. Indeed, it shaped much of the Science and Technology Basic Law in its efforts to build Japan's long-term competitiveness following the bursting of the economic bubble. It is no coincidence that the Basic Law was submitted to the Diet by a group of politicians under the leadership of a former MITI bureaucrat. MITI was also able to influence the details of the First Basic Science and Technology Plan through officials seconded to STA.[17] With the administrative reorganization, however, METI's place in policy making for science and technology has changed. While MITI was able to manipulate STA, METI must now take on the Ministry of Education more directly within the secretariat of the new Council on Science and Technology Policy discussed in chapter 7.

Within the ministry, there have also been changes. The structure of METI differs from that of MITI in several ways, such as the integration of macroeconomic and microeconomic policy functions in the new Economic and Industrial Policy Bureau. The former Machinery and Information Industries Bureau, which oversaw such projects as IMS and RWC, has also become part of a larger entity. In order to deal with manufacturing issues on a more comprehensive basis, three formerly separate bureaus—dealing with basic industries, consumer goods industries, and the machinery and information industries—have been combined to form the Manufacturing Industries Bureau. A second, and more important, change is the realignment of several technology offices under the new Industrial Science and Technology Policy and Environment Bureau. The new bureau brings under its control the technology policy division of the former Industrial Policy Bureau, and oversees the two main research organizations affiliated with the ministry: the New Energy and Industrial Technology Development Organization (NEDO), and a reorganized and renamed Agency of Industrial Science and Technology (AIST). The change in status of these two organizations will have the most far-reaching effect on METI's science and technology policy. While the plans for NEDO are still being developed, the transformation of AIST is already underway.

In 2001, the Agency for Industrial Science and Technology became the National Institute of Advanced Industrial Science and Technology—an independent administrative organization, still referred to in English by its old acronym "AIST." The reorganization has produced a more application-oriented institute with much greater operational autonomy. With 2,400 tenured researchers, and a similar number of visiting researchers, the new AIST will have an annual budget of roughly $1 billion. Although AIST is no longer officially part of the government, it still receives baseline funding from METI, which also establishes its long-term policy goals. Yet, as an independent administrative organization, AIST has much more flexibility than its predecessor in research, financial, and personnel management. AIST now has discretion in deciding its organizational structure, choosing specific research themes, and allocating funds—decisions previously made by MITI bureaucrats. Management of research budgets has also become more straightforward because funds can now be spent on a multiyear basis; this means that surpluses can be carried over from one year to the next. Establishing joint-research projects with industry will also become easier now that AIST institutes can conduct research commissioned by firms. Similarly, discretion in personnel management makes possible fixed-term contracts and greater reliance on a merit rather than a seniority system for promotion of researchers.[18]

The old AIST comprised fifteen research institutes. Today, AIST is built around a network of twenty-two smaller and more focused institutes and twenty-three short-term research centers, although the number of centers may vary over time. According to critics, the size and broad mandate of institutes under the old system led to a "quasi-academic" environment in which senior researchers pursued their own interests rather than the needs of industry. The eight Tsukuba-based institutes under the old system had as many as 500 researchers each; the new institutes will average less than 100 tenured researchers each. The hope is that the smaller size will increase accountability and enhance communication within the institutes. Yet, AIST will have to nurture greater communication among the larger number of institutes in order to avoid inefficiency.[19] The research centers, which did not exist under the former AIST, are the centerpiece of the drive to increase links to industry. Under the leadership of a top researcher, each center will exist for three to seven years and focus on accomplishing a specific objective. Funding from METI will be insufficient to finance the entire research mission, so each center will be forced to raise funds from other sources. In addition, the staff of each center will include recruits from industry and academia as well as career researchers from AIST.[20]

The goal of this reform and reorganization is to increase the quality of research by making the research system more competitive and more responsive to the needs of industry. From METI's perspective, the initial results are promising: The number of projects conducted with outside groups increased by 15 percent in the year following the reforms; but the reform has met resistance from within AIST itself. Many researchers worry that the stress on performance-related targets and vulnerability to cuts in funding will shift priorities too far away from the sort of basic research that can only be performed with government support.[21] Although the reforms concentrate on domestic needs and priorities, they could have important implications for international collaboration. Any increase in the quality of Japanese research will be welcomed by potential collaborators if the new system is open to researchers from overseas. A positive development in this regard is that the directors of the new research centers are being recruited from both Japan and abroad. For example, Fu-kuo Chang, an engineering professor from Stanford University, was chosen to head the Research Center on Smart Structures. Yet, it is still unclear how aggressive individual AIST labs and institutes will be in seeking international partners. The reorganization and quasi-privatization certainly enable change, and the gradual reduction in baseline funding provides a concrete incentive for change.[22]

Collaboration with Japan

The opening of MITI research programs in the early 1990s represented only a small and easy step in the opening of Japan's national system of innovation. In downplaying this shift in policy as nothing but the result of techno-national ideology, however, critics marginalize the importance of many programs that present foreign partners with meaningful, nondiscriminatory research opportunities. Still, foreign participation in most programs remains quite modest. The questions today are whether METI has the will to expand foreign participation in its research programs, and whether the U.S. government has sufficient interest and energy to pursue new opportunities in this area.

Japan's long economic downturn has fundamentally changed the bilateral relationship with the United States. Even though the U.S. economy may slow and the Japanese economy may begin to recover, the two nations will not see again the level of tension in economic relations that defined their relationship during the late 1980s and early 1990s.[23] In today's political climate, trade and technology issues are simply items on a crowded bureaucratic agenda rather than front-page problems demanding immediate attention. The United States is no longer afraid that Japan will leap ahead technologically. In some ways, this could make collaboration easier; Washington will not worry about American firms participating in METI projects in the same way it did in the early 1990s. At the same time, however, there is no sense of urgency in the United States today about accessing Japanese technology, and so little pressure on Japan to move beyond its current policies.

Nevertheless, the possibility of leveraging complementary capabilities still exists in several areas such as energy, nanotechnology, and optoelectronics. The fact that Apple Computer incorporated multimedia search technology from RWC in its Mac OSX operating system suggests that there are such opportunities even in information technology.

The United States recognizes that Japan is striving to revitalize the research infrastructure of its government and university research systems and that this presents a strategic opportunity to engage it in joint research activities that promote greater opening. In 1999, academic and industrial scientists from each country came together as the Joint U.S.–Japan Dialogue Group to examine opportunities for expanding collaboration. A year later, the joint group issued its final report, which identified ten areas that hold promise for bilateral and multilateral collaboration during the first decade of the new century.[24] In mission-oriented research, the joint group pointed to the potential for collaboration in health and medicine, the environment, energy, freshwater management, natural disaster mitigation, and societal aspects of information technology. In frontier research, it identified opportunities for collaboration in the earth sciences, space sciences, life sciences, and nanotechnology. Three of these areas—environment, life sciences, and nanotechnology—are also priorities in Japan's Second Basic Plan.

A major contribution of the joint group was to move beyond the vague highlighting of general themes for cooperation to propose specific research projects in each of the above areas. The joint group hoped that concrete and focused projects in areas with recognized potential would build a strong foundation for expanded collaboration. It also underscored the importance of establishing formal, long-term ties between major research institutions in the United States and Japan. Implicit in this goal is the recognition that choosing suitable research themes requires a knowledge of the capabilities and interests of potential collaborators. Of course, it is easier to build this kind of knowledge base about government research institutes than firms. It is not surprising, then, that most of the joint group's proposals concern public-sector research. In fact, only the energy and nanotechnology themes are singled out as having a strong potential for private-sector collaboration. Since the joint group issued its report, the two nations have initiated projects in several of the targeted fields. In 2002, for example, they agreed to undertake eleven joint projects on climate change. And in 2003, they signed an agreement to proceed with the ten-year Integrated Ocean Drilling Program. These collaborations are between the two governments. While continuing to expand such collaborations, the United States must also consider ways to increase greater access to private-sector research in Japan. This remains a more difficult task.

During the first half of the 1990s, while high-tech remained prominent on the bilateral agenda, the U.S. government energetically monitored and responded to Japanese proposals for collaboration. The Department of Commerce proposed the JOP as part of the RWC program and coordinated the American response to the IMS proposal. In the negotiations leading to the IMS program, for example, the Department of Commerce sponsored workshops where corporate researchers were able to exchange views on the Japanese proposal. The high level of American corporate interest in this program and American success in working with the European Union to reshape Japan's proposal can be attributed, in part, to the grass-roots work of the Department of Commerce in stimulating broader discussion of the issues involved in IMS.

Today, the situation has changed in two ways. While METI continues to establish open, national programs like RWC, it has not made any more innovative proposals along the lines of the HFSP or IMS. Although rooted in complementary scientific and technological capabilities, these two programs were also ambitious responses to foreign pressure during the heady days of the bubble economy. As the Japanese economy soured, MITI became less ambitious and the U.S. government became less resolute in its monitoring of the ministry's research projects. Today, bureaucrats still talk with each other about industrial collaboration but less frequently and at a much lower profile. Impressed with the results of the JOP, for example, the White House OSTP has encouraged that the JOP model be used "for a new cooperative effort in optoelectronic technologies that would be extended to a broader range of application areas in telecommunications, medicine, transportation, and education."[25] The United States will continue to make proposals such as this, but the real initiative for increased opening must come from Japan.

METI will continue to place priority on national needs and interests. As it looks to increase the productivity of its newly reorganized R&D system, however, it could take a few straightforward steps to promote international collaboration. For example, METI could strengthen the research centers of the new AIST by making funding contingent on each center initiating a certain number of projects with foreign partners or meeting quotas for visiting researchers from advanced industrialized countries. Some outreach activities have already begun. In June 2002, AIST held its first ever symposium in Silicon Valley to promote joint research projects and technology transfer opportunities; roughly 200 representatives from the local research community attended. METI could also invite increased foreign participation in the planning of at least a few large-scale projects such as RWC that will be open to foreign firms and research organizations. Like RWC, however, most of these projects will probably be distributed in structure with minimal collaboration between partners. In addition, the working language of open, national programs like RWC and ASET will continue to be Japanese. As the interest in learning Japanese among business and technology professionals has decreased, language has once again become a barrier.

Just as programs to expand international collaboration may promote access to Japan's national system of innovation, so may domestic reforms. The government's efforts to foster more productive linkages between industry, academia, and government research institutes have already produced some unexpected payoffs in foreign access to Japanese technology. In October 2000, Australia's Silex Systems purchased the patent rights to semiconductor material technology developed at Keio University. This marked the first time that a foreign firm acquired patent rights from a Japanese university.[26] Similar deals, it must be admitted, have produced some acrimony. In 2001, the American biotechnology firm Third Wave acquired from the RIKEN SNP Research Center the exclusive rights to all applications emerging from a database of over 3,000 single nucleotide polymorphisms (SNPs) located on genes related to drug metabolism. The Japanese pharmaceutical industry protested this deal loudly because the research had been funded by the Japanese government.[27] Although the industry has been drawing on the work of Western universities and research institutes for years, it was unaccustomed to knowledge flowing in the other direction.

There is no simple way for META to increase foreign participation in its research programs. Drastically expanded budgets are not an option in view of Japan's current economic troubles. Even during the bubble economy, MITI's R&D budget remained relatively consistent. At present, initiatives capitalizing on the mission-oriented reorganization of the Japanese science and technology system present the best opportunity to engage Japan in areas where internationalization is politically expedient for bureaucrats and economically attractive for independent institutions facing potential cuts in government funding. These collaborations will be modest and unlikely to make headlines but will also be a practical way to take advantage of strategic restructuring in one of the world's most advanced research systems. With the shift toward more open forms of government technology promotion throughout the triad, META's techno-globalism is by no means exceptional. Although META's programs remain the only ones to offer subsidized, nondiscriminatory participation to nondomiciled foreign firms, their budgets are smaller than those of comparable U.S. and European programs. META can certainly do more to open its research programs, but what it has accomplished so far should be viewed in the context of change throughout the triad and not dismissed out-of-hand as token responses to foreign pressure or techno-nationalist stratagems to access foreign technology.

Notes

Notes to Chapter 1

1. Richard Katz, *Japanese Phoenix*, pp. 4–5.
2. U.S. National Science Foundation, *Preview of the Second Science and Technology Basic Plan*, pp. 2–3.
3. Philip Hicks, "Science and Technology Overview 2002: Japan," www.infoexport.gc.ca. Viewed August 2003.
4. William W. Keller and Richard J. Samuels, "Innovation and the Asian Economies," p. 10.
5. Structural differences are emphasized in C. Fred Bergsten and Marcus Noland, *Reconcilable Differences?* Deliberate strategies of protectionism are emphasized in Laura D'Andrea Tyson, *Who's Bashing Whom?* pp. 66–71.
6. Michael M. Mochizuki, "The Past in Japan's Future," p. 133.
7. National Research Council, *Maximizing U.S. Interests in Science and Technology Relations with Japan*.
8. Edward J. Lincoln, *Troubled Times*, p. 188.
9. Idem, *Arthritic Japan*, p. 197.
10. Walter Hatch, "Japanese Production Networks in Asia," p. 24.
11. Ulrike Schaede and William Grimes, "The Emergence of Permeable Insulation."
12. Gerald J. Hane, "Innovation in Japan After the Financial Crisis," pp. 3, 21.
13. D.H. Whittaker, "Crisis and Innovation in Japan," pp. 58–59.
14. The term "techno-globalism" has been used variously to describe the global exploitation of technology, the global generation of technology by multinational corporations, and global collaboration in technology development by both firms and governments. See Daniel Archibugi and Jonathan Michie, "The Globalization of Technology."
15. METI does not currently track, or at least does not release, statistics on foreign participation in its programs. I arrived at this figure by surveying all public evaluations of METI programs conducted during 2000–2002. These reports (numbers 50–121) were available in Japanese as of July 2003 at www.meti.go.jp/policy/tech_evaluation/e00/eh130004.html. Because some of the projects were evaluated twice or were "field tests" rather than R&D projects, only 66 of the 71 reports were considered.
16. Chalmers Johnson, "MITI, MPT, and the Telecom Wars," p. 181.
17. Richard J. Samuels, *Rich Nation, Strong Army*, pp. 33–78.
18. Several studies—including Tyson, *Who's Bashing Whom?* and Peter Cowhey and Jonathan Aronson, *Managing the World Economy*—emphasize the role of foreign pressure in opening Japanese research programs. A more systematic treatment of the role of foreign pressure in shaping Japanese economic policy can be found in Leonard Schoppa, *Bargaining with Japan*.

19. There is a voluminous literature in business-management studies on the forces driving corporate alliances. On collaboration in Japan, see Fumio Kodama, *Emerging Patterns of Innovation*.

20. Ministry of International Trade and Industry, Sangyō Gijutsu Shingikai, Kokusai Kenkyū Kyoryoku Bukai, *Shin Gijutsu Rikkoku ni muketa Hōkatsuteki-Senryakutekina Kokusai Sangyō Kenkyū Kyōryoku no Suishin*, pp. 17–19.

21. Intelligent Manufacturing Systems, *Annual Project Monitoring Report, 2002*, p. 2; ibid., *IMS Program: Project Summaries*.

22. Joint U.S.–Japan Dialogue Group, *U.S.–Japan Dialogue on the Role of Science and Technology into the New Millennium*.

23. "METI Expanding New Development Projects," *Japan Chemical Week*, April 17, 2003.

Notes to Chapter 2

1. Robert D. Pearce, *The Internationalization of Research and Development by Multinational Enterprises*, p. 12.

2. Oliver Gassman and Maximilian von Zedwitz, "New Concepts and Trends in International R&D Organization," p. 231.

3. Robert D. Pearce and Satwinder Singh, *Globalizing Research and Development*, p. 189.

4. All facts and figures in this paragraph are from Donald H. Dalton and Manuel G. Serapio, *Globalizing Industrial Research and Development*, pp. 7–8.

5. A foreign R&D facility is defined here as a freestanding R&D site, excluding R&D departments within marketing and manufacturing plants, of which 50 percent or more is owned by a foreign parent company.

6. Marina Papanastassiou and Robert Pearce, "The Internationalization of Research and Development by Japanese Enterprises," p. 158.

7. Ministry of International Trade and Industry, Industrial Technology Council, *Issues and Trends in Industrial-Scientific Technology*, p. 39.

8. Dalton and Serapio, *Globalizing Industrial Research*, pp. 17, 48.

9. Ibid., pp. 25, 38–39.

10. Ibid., p. 24; Eleanor Westney, "Cross-Pacific Internationalization of R&D by U.S. and Japanese Firms," pp. 174–75.

11. Alan Pearson et al., "Decision Parameters in Global R&D Management."

12. Gassman and von Zedwitz, "New Concepts and Trends," pp. 236–48; Kiyonori Sakakibara and Eleanor Westney, "Japan's Management of Global Innovation," pp. 330–31; Jeremy Howells and Michelle Wood, *The Globalization of Production and Technology*, p. 36.

13. Sakakibara and Westney, "Japan's Management of Global Innovation," p. 333.

14. Westney, "Cross-Pacific Internationalization," pp. 171–72.

15. Alexander Gerybadze and Guido Reger, "Globalization of R&D," pp. 251, 257.

16. Dalton and Serapio, *Globalizing Industrial Research*, pp. 28–31; Richard Florida, "The Globalization of R&D," pp. 85–90.

17. Hisayuki Mitsusada, "R&D Goes Abroad for Fresh Twist on Future," *Nikkei Weekly*, June 12, 1995, p. 1.

18. Guido Reger, "How R&D is Coordinated in Japanese and European Multinationals," p. 82.

19. Ministry of Economy, Trade and Industry, *Trends in Japan's Industrial R&D Activities*, pp. 86–89.

20. Ibid., p. 57.

21. Edward M. Graham and Paul R. Krugman, *Foreign Direct Investment in the United States*, ch. 3.

22. Florida, "The Globalization of R&D," p. 94.

23. Pari Patel and Keith Pavitt, "Large Firms in the Production of the World's Technology."

24. John Cantwell, "The International Agglomeration of R&D."

25. Pari Patel and Modesto Vega, "Patterns of Internationalization of Corporate Technology," pp. 148, 154.

26. John H. Dunning, "Governments and Multinational Enterprises."

27. National Research Council, *Maximizing U.S. Interests in Science and Technology Relations with Japan*, pp. 17, 128.

28. Robert B. Reich, *The Work of Nations*, chs. 1, 11, 25.

29. Christopher Freeman, "The National System of Innovation in Historical Perspective," p. 37; Michael Kitson and Jonathan Michie, "The Political Economy of Globalization," p. 176.

30. David C. Mowery, "The Changing Structure of the U.S. National Innovation System," p. 651; National Research Council, *Harnessing Science and Technology for America's Economic Future*, p. 22.

31. Richard Florida, "Technology Policy for a Global Economy," pp. 49–52.

32. Keith Pavitt and Parimal Patel, "Global Corporations and National Systems of Innovation," pp. 94, 97.

33. Yao-Su Hu, "Global or Stateless Corporations Are National Firms with International Operations."

34. Michael Borrus and John Zysman, "Industrial Competitiveness and American National Security," p. 37.

35. Ibid., p. 50.

36. Alan Tonelson, "The Perils of Techno-Globalism," p. 35.

37. Kitson and Michie, "The Political Economy of Globalization," p. 178.

38. Steven Weber and John Zysman, "The Risk that Mercantilism Will Define the Next Security System," p. 180.

39. Michael Borrus, "Foreign Participation in U.S.-Funded R&D," pp. 3–5.

40. William W. Keller and Richard J. Samuels, "Innovation and the Asian Economies," pp. 11–12.

41. Atsushi Yamada, *Neo Tekuno Nashonarizumu*, pp. 21–29.

42. Daniel Archibugi and Jonathan Michie, "The Globalization of Technology," pp. 177–88.

43. Like the Industrial Structure Council, the Industrial Technology Council is essentially a communication channel from MITI to the private sector rather than an open forum for joint policymaking. According to former MITI Vice-Minister Shigeru Sahashi, the Industrial Structure Council is a *kakuremino* or "fairy cape" for creating the appearance of MITI collaboration with industry and academia. See Chalmers Johnson, *Japan, Who Governs?* p. 122.

44. Ministry of International Trade and Industry, Industrial Technology Council, *Tenkanki no R&D*, pp. 3–6.

45. Ministry of International Trade and Industry, Sangyō Kōzō Shingikai Sangyō

Gijutsu Shoiinkai to Sangyō Gijutsu Shingikai Kikaku Iinkai, *Kagaku Gijutsu Sōzō Rikkoku e no Michi o Kirihiraku. Shiteki Shisan no Sōzō Katsuyō ni mukete.*

46. All facts and figures in this paragraph are from U.S. National Science Board, *Science and Engineering Indicators 2002*, pp. A4–77, A4–80.

47. Ministry of International Trade and Industry, Industrial Technology Council, *Framework for R&D in Industrial Science and Technology*, ch. 1.

48. Ministry of International Trade and Industry, Sangyō Gijutsu Shingikai, Kokusai Kenkyū Kyōryoku Bukai, *Shin Gijutsu Rikkoku ni muketa Hōkatsuteki-Senryakutekina Kokusai Sangyō Kenkyū Kyōryoku no Suishin*, pp. 15–19.

49. Ministry of International Trade and Industry, Industrial Technology Division, *National Strategies for Industrial Technology*, pp. 2–5; Hajime Yamada, "Formulation of the Second S&T Basic Plan," *Japan Technology Review* 8, July 16, 2001.

50. Sylvia Ostry and Richard Nelson, *Techno-Nationalism and Techno-Globalism*, p. 88.

51. Organization for Economic Cooperation and Development, *Foreign Access to Technology Programs*, p. 4.

52. Organization for Economic Cooperation and Development, *Spotlight on Public Support to Industry*, p. 206.

53. Organization for Economic Cooperation and Development, *Foreign Access to Technology Programs*, p. 9.

54. "White House Plans Assessment of International Technology Transfer," *Federal Technology Report*, April 23, 1998, p. 3.

55. Thomas H. Lee and Proctor P. Reid, *National Interests in an Age of Global Technology*, p. 8.

56. Rose Marie Ham et al., "The Evolving Role of Semiconductor Consortia in the United States and Japan," pp. 150–51.

57. Richard Perez-Pena, "Albany No Longer a Secret in High-Tech Chip World," *The New York Times* July 19, 2002, p. B5.

58. Paula Doe, "Mask Program Update: Sematech Turns Its Attention to EUV Infrastructure," *Solid State Technology*, February 1, 2003, p. 32.

59. "Asahi Glass, International Sematech to Collaborate in Developing Advanced Mask Technology for EUV," *JCNN*, July 4, 2003.

60. "Tokyo Electron to Add $300 Million R&D Center to Albany Nanotech Project," *Optical Networks Daily*, November 25, 2002.

61. Telephone conversation with Dr. Albert Landgrebe, U.S. Department of Energy, Technology Transportation Lab, May 28, 1996.

62. Jack Keebler, "Battery Group Rebuffs Japan," *Automotive News*, December 2, 1991, p. 1.

63. Harry Stoffer, "U.S.-Funded Programs May Go Global," *Automotive News*, May 10, 1999, p. 4.

64. Neil MacDonald and Bill Loveless, "Execs Discuss Possible Merger of U.S., Foreign Auto Research," *Federal Technology Report*, April 22, 1999, p. 3.

65. Peter Behr, "A Car for the Distant Future," *Washington Post*, March 9, 2003, p. B2; "E.U. and U.S. Sign Partnership Agreement on Fuel Cell Technologies," http://dbs.cordis.lu. Viewed August 2003.

66. "G-8 Leaders Pledge to Develop Cleaner, Efficient Technologies," *State Department Press Releases and Documents*, June 2, 2003.

67. Christopher Hill, "The Advanced Technology Program," p. 143.

68. "Historical Statistics on Awards," www.atp.nist.gov. Viewed August 2003.

69. U.S. Department of Commerce, National Institute of Standards and Technology, *ATP Eligibility Criteria for U.S. Subsidiaries of Foreign-Owned Companies.*

70. Ibid.

71. "Walker Hints Politics at Play in ATP Awards," *Federal Technology Report,* June 22, 1995, p. 1.

72. Vincent Kiernan, "Proposed Royalty Provision for ATP Draws Criticism from Research Community," *Laser Focus World,* June 1, 2002, p. 67; Neil Franz, "Businesses Challenge Bush Plan to Recoup Grant Funding," *Chemical Week,* April 24, 2002, p. 11.

73. Neil Franz, "Bush Proposes to Eliminate ATP," *Chemical Week,* March 5, 2003, p. 29.

74. John Peterson and Margaret Sharp, *Technology Policy in the European Union,* pp. 9–10.

75. www.cordis.lu/fp5. Viewed July 2002. Also U.S. Department of Commerce, *Global Tech Update: The European Union's Sixth Framework Program for Research and Technological Development,* p. 3.

76. Ostry and Nelson, *Techno-Nationalism and Techno-Globalism,* p. 87.

77. Peter Cowhey and Jonathan Aronson, *Managing the World Economy,* p. 154.

78. Peterson and Sharp, *Technology Policy in the European Union,* pp. 102, 226.

79. European Commission, *Five Year Assessment Report Related to the Specific Program,* pp. 38–42.

80. European Commission, *External Monitoring Report on the Specific Program for Research and Technological Development,* p. 11.

81. Unless otherwise noted all statistics concerning Australia, Canada, and the United States are from European Commission, *Five Year Assessment Report Related to the Specific Program,* pp. 24–28.

82. European Commission, *External Monitoring Report,* p. 10.

83. European Commission, *Five Year Assessment Report,* pp. 25–26; "EU/ Research," *Agence Europe,* June 14, 2003.

84. U.S. Department of Commerce, *Global Tech Update,* pp. 2–3.

85. European Commission, *Communication from the Commission,* pp. 4–6, 15–20.

86. Wayne Sandholtz, *High-Tech Europe,* pp. 257, 274.

87. *EUREKA Annual Report 2001/2002,* www.eureka.be. Viewed July 2003.

88. Peterson and Sharp, *Technology Policy in the European Union,* p. 107.

89. Ibid., p. 224.

90. Information supplied by Ms. Nicola Vatthauer, EUREKA Secretariat, August 2003.

91. Japan Economic Institute, *JEI Report* no. 36A, September 29, 1995, p. 16; AIST, "MITI's Technology Policy," (March 1999), pp. 2–3.

92. Kosuke Yamamoto, "Japanese Technology."

93. "International Research and Development," www.aist.go.jp. Viewed May 2000.

94. Organization for Economic Cooperation and Development, *Foreign Access to Technology Programs,* p. 17.

95. Martin Fransman, *Visions of Innovation,* p. 188.

96. Organization for Economic Cooperation and Development, *Foreign Access to Technology Programs*, p. 17.

97. See note 15 in chapter 1 for a fuller explanation of this statistic.

Notes to Chapter 3

1. Personal interview with Dr. Junichi Shimada, Director RWC Research Institute, September 4, 2000.

2. Chalmers Johnson, "MITI, MPT and the Telecom Wars," p. 181. For a broader discussion of bureaucratic politics in Japan see Chalmers Johnson, *Japan, Who Governs?* pp. 117–24.

3. Akifusa Fujioka, *Tsūsanshō no Yomikatta*, pp. 132–35.

4. Gerald J. Hane, "Research and Development Consortia and Innovation in Japan."

5. Hiroyuki Odagiri et al., "Research Consortia as a Vehicle for Basic Research," p. 198.

6. Scott A. Callon, *Divided Sun*, p. 34.

7. Kenkichiro Koizumi, "The Challenge of Joint Research in Japan," *Science*, October 23, 1992, pp. 589–90.

8. "R&D in Japan: Squeezing More from Every Yen," *JEI Report* no. 29, July 1998.

9. Fumio Kodama and Lewis Branscomb, "University Research as an Engine for Growth," p. 4.

10. Gerald Hane, "Comparing University-Industry Linkages in the U.S. and Japan," p. 26.

11. Yuko Harayama, "Japanese Technology Policy," p. 14.

12. U.S. National Science Foundation, *Second Business-Academia-Government Summit*.

13. Organization for Economic Cooperation and Development, Directorate for Science, Technology and Industry, Committee for Science and Technology Policy, *Steering and Funding of Research Institutions*, p. 10.

14. Ministry of Economy, Trade and Industry, *Trends in Japan's Industrial R&D Activities*, p. 128.

15. U.S. National Science Foundation, *Second Business-Academia-Government Summit*.

16. Robert Kneller, "Intellectual Property Rights and University-Industry Technology Transfer in Japan," pp. 323–31.

17. Ministry of Economy, Trade and Industry, *Trends in Japan's Industrial R&D Activities*, p. 127.

18. Personal interview with Yoshiaki Tsukamoto, Frontier Collaborative Research Center, Tokyo Institute of Technology, September 18, 2000.

19. Walter Hatch, "Japanese Production Networks in Asia," pp. 237–38.

20. Ministry of Economy, Trade and Industry, *Trends in Japan's Industrial R&D Activities*, p. 137.

21. See for example Tessa Morris-Suzuki, *The Technological Transformation of Japan from the Seventeenth to the Twenty-First Century*; Chalmers Johnson, *MITI and the Japanese Miracle*; Michael Green, *Arming Japan*.

22. Richard J. Samuels, *Rich Nation Strong Army*, p. 33.

23. Ibid., p. 47.

24. Ibid., pp. 328–29.

25. This criticism of the notion of reciprocal consent is made in Kent Calder, *Strategic Capitalism*, p. 12.

26. Off-the-record interview.

27. Leonard J. Schoppa, *Bargaining with Japan*, pp. 1–18.

28. Quoted in Kenneth B. Pyle, *The Japanese Question*, p. 111.

29. Peter Cowhey and Jonathan Aronson, *Managing the World Economy*, p. 87.

30. Frances Rosenbluth, *Financial Politics in Contemporary Japan*, p. 53.

31. Membership and budget for the science and technology division of the LDP's Policy Affairs Research Council have traditionally been among the lowest of all PARC divisions. The least popular committees, such as science and technology, environment, and justice, are concerned more with public goods and so offer little opportunity for pork. See J. Mark Ramseyer and Frances Rosenbluth, *Japan's Political Marketplace*, pp. 32–33.

32. Clyde V. Prestowitz, *Trading Places*, pp. 458–59.

33. Laura D'Andrea Tyson, *Who's Bashing Whom?* p. 59.

34. *Foreign Broadcast Information Service, Asia-Pacific*, APA-86-067, April 8, 1986, p. C8.

35. Japan Economic Institute, *JEI Report* no. 14B, April 11, 1986, p. 2.

36. U.S. Congress, Senate Committee on Commerce, Science and Transportation, *United States and Japan Science and Technology Agreement*, p. 23.

37. Ibid., p. 18.

38. Ibid., p. 17.

39. U.S. Congress, House Committee on Science, Space, and Technology, *U.S.–Japan Science and Technology Agreement*, p. 53.

40. Ibid., p. 55.

41. See for example Farok Contractor and Peter Lorange, *Cooperative Strategies in International Business*; Bruce Kogut, "Joint Ventures."

42. National Research Council, *U.S.-Japan Strategic Alliances in the Semiconductor Industry*, pp. 18–19.

43. John Hagedoorn, "Understanding the Rationale of Strategic Technology Partnering."

44. Fujio Niwa and Hiroshi Goto, "Japanese Collaborative R&D," p. 215.

45. Mariko Sakakibara, "Evaluating Government-Sponsored R&D Consortia in Japan," p. 456.

46. Fumio Kodama, *Emerging Patterns of Innovation*, pp. 196–99, 212–20.

47. Ibid., p. 226.

48. Fumio Kodama, "Technology Fusion and the New R&D," p. 72.

49. Ibid., p. 72.

50. Lee G. Branstetter and Mariko Sakakibara, "When Do Research Consortia Work Well and Why?" p. 145.

51. Telephone interview with Sir James Gowans, former secretary general of the Human Frontier Science Program Organization, September 28, 1995.

52. IMS Promotion Center, *Joint International Research Programs into an Intelligent Manufacturing System, Version 4*.

53. National Research Council, *R&D Consortia and U.S.-Japan Collaboration*, p. 19.

54. Martin Fransman, *The Market and Beyond*, p. 288.

55. Hane, "Research and Development Consortia and Innovation in Japan," pp. 345–47.

56. Ibid., p. 369.

57. Gerald J. Hane, "The Real Lessons of Japanese Research Consortia," p. 60.

58. Branstetter and Sakakibara, "When Do Research Consortia Work Well and Why?" p. 144.

59. Sakakibara, "Evaluating Government-Sponsored R&D Consortia in Japan," pp. 447, 461.

60. National Research Council, *R&D Consortia and U.S.-Japan Collaboration*, p. 21.

61. Sully Taylor and Kozo Yamamura, "Japan's Technological Capabilities and Its Future," pp. 33–34.

62. Daniel I. Okimoto, *Between MITI and the Market*, pp. 67–73.

63. Cited in Hiroyuki Odagiri and Akira Goto, "The Japanese System of Innovation," p. 88.

64. Callon, *Divided Sun*, chs. 5 and 6.

65. D.H. Whittaker, "Crisis and Innovation in Japan," p. 75.

66. Marie Anchordoguy, "Japan at a Technological Crossroads," pp. 371, 385.

67. Ministry of Economy, Trade and Industry, "Key Points, 2003 Economic and Industrial Policy."

Notes to Chapter 4

1. "Tsūsanshō no Tōsho Keikaku Hyuman Frontia Kōsō" (The Human Frontier Concept, A Japanese Plan at the Beginning), *Nihon Keizai Shimbun*, July 23, 1988, p. 11.

2. Human Frontier Science Program, "Report of the International Scientific Committee," p. 8.

3. Ibid., p. 9.

4. As of 2003, the members of the HFSP included the G7 nations, Switzerland, and the non-G7 members of the European Union, who are represented by the European Commission.

5. Human Frontier Science Program, *Annual Report FY 2002*, p. 11; "Intercontinentality" and "Supporting International Projects" in Human Frontier Science Program, *Tenth Anniversary Brochure, Human Frontier*.

6. Torsten Wiesel, *The Human Frontier Science Program*; Human Frontier Science Program *Annual Report FY 2002*, p. 15.

7. Human Frontier Science Program, *Annual Report FY 2002*, p. 24; Human Frontier Science Program, *Balancing Biomedicine's Postdoc Exchange Rate*.

8. Wiesel, *The Human Frontier Science Program*.

9. Many Japanese academics opposed the HFSP as unnecessary "international philanthropy" at a time when domestic infrastructure and research support for academic scientists were severely lacking. These concerns are not addressed in this analysis, however, because these academics did not form any organized opposition to the HFSP and because their criticisms were rebuffed by several elite members of the Japanese science community. The elite argument was that increased support was no guarantee of better science without rigorous peer review of research proposals. Thus, money was better spent integrating Japanese researchers with the international science community than investing more in the rigid *kōza* system of Japanese universities.

10. Personal interview with Tateo Arimoto, director of Planning Department, STA Marine Science and Technology Center, April 19, 1995.

11. Personal interview with Katsuhiko Umehara, director of the General Planning and Coordination Division, NEDO, March 30, 1995.

12. Personal interview with Tateo Arimoto, April 19, 1995.

13. Off-the-record interview.

14. Personal interview with Dr. Kozo Iizuka, chairman of the HFSP Board of Trustees, April 18, 1995.

15. Personal interview with Tateo Arimoto, April 19, 1995.

16. "Sekai no Kiso Kagaku e Kokusai Kōken: HFSP," p. 32.

17. Personal interview with Katsuhiko Umehara, March 30, 1995.

18. Scott Callon, *Divided Sun*, p. 34.

19. Personal interview with Dr. Masao Ito, president of the Science Council of Japan, April 6, 1995.

20. David Swinbanks, "Revenge of the Taxmen on Grant Recipients," *Nature*, June 21, 1990, p. 649.

21. David Swinbanks, "Bureaucracy Denies Grants," *Nature*, January 17, 1991, p. 185.

22. David Swinbanks, "A Foray into Red Tape," *Nature*, April 25, 1991, p. 644.

23. Personal interview with Katsuhiko Umehara, March 30, 1995.

24. Ibid.

25. Jun Oriyama, "Hyuman Frontia Saiensu Puroguramu Kōsō."

26. Ministry of International Trade and Industry, AIST, *21 Seiki ni muketa Gijutsu Kaihatsu to Kokusai Kōryū no Arikata*, pp. 14–18.

27. "Sekai no Kiso Kagaku e Kokusai Kōken: HFSP," p. 26.

28. Telephone interview with Dr. Mary Clutter, assistant director of biological sciences, U.S. National Science Foundation, November 11, 1994.

29. Telephone interview with Dr. Joseph Rall, former director of intramural research at the U.S. National Institutes of Health, September 28, 1995.

30. Quoted in William Lepowski, "Japan Sets Up Program for Biological Research," *Chemical & Engineering News*, May 16, 1988, pp. 21–22.

31. Human Frontier Science Program, "Feasibility Study Committee Report," p. 7.

32. "Sekai no Kiso Kagaku e Kokusai Kōken: HFSP," p. 26.

33. Personal interviews with Katsuhiko Umehara, March 30, 1995, and Dr. Akiyoshi Wada, former dean of natural sciences at Tokyo University and chairman of the HFSP International Feasibility Study Committee, March 28, 1995.

34. Personal interview with Dr. Akiyoshi Wada, March 28, 1995.

35. "Sekai no Kiso Kagaku e Kokusai Kōken: HFSP," p. 26.

36. "HFSP Seifu aida Kaigō Kaisai" (Meeting Opens between HFSP Governments), *Nihon Keizai Shimbun*, June 16, 1989, p. 2.

37. "Raishū HFSP Seifu Kaigō Kaisai" (HFSP Government Meeting Opens Next Week), *Nikkei Sangyō Shimbun*, July 25, 1989, p. 5.

38. Edmund Klamann, "U.S. Offers Symbolic Gift to Japan Project," *Nikkei Weekly*, February 1, 1993, p. 7.

39. "Bei no Ōgata Kasokuki muke Shikin Kyōyoku" (Financial Cooperation with America's Supercollider), *Nihon Keizai Shimbun*, November 26, 1991, p. 9.

40. Off-the-record interview.

41. Telephone interview with Sir James Gowans, former secretary-general of the HFSP Organization, September 28, 1995.

42. The results of the survey are based on 33 responses to 80 distributed questionnaires. Nomura Research Institute, "Study Concerning Promotion of Research Overseas as Reference Material for the HFSP," pp. 66–76.

43. "HFSP Chronology," NSF Tokyo Office, internal memo, September 27, 1991.

44. "Nihon Teishō no Seimei Kiso Kenkyū Bei mo Shikin Kyoshutsu" (America will also Contribute Funds to Life-Science Basic Research Advocated by Japan), *Nihon Keizai Shimbun*, March 18, 1991, p. 17.

45. Human Frontier Science Program, *Annual Report FY 2002*, pp. 17, 47.

46. "HFSP Honkaku Dankai Ikō e Kyōgi" (Conference Shifts to Setting-up Stage of HFSP), *Nihon Keizai Shimbun*, January 21, 1991, p. 17.

47. David Swinbanks, "Human Frontier Program Gets Promise from NIH," *Nature*, March 14, 1991, p. 97.

48. Telephone interview with Dr. Joseph Rall, September 28, 1995.

49. Akiyoshi Wada, "What Frontiers for Frontier?" *Nature*, June 4, 1992, p. 356.

50. "Sekai no Kiso Kagaku e Kokusai Kōken: HFSP," p. 28.

51. Telephone interview with Sir James Gowans, September 28, 1995. Gowans's view is supported in personal correspondence he received from several council members.

52. Personal interview with Dr. Akiyoshi Wada, March 28, 1995.

53. Off-the-record interview.

54. "Sekai no Kiso Kagaku e Kokusai Kōken: HFSP," p. 23.

55. "Publicity, Jobs Needed to Woo Foreign Researchers," *Japan Economic Journal*, December 17, 1988, p. 11.

56. Off-the-record interview.

57. "Across the World and Back" in Human Frontier Science Program, *Tenth Anniversary Brochure, Human Frontier*.

58. Telephone interview with Dr. Mary Clutter, November 3, 1994.

59. ARA Consulting (Canada) and the University of Manchester Policy Research Group in Engineering, Science, and Technology (PREST), "General Review of the Human Frontier Science Program 1996," p. 2; KMPG Consulting (Canada) and the University of Manchester Policy Research Group in Engineering, Science and Technology (PREST); "Human Frontier Science Program Review 2001," p. 41.

60. KMPG Consulting (Canada) and the University of Manchester Policy Research Group in Engineering, Science and Technology (PREST), "Human Frontier Science Program Review 2001," pp. 6–7, 19–21.

61. Telephone interview with Dr. Elizabeth Neufeld, Department of Biochemistry UCLA, September 21, 1995.

Notes to Chapter 5

1. Like EUREKA, the IMS program is an ad hoc intergovernmental bargain with a distributed funding structure. In contrast, the Framework Program took shape around an existing regional organization and its funds come from a central pool. The review process in IMS, however, more closely resembles that of the Framework Program.

2. Gregory Rutchik, *Japanese Research Projects and Intellectual Property Laws*, pp. 44–45.

3. U.S. Department of Commerce, *IMS: A Program for International Cooperation in Advanced Manufacturing*, Part I-5.1.

4. Ibid., Part II-3.

5. Rutchik, *Japanese Research Projects*, p. 46.

6. Telephone interview with Dr. Odo Struger, vice president for technology development, Allen-Bradley, February 16, 1995.

7. Intelligent Manufacturing Systems, *Annual Project Report, 2002*; Intelligent Manufacturing Systems, *IMS Program: Project Summaries*. Also www.ims.org/index_faq.html. Viewed August 2003.

8. Intelligent Manufacturing Systems, "Project Portfolio and Monitoring, 2001," p. 6.

9. Intelligent Manufacturing Systems, *Annual Report 2000*, p. 12.

10. Michael Parker, "The Intelligent Manufacturing System Initiative," p. 222.

11. Ibid., p. 222; Intelligent Manufacturing Systems, *Annual Report 2001*, pp. 28–29.

12. Parker, "The Intelligent Manufacturing System Initiative," pp. 220–22.

13. Personal interviews with Professor Ichiro Inasaki, Faculty of Science and Technology, Keio University, July 5, 1995; and Professor Fumihiko Kimura, Department of Precision Machinery Engineering, Tokyo University, July 18, 1995.

14. Personal interview with Mr. Yuichi Tanioka, manager Planning Department, Corporate Planning Division, Shimizu Corporation, June 6, 1995.

15. David Swinbanks, "Counterpart to Frontiers," *Nature*, February 8, 1990, p. 496.

16. "Dai Ni Bu FA Tokushū," p. 3.

17. George R. Heaton, *International R&D Cooperation*, p. 10.

18. Personal interview with Professor Yuji Furukawa, dean, Faculty of Engineering, Tokyo Metropolitan University, June 27, 1995.

19. Off-the-record interview.

20. Personal interview with Mr. Katsuhiko Umehara, director, General Planning and Coordination Division, NEDO, March 30, 1995.

21. Personal interview with Mr. Hideyuki Hayashi, senior executive director, IMS Promotion Center, April 3, 1995.

22. Noboyuki Oishi, "Suspicions Slow Implementation of IMS Standard," p. 1.

23. Heaton, *International R&D Cooperation*, p. 10.

24. IMS Promotion Center, *Joint International Research Programs into an Intelligent Manufacturing System, Version 4*, p. 16.

25. Personal interview with Mr. Hideyuki Hayashi, April 3, 1995.

26. Oishi, "Suspicions Slow Implementation of IMS Standard."

27. IMS Promotion Center, *Joint International Research Programs*, p. 6.

28. "Dai Ni Bu FA Tokushū," p. 2.

29. David Swinbanks, "Two Sides of the Coin," *Nature*, September 27, 1990, p. 320.

30. Makoto Ishizuka, "International Collaborative Research," p. 51.

31. Ibid.

32. Nick Garnett, "Suspicions of a Link Up," *Financial Times*, January 4, 1990, p. 12.

33. "Conference Urges Europe to Devise Standards for CIM or Risk Losing Out to Japan," *Computer Weekly*, June 4, 1992.

34. National Research Council, *Manufacturing Research Exchange*, p. 1.

35. Ministry of International Trade and Industry, Machinery and Information Industries Bureau, *FA Bijon: FA kara IMS e*, pp. 63–64.

36. "Dai Ni Bu FA Tokushū," p. 2.

37. On foreign pressure see "Tsugi Sedai Seisan Shisutemu IMS no Mosaku" (Groping Towards the Next Generation Manufacturing System IMS), *Nikkei Sangyō Shimbun*, January 22, 1993, p. 4. For the statement that reducing trade friction is a more important motivation than international contribution, see "Denshi Gijutsu 90 Nendai no Chōryū Saizensen no Kenkyūsha ni Kiku" (Listening to Researchers at the Forefront of Electronics Technology in the 1990s), *Nikkei Sangyō Shimbun*, August 24, 1992, p. 5.

38. Off-the-record interview.

39. Detailed chronologies of domestic discussions in the United States and European Union can be found in Heaton, *International R&D Cooperation*, pp. 10–12; and Ishizuka, "International Collaborative Research," pp. 41–53.

40. Ronald K. Jurgen, "Global R&D for a 21st Century Manufacturing System," *IEEE Spectrum*, November 1990, p. 123.

41. Commission of the European Communities, "Draft Terms of Reference for a Feasibility Study on Future Generation Manufacturing Systems," (July 1990), p. 2. Photocopy provided by IMS Promotion Center.

42. IMS Promotion Center, *Joint International Research Programs*, pp. 3–4.

43. Personal interview with Professor Yuji Furukawa, June 27, 1995.

44. Personal interview with Mr. Hideyuki Hayashi, April 3, 1995.

45. "News from the Regions," in *Impressions: IMS Newsletter* no. 17, July 17, 2000, www.ims.org. Viewed July 2001.

46. IMS Promotion Center, *Joint International Research Programs*, p. 6.

47. Personal interview with Mr. Takayoshi Ozaki, deputy director, Industrial Machinery Division, Machinery and Information Industries Bureau, MITI, March 6, 1995.

48. "IMS Susumuka" (Will IMS Advance?), *Nikkei Sangyō Shimbun*, February 9, 1990, p. 12.

49. Ishizuka, "International Collaborative Research," p. 31.

50. Oishi, "Suspicions Slow Implementation of IMS Standard."

51. "Chiteki Seisan Shisutemu IMS, Nichibei Kyōdō Purojekuto Shidō e" (IMS: Towards the Start of a Japan-U.S.-Europe Cooperative Project), *Nikkei Sangyō Shimbun*, April 16, 1991, p. 5.

52. Personal interview with Mr. Hideyuki Hayashi, April 3, 1995.

53. David Swinbanks, "Gift Horse Arouses Suspicion," *Nature*, June 14, 1990, p. 563.

54. "IMS no Kokusai Kyōdō Kaihatsu" (The Development of International Cooperation in IMS), *Nikkei Sangyō Shimbun*, October 17, 1991, p. 11.

55. Quoted in "The Human Factory," *Far Eastern Economic Review*, July 5, 1990, pp. 56–58.

56. Quoted in Ishizuka, "International Collaborative Research," p. 40.

57. Telephone interview with Mr. Richard Aubin, United Technologies Research Center, February 7, 1995.

58. Oishi, "Suspicions Slow Implementation of IMS Standard."

59. Quoted in Ishizuka, "International Collaborative Research," p. 57.

60. Off-the-record interview.

61. Ishizuka, "International Collaborative Research," p. 60.

62. "Fundamentals of IMS," pp. 2–3, www.ims.org. Viewed July 2001.

63. Intelligent Manufacturing Systems, *Annual Project Report*, 2002, pp. 1–3.

64. Intelligent Manufacturing Systems, "Final International Technical Committee Report to the International Steering Committee," p. 599.

65. Tetsuo Tomiyama, "The Technical Concept of IMS," p. 180.

66. Off-the-record interview.

67. GNOSIS Consortium, *Knowledge Systematization: Configuration Systems for Design and Manufacturing*. Final report, March 2000, p. 16.

68. Off-the-record interview.

69. Personal interview with Dr. Niall Murtagh, Industrial Electronics and Systems Lab, Mitsubishi Electric, May 4, 1995, and telephone interview October 27, 2000.

70. Personal interviews with Mr. Yuichi Tanioka, planning department manager, and Mr. Kobun Araki, engineering division manager, Shimizu Corporation, June 6, 1995; and Mr. Hiroyuki Nakamura, chief research engineer, Building Design and Construction R&D, Institute of Technology, Shimizu Corporation, October 31, 2000.

71. Personal interview with Mr. Kikuo Nakazawa, assistant general manager, Logistics Engineering Department, Engineering Division, Kajima, November 7, 2000.

72. Robert H. Brown and Hannu Syntera, *Globeman 21, Global Manufacturing in the 21st Century: Final Report*, p. 22.

73. Personal interviews with Mr. Tetsuya Oishi, senior advisor, Toyo Business Engineering Corporation, April 28, 1995 and October 27, 2000; and Mr. Yoichi Kamio, IMS project manager, Technology R&D Center, Toyo Engineering, October 27, 2000.

74. Brown and Syntera, *Globeman 21, Global Manufacturing in the 21st Century*, p. 13.

75. Ibid., p. 22.

76. Consortium for Advanced Manufacturing International, *NGMS-IMS Interim Report*, pp. 3–6.

77. Ibid., p. 28.

78. Idem, *NGMS-IMS Project Phase II*, p. 11.

79. Idem, *NGMS-IMS Interim Report*, p. 27; idem, *NGMS-IMS Project Phase II*, p. 34.

80. Otis Port, "Factories Get a Lot Smarter," *Business Week*, May 29, 2000, p. 42; "Honda Reduces Manufacturing Costs by 87 Percent with Prototype Biological Manufacturing System," *Manufacturing News*, May 12, 2000, p. 1.

81. Consortium for Advanced Manufacturing International, *NGMS-IMS Interim Report*, p. 19.

82. Otis Port, "Thinking Machines," *Business Week Asia*, August 7, 2000, p. 66.

83. Adam Ashton, "A Global Think-Tank Targets the Factory," *Business Week Asia*, August 7, 2000, p. 72.

84. Intelligent Manufacturing Systems, *Annual Report*, 2000, p. 24.

Notes to Chapter 6

1. Personal interview with Mr. Kenichi Fukuda, deputy director, Electronics Policy Division, Machinery and Information Industries Bureau, MITI, September 27, 2000.

2. "RWC Project as Proved by Data," *RWC News* 7 (June 2000), p. 19.

3. Akinori Yonezawa, "The RWC Program: MITI's Next Computer Research Initiative," *Science*, October 23, 1992, p. 581.

4. Ministry of International Trade and Industry, Machinery and Information Industries Bureau, *The Master Plan for the Real World Computing Program*.

5. Atsushi Senda, "Tokushū: Yawarakana Jōhō Shori e no Chōsen," p. 49.

6. "Overview of the Project for the Fundamental Information Technology of the Next Generation," *RWC News* 5 (February 1999), pp. 4–8.

7. Junichi Shimada, "RWC Technologies Enter Actual Use," *RWC News* 7 (June 2000), p. 8.

8. Personal interview with Dr. Junichi Shimada, research director, RWC Partnership, September 4, 2000.

9. The FGCP is discussed in Scott A. Callon, *Divided Sun*, p. 34; the information regarding the RWC comes from a personal interview with Mr. Toshinori Saeki, deputy director, Industrial Electronics Division, Machinery and Information Industries Bureau, MITI, March 6, 1995.

10. Personal interview with Dr. Junichi Shimada, September 4, 2000.

11. Organization for Economic Cooperation and Development, *Steering and Funding of Research Institutions, Country Report on Japan*, p. 13.

12. David Swinbanks, "Computing in the Real World," *Nature*, April 30, 1992, p. 734.

13. Asian Technology Information Program, *Summary of Parallel Computer Installations in Japan*, p. 1.

14. Tatsuro Fuji, "Controversy Surrounds 4-D Computer Project," *Nikkei Weekly*, August 29, 1992, p. 8.

15. Quoted in Andrew Pollack, "Japan Plans Computer to Mimic Human Brain," *The New York Times*, August 25, 1992, p. C1.

16. Telephone interview with Mr. Judson French, director, Electronics and Electrical Engineering Laboratory, National Institute of Standards and Technology, December 9, 1994.

17. Evelyn Richards, "U.S. Protests Japan's Overtures to Computer Researchers," *Washington Post*, May 21, 1991, p. D1.

18. David Swinbanks, "Japan Courts U.S. on Joint Project," *Nature*, May 30, 1991, p. 336.

19. Telephone interview with Judson French, December 9, 1994.

20. Telephone interview with Dr. Eugene Wong, formerly associate director for Industrial Technology, Office of Science and Technology Policy, February 16, 1995.

21. U.S. National Science Foundation, "MITI's New Patent Rules for International R&D Projects."

22. "Zadankai: Yojigen Konpyutaa, RWC no Tenbō" (Roundtable Discussion: The Four Dimensional Computer, Prospects for the RWC), *Kikai Shinkō* 25, no. 6 (June 1992): 29.

23. Ibid., p. 7.

24. Quoted in Swinbanks, "Computing in the Real World," p. 734.

25. Off-the-record interview.

26. Christine Tomovich, "MOSIS—A Gateway to Silicon," p. 23.

27. U.S. Department of Commerce, National Institute of Standards and Technology, *Consignment Agreement between NIST and the RWC Partnership*, p. 4.

28. Idem, *U.S.-Japan Joint Optoelectronics Project Implementation Plan*, p. 2.

29. Off-the-record interview.

30. Telephone interview with Dr. Eugene Wong, February 16, 1995.

31. Ibid.

32. "RWC Puroguramu e no Kitai" (Expectations for the RWC Program), *Kikai Shinkō* 25, no. 6 (June 1992): 8.

33. U.S. Department of Commerce, National Institute of Standards and Technology, *U.S.–Japan Joint Optoelectronics Project Implementation Plan*, p. 2.

34. The American interest in prototyping for optoelectronic devices was evident in the DARPA-sponsored Consortium for Optical and Optoelectronic Technologies in Computing (CO-OP), which was established at the same time as the RWC.

35. In this paragraph and the next, all statistics on the FGCP are from Hiroyuki Odagiri et al., "Research Consortia as a Vehicle for Basic Research," p. 201; all statistics on the RWC are from "RWCP Kenkyū Gyōseki Ichiran" (Summary of RWC Research Achievements), www.rwcp.or.jp. Viewed February 2002. The argument that RWC papers have been more influential than FGCP papers is found in Yoshiaki Nakamura, "Effectiveness of Japan's Government Sponsored Research Project-The Real World Computing Program," pp. 109-11.

36. U.S. Department of Commerce, National Institute of Standards and Technology, *U.S.–Japan Joint Optoelectronics Project 1992–2001: Final Report*, pp. 9–15.

37. Edward Feigenbaum et al., *JTEC Panel Report on Knowledge-Based Systems in Japan*, p. 103.

38. Callon, *Divided Sun*, p. 67.

39. Ibid., pp. 66–74.

40. Martin Fransman in *The Market and Beyond* offers a much more positive evaluation of the FGCP. He argues that the FGCP form of organization, together with the tacitness inherent in the creation of technical knowledge, provided firms with an incentive to participate in the program, and that the FGCP produced economies of scale and standardization. His analysis is less compelling than Callon's for several reasons. Fransman takes as given that knowledge processing is an important area of research that requires active government support. Callon's field research is convincing in suggesting that firms did not share this assumption. Fransman also tends to rely more on theoretical deductions about the relative efficiency of various forms of collaborative research rather than concrete examples of the benefits of the FGCP to firms.

41. "Zadankai: RWC Puroguramu e no Kitai" (Roundtable Discussion: Expectations for the RWC Program), *Kikai Shinkō* 27, no. 1 (January 1994): 13.

42. Pollack, "Japan Plans Computer to Mimic Human Brain," p. C1.

43. Quoted in Senda, "Tokushū: Yawarakana Jōhō Shori e no Chōsen," p. 40.

44. Personal interview with Mr. Hajime Irisawa, March 20, 1995.

45. David Kahaner, "MITI's RWC Program," p. 71.

46. Callon, *Divided Sun*, pp. 129–45.

47. Hiroyuki Odagiri et al., "Research Consortia as a Vehicle for Basic Research," p. 206.

48. Personal interview with Dr. Junichi Shimada, September 4, 2000.

49. Ibid.

50. *Seamless*. Promotional video. Tokyo: RWC Partnership, 1999.

51. "Japan Group's 1,024-PC Parallel Computer Achieves 11th Highest Speed," *Asia Pulse*, April 23, 2001.

52. Beckman and Gannon are quoted in "Toward Seamless Computing: RWC Research Results at SC98," *RWC News* 7 (June 2000), pp. 25–27.

53. "RWC Technologies Enter Actual Use," *RWC News* 7 (June 2000), p. 8.

54. "Fujitsu Laboratories Announces World's First Complete Linux Cluster System," *Japan Corporate News Network*, October 29, 2001.

55. Yutaka Akiyama, "PAPIA System," *RWC News* 5 (February 1999), p. 20.

56. Quoted in "RWCP High Performance Computing for Structural Biology," *RWC News* 7 (June 2000), p. 27.

57. "Press Releases on Recent Research Results of RWC," *RWC News* 2 (December 1996), p. 9.

58. "Media Drive Unveils CrossMediator for Video 2.0," *Asia Pulse,* July 19, 2001; Kuriko Miyake, "Future-Watching at Japan's RWC," *CNN.com*, October 11, 2001.

59. Junichi Shimada, "Setting a Trend," *RWC News* 4 (December 1997), pp. 9–11.

60. Personal interview with Dr. Junichi Shimada, September 4, 2000.

61. Personal interviews with Mr. Shintaro Komiya, research director, Planning and Accounting Division, and Mr. Shinichi Kobayashi, research director and general manager, Information Technologies Department, Mitsubishi Research Institute, June 2, 1995.

62. Senda, "Tokushū: Yawarakana Jōhō Shori e no Chōsen," p. 47.

63. Personal interviews with Mr. Norio Tsubouchi, associate chief specialist, R&D Group, NEC, May 10, 1995, and Mr. Michio Kawade, manager, External Relations Division and National Projects, NEC, October 11, 2000.

64. "NEC Develops Computer Screening Tech for New Drug Development," *Dow Jones International News,* June 25, 2001.

65. Personal interviews with Mr. Tadashi Matsuda, general manager, R&D Administration Division, Fujitsu, May 16, 1995, and Mr. Kenji Tomizawa, general manager, Planning Division, External Affairs Group, Fujitsu, October 16, 2000.

66. Personal interviews with Mr. Atsushi Otomo, attached to the general manager, Corporate R&D Promotion Office, Hitachi, May 11, 1995, and Mr. Seishi Hara, chief engineer, Technical Coordination Department, R&D Group, and Mr. Yasuhiro Inagami, department manager, Enterprise Server Systems, October 17, 2000.

67. "Hitachi Info Systems Turns Text into Animated Sign Language," *Nikkei Report*, October 29, 2002.

68. Personal interviews with Dr. Okio Yoshida, senior manager, Corporate Planning Division, Toshiba, February 7, 1995, and Mr. Keijiro Hirahara, chief specialist, Research Planning Group, Corporate R&D Center, and Dr. Shigeru Oyanagi, chief research scientist, Laboratory III, Communication and Information Systems Research Labs, Toshiba, November 16, 2000.

69. Personal interviews with Mr. Shozo Morita, manager, R&D Planning Administration Department, Headquarters R&D, Mitsubishi Electric, May 25, 1995, and Mr. Shunichi Adegawa, manager, National Project Group, Corporate Research and Development, Mitsubishi Electric, October 10, 2000.

70. Personal interviews with Dr. Takeshi Kamijoh, Strategic Planning, Advanced Devices Laboratories, R&D Group, and Mr. Shinichi Ito, senior manager, Engineering Relations Division, Oki Electric, November 7, 2000.

71. "METI Expanding New Development Projects," *Japan Chemical Week*, April 17, 2003.

72. Personal interviews with Dr. Thomas Hagemann, director, GMD Tokyo Office, May 17, 1995, and Mr. Fahim Nawabi, director, GMD Tokyo Office, November 1, 2000.

73. All discussion of SICS's involvement in RWC is based on e-mails from Dr. Janusz Launberg, information and planning manager, Swedish Institute of Computer Science, June 1, 1995, and Dr. Martin Nilsson, Autonomous Learning Functions Lab, March 9, 2001.

74. Telephone interviews with Dr. Bert Kappen, program manager, Foundation for Neural Networks, October 9, 1995 and December 7, 2000.

75. Ibid.

76. Telephone interviews with Dr. Lui Ho Chung, program manager, Institute of Systems Science, National University of Singapore, May 24, 1995, and Dr. Jiankang Wu, principal investigator, Multi-Modal Functions KRDL Lab, January 15, 2001.

Notes to Chapter 7

1. Annabel Wells, "Supersonic Rising Sun: Japan Plans to Get its Foot in the Door of International Collaboration on New Supersonic Aircraft," *Flight International*, June 17, 1998.

2. Michael A. Dornheim, "Japan Pushes High Speed Research," *Aviation Week & Space Technology*, August 17, 1992, p. 48.

3. Stanley Kandebo, "GE Tests Japanese Engine Aimed at Future SSTs," *Aviation Week & Space Technology*, January 20, 1997, p. 30.

4. "Japan Pushes High Speed Research International Group to Build Combined-Cycle Hypersonic Engine," *Aviation Week & Space Technology*, August 17, 1992, p. 50.

5. "Editorial: MITI's Worthwhile Learning Experiment," *Aviation Week & Space Technology*, August 17, 1992, p. 9.

6. National Research Council, *High-Stakes Aviation*, p. 141.

7. Ibid., p. 140.

8. Ai Nakajima, "MITI Casts R&D Bait to Lure Foreigners," *Nikkei Weekly*, June 29, 1991, p. 3.

9. Kanichi Amano, "Moving Swiftly," *Flight International*, December 23, 1998.

10. Ministry of International Trade and Industry, *Industrial Science and Technology Frontier Program, 1994*, p. 5.

11. All discussion of Crucible Materials' participation in the project is taken from a telephone interview with Dr. Bill Eisen, Crucible Materials Corporation, April 24, 1996.

12. Asian Technology Information Program, *An Overview of Micromachining in Japan*, p. 4.

13. U.S. National Science Foundation, *Emerging Manufacturing Technologies and Research Activities in Japan*; Asian Technology Information Program, *MITI's Micromachine Project—What Comes Next?* pp. 5, 8.

14. Yuko Harayama, "Technological Paradigm Change and the Role of the University," p. 7.

15. Karen Lowry Miller et al., "Japan Pours Big Bucks into Very Little Machines," *Business Week*, August 27, 1990, p. 83.

16. Bob Johnstone, "Shrinking Technology," *Far Eastern Economic Review*, February 4, 1993, p. 34.

17. Unless otherwise indicated all discussion of SRI's involvement in the Micromachine project is based on telephone interviews and e-mail exchanges with Dr. Paul Jorgensen, executive vice president, and Dr. Ronald Pelrine, senior research engineer, SRI International, April 29, 1996 and May 1, 1996.

18. Seiki Chiba, "The Advanced Automation Technology Center of SRI International: Laboratory Introduction," *Micromachine* 34, February 2001, p. 4.

19. Telephone interview with Dr. Pavlo Rudakevych, IS Robotics, April 23, 1996; www.irobot.com. Viewed July 2003.

20. Harayama, "Technological Paradigm Change," p. 24.

21. Peter Hadfield, "Japan's Latest Micromachines Can Hunt in Packs," *New Scientist*, July 3, 1999, p. 20.

22. "Bonsai Factory," *The Economist*, November 13, 1999.

23. E-mail from Mr. Etsuro Shimizu, Research Department, Micromachine Center, August 7, 2003; Asian Technology Information Program, *An Overview of Micromachining in Japan*, p. 24.

24. Miwako Waga, "MITI Assesses the Ten-Year Japanese Micromachine Project," p. 4.

25. www.medea.org. Viewed August 2003.

26. Rose Marie Ham et al., "The Evolving Role of Semiconductor Consortia in the United States and Japan," pp. 139–40.

27. Kenneth Flamm, *Japan's New Semiconductor Technology Programs*, p. 3.

28. Hajime Sasaki, "Japanese Chip Industry in Jeopardy without a National Policy," *Solid State Technology*, February 1, 2001, p. 56.

29. Ham et al., "The Evolving Role of Semiconductor Consortia," pp. 151–52.

30. Flamm, *Japan's New Semiconductor Technology Programs*, pp. 11–12.

31. Ham et al., "The Evolving Role of Semiconductor Consortia," p. 160.

32. Ibid., p. 145; Flamm, *Japan's New Semiconductor Technology Programs*, p. 8.

33. Ham et al., "The Evolving Role of Semiconductor Consortia," pp. 145–49.

34. Peter Dunn, "Globalization to be a Reality at Sematech," *Solid State Technology*, May 1, 1998, p. 50.

35. Elias Carayannis and Jeffrey Alexander, "Revisiting Sematech: Profiling Public and Private-Sector Cooperation," *Engineering Management Journal*, December 1, 2000, pp. 33–42.

36. Quoted in David Lammers, "Chip Industry to Hammer Out Technology Plan," *CMP Tech Web*, July 5, 1999.

37. Peter Singer, "300 mm Equipment Software Requirements Defined," *Semiconductor International*, July 1, 2000, p. 78.

38. "International Sematech and JEITA/SELETE Expand Global Partnership," *Dow Jones Business Wire*, July 20, 2001.

39. Paul Kallender, "EUV Push Sends Japanese Group to Alliance Camp," *Electronic Engineering Times*, May 28, 2001, p. 6.

40. Idem, "Japan to Launch Separate Nanometer-Gate Project," February 23, 2001. http://siliconstrategies.com. Viewed July 2003.

41. "Japanese Chip Makers Band Together to Develop Advanced Semiconductors," *Dow Jones Business Wire*, September 29, 2000; "Consortium Plans to Develop Innovative Chip Technologies," *New Materials Japan*, May 1, 2001, p. 2.

42. "IMEC and STARC Will Partner on SoC Design," *Solid State Technology*, August 1, 2002, p. 20.

43. Masahide Kimura, "Ohmi Heads New Japanese Research Consortia," *Solid State Technology*, February 1, 2002, p. 36.

44. www.miraipj.jp. Viewed August 2003.

45. Chiang Yang, "Intel's Two-Pronged Approach," *Solid State Technology*, June 1, 2003.

46. Off-the-record interview.

47. "Private-Public Collaboration to Begin in Advanced Chip Development," *Nikkei Report*, January 19, 2003.

48. Paula Doe, "Asian Focus," p. 30.

49. www.aspla.com. Viewed August 2003.

50. Doe, "Asian Focus," p. 30.

51. "Chipmakers Urged to Tap Wide Range of Expertise," *Nikkei Weekly*, August 5, 2002.

52. "Nikon and SELETE Solve Problem for E-Beam Steppers," *Nikkei Report*, February 6, 2003; "Optical connector," *Nikkei Weekly*, June 23, 2003; "Japan's ASET Develops High-Performance Mask for EUV Lithography," *Asia Pulse*, July 6, 2003.

53. Paula Doe, "Japan Opens National Tsukuba Research Fab," *Solid State Technology*, August 1, 2002, p. 42.

54. Doe, "Asian Focus," p. 30.

55. Ministry of Economy, Trade and Industry, *Trends in Japan's Industrial R&D Activities*, p. 160.

56. Yoshiyuki Ohtawa, "Public Financing of University Research in Japan," pp. 157–58, 169.

57. "Quantity Outpaces Quality of Japan's Scientific Research," and "Rigid Funding Hobbles Scientific Research," *Nikkei Weekly*, June 25, 2001.

58. "Reorganization of Japan's Ministries and Agencies," *Japan Echo* 28, no. 1, pp. 57–58.

59. Edward J. Lincoln, *Arthritic Japan*, p. 167.

60. Organization for Economic Cooperation and Development, Directorate for Science, Technology and Industry, Committee for Science and Technology Policy, *Steering and Funding of Research Institutions, Country Report on Japan*, p. 4; U.S. National Science Foundation, *A New System for Promoting Science and Technology in Japan*, pp. 1–3.

61. Organization for Economic Cooperation and Development, *Steering and Funding of Research Institutions*, p. 7.

62. "Panel Says R&D Bodies Should Be Privatized," *Daily Yomiuri*, October 23, 2001.

63. "SCJ Fends Off Motions for Reforms," *Daily Yomiuri*, December 30, 2002.

64. U.S. National Science Foundation, *Japan's Basic Law for Science and Technology*, p. 2.

65. U.S. National Science Foundation, *The Government of Japan's Reorganization and Reform Plan*, p. 5.

66. U.S. Department of Commerce, U.S. Foreign and Commercial Service, *Japan —Impact of Government Administrative Reform on S&T Issues*.

67. "STA Bid to Keep Independence Quashed by PNC Oversight Failure," *Nucleonics Week*, August 21, 1997, p. 6.

68. U.S. Department of Commerce, *Japan—Impact of Government Administrative Reform*.

69. Dennis Normille, "Researchers Fear Merger Could Muffle Their Voice," *Science*, January 4, 2002, p. 37.

70. Organization for Economic Cooperation and Development, *Steering and Funding of Research Institutions*, pp. 11–13.

71. Japan Society for the Promotion of Science, *JSPS Annual Report 2003*, p. 33.

72. Ibid., appendix 4.

73. Ibid.

74. Dennis Normille, "New Faculty Grants Program Expands Role of STA," *Science*, May 3, 1996, p. 645; U.S. National Science Foundation, *Japan's Science and Technology Policy*, p. 6.

75. "Disaster Threatens Space Station," *New Zealand Herald*, February 7, 2003.

76. Personal interview with Mr. Gilbert Kirkham, NASA Japan representative, September 27, 2000.

77. "Government to Outsource Management of Space Module Kibo," *Kyodo News*, June 24, 2003.

78. "DOE's Projected Costs for Ending Its Participation in ITER," *Inside Energy*, June 7, 1999, p. 6.

79. "Japan to Propose Shouldering 22%–47% of ITER Building Cost," *Nikkei Report*, September 15, 2002.

80. U.S. Congress, Office of Technology Assessment, *International Partnerships in Large Science Projects*, p. 56.

81. All comments by Professor Kimura are taken from Kenneth Pechter, *Assessment of Japanese Attitudes Toward International Collaboration in Big Science*, pp. 25–27.

82. U.S. Congress, Office of Technology Assessment, *International Partnerships in Large Science Projects*, p. 57.

83. U.S. National Science Foundation, *Japan's High Energy Accelerator Research Organization*.

84. Joan Johnson-Freese, *Over the Pacific*, pp. 107–8.

85. U.S. Congress, Office of Technology Assessment, *International Partnerships in Large Science Projects*, p. 96.

86. All comments by Professor Kodaira are taken from Kenneth Pechter, *Assessment of Japanese Attitudes*, pp. 27–31.

Notes to Chapter 8

1. Richard Katz, *Japanese Phoenix*, pp. 147–48.

2. Human Frontier Science Program, *Annual Report FY 2002*.

3. Intelligent Manufacturing Systems, *Annual Project Monitoring Report, 2002*.

4. Karl Zinsmeister, "MITI Mouse."

5. Scott Callon, *Divided Sun*, p. 189.

6. Personal interview with Mr. Kenichi Fukuda, deputy director, Electronics Policy Division, Machinery and Information Industries Bureau, MITI, September 27, 2000.

7. "R&D Budget Focuses on End Product," *Nikkei Weekly*, January 20, 2003.

8. "METI to Cut 40% in Existing R&D Budget to Focus on Four Areas," *Japan Weekly Monitor*, September 2, 2002.

9. "METI Expanding New Development Projects," *Japan Chemical Week*, April 17, 2003.

10. Edward J. Lincoln, *Troubled Times*; C. Fred Bergsten et al., *No More Bashing*.

11. Richard J. Samuels, *Rich Nation Strong Army*, p. 48; Shigeru Nakayama, *Science, Technology, and Society in Postwar Japan*, p. 200.

12. Ministry of International Trade and Industry, Industrial Technology Division, Industrial Policy Bureau, *National Strategies for Industrial Technology*, pp. 3–4.

13. U.S. National Science Foundation, *The Government of Japan's Reorganization and Reform Plan*, p. 2.

14. "Japan Ministries Report," *Capital Markets Report*, August 29, 1996.

15. "MITI, MOT Oppose Restructuring," *Jiji Press*, June 5, 1997.

16. Mark Elder, "METI and Industrial Policy in Japan," p. 168.

17. U.S. Department of Commerce, U.S. Foreign and Commercial Service, *Japan—Impact of Government Administrative Reform on S&T Issues*.

18. Hiroyuki Yoshikawa, "International Society and the Goals of the National Institute of Advanced Industrial Science and Technology."

19. U.S. National Science Foundation, Tokyo Office, *National Institute of Advanced Industrial Science and Technology*, pp. 5–6; David Cyranoski, "Goal-Directed Revamp for Japanese Research," *Nature*, March 1, 2001.

20. U.S. National Science Foundation, Tokyo Office, *National Institute of Advanced Industrial Science and Technology*, pp. 6–7.

21. "Unleashing R&D in Japan," *Chemical & Engineering News*, December 9, 2002.

22. I am grateful to Richard Dasher, director of the U.S.-Asia Technology Management Center at Stanford University for sharing his thoughts on this topic.

23. Steven K. Vogel, "Final Thoughts," in idem, ed., *U.S.-Japan Relations in a Changing World*, p. 265.

24. Joint U.S.-Japan Dialogue Group, *U.S.-Japan Dialogue on the Role of Science and Technology in Society into the New Millennium*.

25. U.S. Department of Commerce, National Institute of Standards and Technology, *U.S.–Japan Joint Optoelectronics Project 1992–2001: Final Report*, p. 18.

26. D.H. Whittaker, "Crisis and Innovation in Japan," p. 79.

27. Robert Triendl, "Japanese Rules Hinder Commercialization of Publicly Funded Projects," *Nature Biotechnology*, April 2002, p. 325.

Bibliography

Anchordoguy, Marie. "Japan at a Technological Crossroads: Does Change Support Convergence Theory?" *Journal of Japanese Studies* 23, no. 2 (1997): 363–97.

ARA Consulting (Canada) and the University of Manchester Policy Research Group in Engineering, Science, and Technology (PREST). "General Review of the Human Frontier Science Program 1996." Strasbourg: HFSP Organization, 1996.

Archibugi, Daniele, Jeremy Howells, and Jonathan Michie, eds. *Innovation Policy in a Global Economy.* Cambridge, UK: Cambridge University Press, 1999.

Archibugi, Daniele, and Simona Iammarino. "The Globalization of Technological Innovation: Definition and Evidence." *Review of International Political Economy* 9, no. 1 (March 2002): 98–122.

Archibugi, Daniel, and Jonathan Michie. "The Globalization of Technology." In Archibugi and Michie, eds., *Technology, Globalization and Economic Performance*, pp. 172–97.

Archibugi, Daniele, and Jonathan Michie, eds. *Technology, Globalization and Economic Performance.* Cambridge, UK: Cambridge University Press, 1997.

Arrison, Thomas, et al., eds. *Japan's Growing Technological Capability.* Washington, DC: National Academy Press, 1992.

Asian Technology Information Program. *MITI's Micromachine Project—What Comes Next?* Report No. 99.077. Tokyo: ATIP, 1999.

———. *An Overview of Micromachining in Japan.* Report No. 99.086. Tokyo: ATIP, 1999.

———. *Summary of Parallel Computer Installations in Japan.* Report No. 93.011. Tokyo: ATIP, 1993.

Bergsten, C. Fred, Takatoshi Ito, and Marcus Noland. *No More Bashing: Building a New Japan–United States Economic Relationship.* Washington, DC: Institute for International Economics, 2001.

Bergsten, C. Fred, and Marcus Noland. *Reconcilable Differences? United States–Japan Economic Conflict.* Washington, DC: Institute for International Economics, 1993.

Borrus, Michael. "Foreign Participation in U.S.-Funded R&D: The EUV Project as a New Model for a New Reality." Berkeley Roundtable on the International Economy, Working Paper No. 118. Berkeley, CA: BRIE, 1998.

Borrus, Michael, and John Zysman. "Industrial Competitiveness and American National Security." In Sandholtz et al., eds., *The Highest Stakes*, pp. 7–52.

Branscomb, Lewis M., Fumio Kodama, and Richard Florida. *Industrializing Knowledge: University-Industry Linkages in Japan and the United States.* Cambridge, MA: MIT Press, 1999.

Branstetter, Lee G., and Mariko Sakakibara. "When Do Research Consortia Work Well and Why? Evidence from Japanese Panel Data." *American Economic Review* 92, no. 1 (March 2002): 143–59.

Brown, Robert H., and Hannu Syntera, eds. *Globeman 21, Global Manufacturing in the 21st Century: Final Report*. 1999. Report by Tetsuya Oishi, Toyo Engineering.

Calder, Kent. *Strategic Capitalism: Private Business and Public Purpose in Japanese Industrial Finance*. Princeton, NJ: Princeton University Press, 1993.

Callon, Scott A. *Divided Sun: MITI and the Breakdown of Japanese High-Tech Industrial Policy, 1975–93*. Stanford, CA: Stanford University Press, 1995.

Cassidy, Janice H. "Enhancing Future Competitiveness: The Japanese Government's Promotion of Basic Research." Tokyo: National Institute of Science and Technology Policy, October 1990.

Cantwell, John. "The International Agglomeration of R&D." In *Global Research Strategy and International Competitiveness,* ed. Mark Casson, pp. 104–32. Cambridge, MA: Basil Blackwell, 1991.

Coleman, Samuel. *Japanese Science: From the Inside*. London, UK: Routledge, 1999.

Consortium for Advanced Manufacturing International. *NGMS-IMS Interim Report*. R-00-NGMS-01, Bedford, TX, April 2000.

———. *NGMS-IMS Project Phase II: Synergistic Integration of Distributed Manufacturing and Enterprise Information*. Reference Manual P-00-NGMS-01.1, Bedford, TX, May 2000.

Contractor, Farok, and Peter Lorange, eds. *Cooperative Strategies in International Business*. New York: Macmillan, 1988.

Cowhey, Peter, and Jonathan Aronson. *Managing the World Economy: The Consequences of Corporate Alliances*. New York: Council on Foreign Relations Press, 1993.

"Dai Ni Bu FA Tokushū" (FA Special Feature, Part Two). *Nikkei Sangyō Shimbun,* April 16, 1991, 1–5.

Dalton, Donald H., and Manuel G. Serapio. *Globalizing Industrial Research and Development*. Washington, DC: U.S. Department of Commerce, Office of Technology Policy, 1999.

Doane, Donna L. *Cooperation, Technology, and Japanese Development: Indigenous Knowledge, the Power of Networks, and the State*. Boulder, CO: Westview Press, 1998.

Doe, Paula. "Asian Focus" (Interview with Director of IT Industry Division, Commerce and Information Policy Bureau, METI). *Solid State Technology* (November 1, 2000): 30.

Dunning, John H. "Governments and Multinational Enterprises." In *Multinationals in the Global Economy*, eds. Lorraine Eden and Evan H. Potter, pp. 59–83. New York: St. Martin's Press, 1993.

Dunning, John H., ed. *Governments, Globalization, and International Business*. New York: Oxford University Press, 1997.

Elder, Mark. "METI and Industrial Policy in Japan." In Schaede and Grimes, eds., *Japan's Managed Globalization*, pp. 159–90.

European Commission. *Communication from the Commission: The International Dimension of the European Research Area*. COM 346 Final Report, Brussels, June 2001.

———. *External Monitoring Report on the Specific Program for Research and Technological Development: Confirming the International Role of Community Research*. Brussels, 2001.

———. *Five Year Assessment Report Related to the Specific Program: Confirming the International Role of Community Research, 1995–2000*. INCO 5YA Final Report, Brussels, May 2000.

European IMS Secretariat. *First Assessment of the IMS Scheme and IMS Projects Overview and Results*. Helsinki, November 1999.

Feigenbaum, Edward et al., eds. *JTEC Panel Report on Knowledge-Based Systems in Japan*. Baltimore, MD: International Technology Research Institute, Loyola College, 1993.

Flamm, Kenneth. *Japan's New Semiconductor Technology Programs*. ATIP Report No. 96.091. Tokyo: Asian Technology Information Program, 1996.

Florida, Richard. "The Globalization of R&D: Results of a Survey of Foreign-Affiliated R&D Laboratories in the USA." *Research Policy* 26 (1997): 85–103.

———. "Technology Policy for a Global Economy." *Issues in Science and Technology* (Spring 1995): 49–56.

Fong, Glenn R. "Follower at the Frontier: International Competition and Japanese Industrial Policy." *International Studies Quarterly* 42 (June 1998): 339–66.

Fransman, Martin. *Japan's Computer and Communications Industry: The Evolution of Industrial Giants and Global Competitiveness*. New York: Oxford University Press, 1995.

———. *The Market and Beyond: Information Technology in Japan*. New York: Cambridge University Press, 1993.

———. *Visions of Innovation: The Firm and Japan*. Oxford, UK: Oxford University Press, 1999.

Freeman, Christopher. "The National System of Innovation in Historical Perspective," in *Technology, Globalization and Economic Performance*, Archibugi and Michie, eds., pp. 24–49.

Fujioka, Akifusa. *Tsūsanshō no Yomikatta* (How to Read MITI). Tokyo: OS Publishers, 1994.

Gassman, Oliver, and Maximilian von Zedwitz. "New Concepts and Trends in International R&D Organization." *Research Policy* 28 (1999): 231–50.

Georghiou, Luke, and David Roessner. "Evaluating Technology Programs: Tools and Methods." *Research Policy* 29 (2000): 657–78.

Gerybadze, Alexander, and Guido Reger. "Globalization of R&D: Recent Changes in the Management of Innovation in Transnational Corporations." *Research Policy* 28 (1999): 251–74.

Goto, Akira, and Hiroyuki Odagiri, eds. *Innovation in Japan*. Oxford, UK: Clarendon Press, 1997.

Graham, Edward M., and Paul R. Krugman. *Foreign Direct Investment in the United States*. Washington, DC: Institute for International Economics, 1991.

Green, Michael. *Arming Japan: Defense Production, Alliance Politics, and the Postwar Search for Autonomy*. New York: Columbia University Press, 1995.

Hagedoorn, John. "Understanding the Rationale of Strategic Technology Partnering." *Strategic Management Journal* 14 (1993): 371–85.

Ham, Rose Marie, Greg Linden, and Melissa Appleyard. "The Evolving Role of Semiconductor Consortia in the United States and Japan." *California Management Review* 41, no. 1 (Fall 1998): 137–63.

Hane, Gerald J. "Comparing University-Industry Linkages in the U.S. and Japan." In Branscomb, Kodama, and Florida, eds., *Industrializing Knowledge*, pp. 20–61.

————. "Innovation in Japan after the Financial Crisis: The Transition from Techno-Nationalism to Techno-Realism." MIT Japan Program, Working Paper 02.01, 2002.

————. "The Real Lessons of Japanese Research Consortia." *Issues in Science and Technology* (Winter 1993): 56–62.

————. "Research and Development Consortia and Innovation in Japan: Case Studies in Superconductivity and Engineering Ceramics." Ph.D. dissertation, Harvard University, 1992.

Harayama, Yuko. *Japanese Technology Policy: History and a New Perspective.* Tokyo: Research Institute of Economy, Trade, and Industry. Discussion Paper Series 01-E-001, 2001.

————. "Technological Paradigm Change and the Role of the University: The Case of the Micromachine in Japan." Unpublished paper, 2000.

Hatch, Walter. "Japanese Production Networks in Asia." In Keller and Samuels, eds., *Crisis and Innovation in Asian Technology*, pp. 23–56.

Heaton, George R., Jr. *International R&D Cooperation: Lessons from the IMS Proposal.* Washington, DC: National Academy of Sciences, Manufacturing Forum, Discussion Paper No. 2, 1991.

Hill, Christopher. "The Advanced Technology Program." In *Investing in Innovation: Creating an Innovation Policy That Works*, ed. Lewis Branscomb and James Keller, pp. 143–73. Cambridge, MA: MIT Press, 1998.

Howells, Jeremy, and Michelle Wood. *The Globalization of Production and Technology.* New York: Belhaven Press, 1992.

Hu, Yao-Su. "Global or Stateless Corporations Are National Firms with International Operations." *California Management Review* (Winter 1992): 107–26.

Human Frontier Science Program. *Annual Report FY 2002.* Strasbourg: HFSP Organization, 2002.

————. *Balancing Biomedicine's Postdoc Exchange Rate.* Strasbourg: HFSP Organization, 2000.

————. "Feasibility Study Committee Report." Unpublished report, 1989.

————. *Tenth Anniversary Brochure, Human Frontier: A Decade of Intercontinental Research in Life and Brain Sciences, 1989–1999.* Strasbourg: HFSP Organization, 1999.

————. "Report of the International Scientific Committee." Unpublished report, 1989.

Intelligent Manufacturing Systems. *Annual Project Monitoring Report, 2002.* IMS Inter-Regional Secretariat, May 2003.

————. *Annual Report, 2000.* IMS Inter-Regional Secretariat, 2000.

————. *Annual Report, 2001.* IMS Inter-Regional Secretariat, 2001.

————. "Final International Technical Committee Report to the International Steering Committee." Unpublished report provided by the Coalition for IMS, Washington, DC, 1994.

————. *IMS Program: Project Summaries.* Internal memo provided by the IMS Inter-Regional Secretariat, July 2003.

————. "Project Portfolio and Project Monitoring." Internal memo provided by the IMS Inter-Regional Secretariat, October 2001.

IMS Promotion Center, Tokyo. *Joint International Research Programs into an Intelligent Manufacturing System, Version 4.* Pamphlet, 1990.

————. *Outline of IMS Domestic Feasibility Study Projects.* Pamphlet, 1993.

Ishizuka, Makoto. "International Collaborative Research: A Case Study of the IMS Program." Masters thesis, MIT, 1993.

Iwasa, Tomoko, and Hiroyuki Odagiri. 2002. *The Role of Overseas R&D Activities in Technological Knowledge Sourcing: An Empirical Study of Japanese R&D Investment in the United States.* First Theory-Oriented Research Group, NISTEP and MEXT. Discussion Paper No. 23 (June).

Japan Society for the Promotion of Science. "JSPS Annual Report 2003." Tokyo, 2003.

Johnson, Chalmers. *Japan, Who Governs? The Rise of the Developmental State.* New York: W.W. Norton, 1995.

————. *MITI and the Japanese Miracle: The Growth of Industrial Policy, 1925–1975.* Stanford, CA: Stanford University Press, 1982.

————. "MITI, MPT, and the Telecom Wars." In *Politics and Productivity: How Japan's Development State Works,* ed. Chalmers Johnson et al., pp. 177–240. New York: Harper Collins, 1989.

Johnson-Freese, Joan. *Over the Pacific: Japanese Space Policy into the Twenty-First Century.* Dubuque, IA: Kendall-Hunt, 1993.

Joint U.S.–Japan Dialogue Group. *U.S.–Japan Dialogue on the Role of Science and Technology into the New Millennium.* Washington, DC: U.S.–Japan High Level Advisory Committee, 2000.

Kahaner, David. "MITI's Real World Computing Program." *IEEE Micro* (August 1992): 70–80.

Katz, Richard. *Japanese Phoenix: The Long Road to Economic Revival.* Armonk, NY: M.E. Sharpe, 2003.

Keller, William W., and Richard J. Samuels, eds. *Crisis and Innovation in Asian Technology.* New York: Cambridge University Press, 2003.

————. "Innovation and the Asian Economies." In Keller and Samuels, eds., *Crisis and Innovation in Asian Technology,* pp. 1–22.

Kitson, Michael, and Jonathan Michie. "The Political Economy of Globalization." In Archibugi, Howells, and Michie, eds., *Innovation Policy in a Global Economy,* pp. 163–83.

KMPG Consulting (Canada) and the University of Manchester Policy Research Group in Engineering, Science, and Technology (PREST). "Human Frontier Science Program Review 2001."

Kneller, Robert. "Intellectual Property Rights and University-Industry Technology Transfer in Japan." In Branscomb, Kodama, and Florida, eds., *Industrializing Knowledge,* pp. 307–47.

Kodama, Fumio. *Emerging Patterns of Innovation: Sources of Japan's Technological Edge.* Boston: Harvard Business School Press, 1995.

————. "Technology Fusion and the New R&D." *Harvard Business Review* (July–August 1992): 70–78.

Kodama, Fumio, and Lewis Branscomb. "University Research as an Engine for Growth." In Branscomb, Kodama, and Florida, eds., *Industrializing Knowledge,* pp. 3–19.

Kogut, Bruce. "Joint Ventures: Theoretical and Empirical Perspectives." *Strategic Management Journal* 9 (1988): 319–32.

Laredo, Philippe, and Philippe Mustar, eds. *Research and Innovation Policies in the New Global Economy.* Northampton, MA: Edward Elgar, 2001.

Lee, Thomas H., and Proctor P. Reid, eds. *National Interests in an Age of Global Technology.* Washington, DC: National Academy Press, 1991.

Lincoln, Edward J. *Arthritic Japan: The Slow Pace of Economic Reform.* Washington, DC: Brookings Institution Press, 2001.

————. *Troubled Times: U.S.–Japan Trade Relations in the 1990s*. Washington, DC: Brookings Institution Press, 1999.

Mani, Sunil. *Government, Innovation and Technology Policy: An International Comparative Analysis*. Northampton, MA: Edward Elgar, 2001.

Ministry of Economy, Trade and Industry. "Key Points, 2003 Economic and Industrial Policy" (Provisional Translation). Tokyo: METI, August 2002.

————. *Trends in Japan's Industrial R&D Activities: Principal Indicators and Survey Data, No. 3*. Tokyo: METI, November 2002.

Ministry of Education. *Research Cooperation Between Universities and Industry in Japan*. Tokyo: MESC, 1994.

Ministry of International Trade and Industry. AIST. International Cooperation Division. *Overview of MITI's Technology Policy*. Tokyo: MITI, 2000.

————. AIST. Gijutsu to Kokusai Kōryū ni kansuru Kenkyūkai (Research Group on Technology and International Exchange). *21 Seiki ni muketa Gijutsu Kaihatsu to Kokusai Kōryū no Arikata* (Toward the Twenty-first Century: Technology Development and International Exchange). Tokyo: MITI, 1986.

————. *Industrial Science and Technology Frontier Program, 1994*. Tokyo: MITI, 1994.

————. Industrial Technology Council. *Framework for R&D in Industrial Science and Technology*. Tokyo: MITI, 1994.

————. Industrial Technology Council. *Issues and Trends in Industrial-Scientific Technology*. Tokyo: MITI, 1992.

————. Industrial Technology Council. *Tenkanki no R&D* (R&D at a Turning Point). Tokyo: MITI, 1992.

————. Industrial Technology Division, Industrial Policy Bureau. *National Strategies for Industrial Technology*. Tokyo: MITI, April 2000.

————. Kikai Jōhō Sangyō Kyoku, Kokusai Haiteku Gijutsu Kyōryoku Kondankai (Machinery and Information Industries Bureau. Roundtable on International Cooperation in High-Technology). *Kokusai Haiteku Gijutsu Kyōryoku no Sokushin ni mukete* (Aiming Toward Promotion of International Cooperation in High-Technology). Tokyo: MITI, 1990.

————. Kikai Jōhō Sangyō Kyoku, Sangyō Kikaika (Machinery and Information Industries Bureau, Industrial Machinery Division). *FA Bijon: FA kara IMS e.* (FA Vision: From FA to IMS). Tokyo: Keibun Press, 1989.

————. Machinery and Information Industries Bureau. *The Master Plan for the Real World Computing Program*. Tokyo: MITI, 1992.

————. Sangyō Gijutsu Shingikai, Kokusai Kenkyū Kyōryoku Bukai (Industrial Technology Council, International Research and Development Cooperation Committee). *Shin Gijutsu Rikkoku ni muketa Hōkatsuteki-Senryakutekina Kokusai Sangyō Kenkyū Kyōryoku no Suishin* (Promotion of Comprehensive and Strategic International Research and Development Cooperation: Aiming toward a New Technology-Based Nation). Tokyo: MITI, 1994.

————. Sangyō Kōzō Shingikai Sangyō Gijutsu Shoiinkai to Sangyō Gijutsu Shingikai Kikaku Iinkai (Industrial Structure Council, Industrial Technology Subcommittee and the Industrial Technology Council, Planning Committee). *Kagaku Gijutsu Sōzō Rikkoku e no Michi o Kirihiraku, Shiteki Shisan no Sōzō, Katsuyō ni mukete* (Clearing a Path Toward a Nation Built on Creative Science and Technology: Toward Creation and Utilization of Intellectual Assets). Tokyo: MITI, June 1995.

Mochizuki, Michael M. "The Past in Japan's Future." *Foreign Affairs* (September/ October 1994): 126–34.

Morris-Suzuki, Tessa. *The Technological Transformation of Japan from the Seventeenth to the Twenty-First Century.* New York: Cambridge University Press, 1994.

Mowery, David C. "The Changing Structure of the U.S. National Innovation System: Implications for International Conflict and Cooperation in R&D." *Research Policy* 27 (1998): 639–54.

Mytelka, Lynn Krieger, ed. *Strategic Partnerships.* Madison, NJ: Fairleigh Dickinson University Press, 1991.

Nakamura, Yoshiaki. "Effectiveness of Japan's Government Sponsored Research Project-The Real World Computing Program." *International Journal of Entrepreneurship and Innovation Management* 2, no. 1 (2002): 100–116.

Nakayama, Shigeru. *Science, Technology, and Society in Postwar Japan.* Melbourne: Kegan Paul International, 1991.

National Research Council. *Global Economy, Global Technology, Global Corporations.* Washington, DC: National Academy Press, 1998.

———. *Harnessing Science and Technology for America's Economic Future: National and Regional Priorities.* Washington, DC: National Academy Press, 2000.

———. *High-Stakes Aviation: U.S.–Japan Technology Linkages in Transport Aircraft.* Washington, DC: National Academy Press, 1994.

———. *Manufacturing Research Exchange: Foundation of a Japan–U.S. Cooperative Research Program.* Washington, DC: National Academy Press, 1989.

———. *Maximizing U.S. Interests in Science and Technology Relations with Japan.* Washington, DC: National Academy Press, 1997.

———. *R&D Consortia and U.S.–Japan Collaboration: Report of a Workshop.* Washington, DC: National Academy Press, 1991.

———. *U.S.–Japan Strategic Alliances in the Semiconductor Industry.* Washington, DC: National Academy Press, 1992.

Nikkan Kōgyō Shimbun, Tokubetsu Shuzai Han (Nikkan Kogyo Newspaper, Special Research Group). *Shin Maekawa Ripoto ga Shimesu Michi (The Road Ahead Shown in the New Maekawa Report).* Tokyo: Nikkan Press, 1987.

Nomura Research Institute. "Study Concerning Promotion of Research Cooperation Overseas as Reference Material for the HFSP." Unpublished report, 1998.

Niwa, Fujio, and Hiroshi Goto. "Japanese Collaborative R&D." In *R&D Strategies in Japan: The National, Regional, and Corporate Approach,* ed. Hajime Eto, pp. 207–24. New York: Elsevier Press, 1993.

Odagiri, Hiroyuki, and Akira Goto. "The Japanese System of Innovation." In *National Innovation Systems,* ed. Richard R. Nelson, pp. 76–114. New York: Oxford University Press, 1993.

Odagiri, Hiroyuki, Yoshiaki Nakamura, and Minoru Shibuya. "Research Consortia as a Vehicle for Basic Research: The Case of the Fifth Generation Computer Project in Japan." *Research Policy* 26 (1997): 197–207.

Ohtawa, Yoshiyuki. "Public Financing of University Research in Japan." In Branscomb, Kodama, and Florida, eds., *Industrializing Knowledge,* pp. 157–79.

Oishi, Noboyuki. "Suspicions Slow Implementation of IMS Standard." *Japan Economic Journal* (July 21, 1990).

Okimoto, Daniel I. *Between MITI and the Market: Industrial Policy for High-Technology.* Stanford, CA: Stanford University Press, 1989.

Organization for Economic Cooperation and Development. *Foreign Access to Technology Programs*. OECD/GD (97) 209. Paris: OECD, 1997.

————. *Spotlight on Public Support to Industry*. Paris: OECD, 1998.

————. Directorate for Science, Technology and Industry, Committee for Science and Technology Policy. *Steering and Funding of Research Institutions, Country Report on Japan*. Paris: OECD, 2003.

Oriyama, Jun. "Hyuman Frontia Saiensu Puroguramu Kōsō: Aratana Kagaku Gijutsu Taikei no Sōzō" (The Concept of HFSP: Creation of a New Science and Technology System). *Kikai Shinkō* (Promotion of the Machine Industry) 19, no. 9 (1986).

Ostry, Sylvia, and Richard R. Nelson. *Techno-Nationalism and Techno-Globalism*. Washington, DC: Brookings Institution Press, 1995.

Papanastassiou, Marina, and Robert D. Pearce. "The Internationalization of Research and Development by Japanese Enterprises." *R&D Management* 24 (April 1994): 155–65.

Parker, Michael. "The Intelligent Manufacturing Systems Initiative: An International Partnership Between Industry and Government." *STI Review* 23 (December 1998): 214–37.

Patel, Pari, and Keith Pavitt. "Large Firms in the Production of the World's Technology." In *Technology Management and International Business*, ed. Ove Granstrand, et al., pp. 53–73. New York: John Wiley & Sons, 1992.

Patel, Pari, and Modesto Vega. "Patterns of Internationalization of Corporate Technology: Location vs Home Country Advantages." *Research Policy* 28 (1999): 145–55.

Pavitt, Keith, and Parimal Patel. "Global Corporations and National Systems of Innovation." In Archibugi, Howells, and Michie, eds., *Innovation Policy in a Global Economy*, pp. 94–119.

Pearce, Robert D. *The Internationalization of Research and Development by Multinational Enterprises*. London: Macmillan, 1989.

Pearce, Robert D., and Satwinder Singh. *Globalizing Research and Development*. London: Macmillan, 1992.

Pearson, Alan, et al. "Decision Parameters in Global R&D Management." *R&D Management* 23 (July 1993): 249–62.

Pechter, Kenneth G. *Assessment of Japanese Attitudes Toward International Collaboration in Big Science*. Contractor report prepared for the U.S. Congress, Office of Technology Assessment, 1995.

Peterson, John, and Margaret Sharp. *Technology Policy in the European Union*. New York: St. Martin's Press, 1998.

Prestowitz, Clyde V. *Trading Places: How We Are Giving Our Future to Japan and How to Reclaim It*. New York: Basic Books, 1989.

Pyle, Kenneth B. *The Japanese Question: Power and Purpose in a New Era*. 2d ed. Washington, DC: American Enterprise Institute Press, 1996.

Ramseyer, J. Mark, and Frances Rosenbluth. *Japan's Political Marketplace*. Cambridge, MA: Harvard University Press, 1993.

Reger, Guido. "How R&D is Coordinated in Japanese and European Multinationals." *R&D Management* 29, no. 1 (1999): 71–88.

Reich, Robert B. *The Work of Nations*. New York: Vintage Books, 1992.

Rosenbluth, Frances. *Financial Politics in Contemporary Japan*. Ithaca, NY: Cornell University Press, 1989.

Ruberti, Antonio, and Michel Andre. "The European Model of Research Cooperation." *Issues in Science and Technology* (Spring 1995): 17–21.

Rutchik, Gregory. *Japanese Research Projects and Intellectual Property Laws*. Washington, DC: U.S. Department of Commerce, Office of Technology Policy, 1996.

"RWC Project as Proved by Data." *RWC News* June 2000, p. 19. Tokyo: Real World Computing Partnership.

Sakakibara, Kiyonori, and Eleanor Westney. "Japan's Management of Global Innovation: Technology Management Crossing Borders." In *Technology and the Wealth of Nations*, ed. Nathan Rosenberg et al., pp. 327–43. Stanford, CA: Stanford University Press, 1992.

Sakakibara, Mariko. "The Diversity of R&D Consortia and Firms Behavior: Evidence from Japanese Panel Data." *Journal of Industrial Economics* 49, no. 2 (June 2001): 181–96.

———. "Evaluating Government-Sponsored R&D Consortia in Japan: Who Benefits and How?" *Research Policy* 26 (1997): 447–73.

Samuels, Richard J. *The Business of the Japanese State: Energy Markets in Comparative and Historical Perspective*. Ithaca, NY: Cornell University Press, 1987.

———. "Japan as a Technological Superpower." Japan Policy Research Institute, Working Paper No. 15 (January 1996).

———. *Rich Nation, Strong Army: National Security and the Technological Transformation of Japan*. Ithaca, NY: Cornell University Press, 1994.

Sandholtz, Wayne. *High-Tech Europe: The Politics of International Cooperation*. Berkeley, CA: University of California Press, 1992.

Sandholtz, Wayne, et al., eds. *The Highest Stakes: The Economic Foundations of the Next Security System*. New York: Oxford University Press, 1992.

Schaede, Ulrike, and William Grimes. "The Emergence of Permeable Insulation." In Schaede and Grimes, eds., *Japan's Managed Globalization*, pp. 3–16.

———, eds. *Japan's Managed Globalization: Adapting to the Twenty-First Century*. Armonk, NY: M.E. Sharpe, 2003.

Schoppa, Leonard J. *Bargaining with Japan: What American Pressure Can and Cannot Do*. New York: Columbia University Press, 1997.

Science and Technology Agency. National Institute of Science and Technology Policy, ed. *Historical Review of Japanese Science and Technology Policy*. Tokyo: STA, 1991.

———. *Kagaku Gijutsu Shihyō: Nihon no Kagaku Gijutsu Katsudō no Taiketeki Bunseki, Heisei Roku Nenban* (Science and Technology Indicators 1994: A Systematic Analysis of Science and Technology Activities in Japan). Tokyo: STA, 1995.

"Sekai no Kiso Kagaku e Kokusai Kōken: HFSP" (HFSP: International Contribution to Global Basic Science). *Nikkei Saiensu* (Nikkei Science), December 1993.

Senda, Atsushi. "Tokushū: Yawarakana Jōhō Shori e no Chōsen" (Special Feature: Toward the Challenge of Flexible Information Processing). *Nikkei Computer,* April 5, 1993, 49–52.

Simon, Dennis Fred, ed. *Techno-Security in an Age of Globalization: Perspectives from the Pacific Rim*. Armonk, NY: M.E. Sharpe, 1997.

Taylor, Sully, and Kozo Yamamura. "Japan's Technological Capabilities and Its Future." In *Technological Competition and Interdependence*, ed. Gunter Heiduk and Kozo Yamamura, pp. 25–63. Seattle, WA: University of Washington Press, 1990.

Tomiyama, Tetsuo. "The Technical Concept of IMS." Unpublished paper, Tomiyama Laboratory, Department of Precision Machinery Engineering, Tokyo University, 1993.

Tomovich, Christine. "MOSIS—A Gateway to Silicon." *IEEE Circuits and Devices Magazine* (March 1988).

Tonelson, Alan. "The Perils of Techno-Globalism." *Issues in Science and Technology* (Summer 1995): 31–38.

Tyson, Laura D'Andrea. *Who's Bashing Whom? Trade Conflict in High-Technology Industries.* Washington, DC: Institute for International Economics, 1992.

U.S. Congress. House Committee on Science, Space, and Technology. *U.S./Japan Science and Technology Agreement.* 100th Cong., 2d sess., 1988.

———. Office of Technology Assessment. *International Partnerships in Large Science Projects.* Washington, DC: Government Printing Office, 1995.

———. Senate Committee on Commerce, Science and Transportation. *United States and Japan Science and Technology Agreement: Hearing before the Subcommittee on Science, Space, and Technology.* 100th Cong., 1st sess., 1987.

U.S. Department of Commerce. *Global Tech Update: The European Union's Sixth Framework Program for Research and Technological Development.* Washington, DC: Office of Technology Policy, 2002.

———. National Institute of Standards and Technology. *ATP Eligibility Criteria for U.S. Subsidiaries of Foreign-Owned Companies: Legislation, Implementation and Results.* NISTIR-6099, 1998.

———. National Institute of Standards and Technology. *Consignment Agreement between NIST and the RWC Partnership,* 1995.

———. National Institute of Standards and Technology. *U.S.–Japan Joint Optoelectronics Project Implementation Plan,* 1994.

———. Office of Technology Policy. *IMS: A Program for International Cooperation in Advanced Manufacturing (Final Report of the International Steering Committee),* 1994.

———. U.S. Foreign and Commercial Service. *Japan—Impact of Government Administrative Reform on S&T Issues.* Report from the American embassy in Tokyo, October 1997.

U.S. National Science Board. *Science and Engineering Indicators 2002.* NSB-02-01C. Arlington, VA: National Science Foundation, 2002.

U.S. National Science Foundation, Tokyo Office. *Emerging Manufacturing Technologies and Research Activities in Japan.* Report Memorandum No. 96–2, 1996.

———. *The Government of Japan's Reorganization and Reform Plan.* Report Memorandum No. 99-11, 1999.

———. *Japanese Ministry of Education Grants-in-Aid for Scientific Research.* Research Memorandum No. 95-18, 1995.

———. *Japanese Programs for Promoting Centers of Excellence.* Report Memorandum No. 96-6, 1996.

———. *Japan's Basic Law for Science and Technology.* Report Memorandum No. 96-11, 1996.

———. *Japan's High-Energy Accelerator Research Organization.* Report Memorandum No. 01-14, 2001.

———. *Japan's Science and Technology Policy: Retooling for the Future.* Report Memorandum No. 98-06, 1998.

———. *MITI's New Patent Rules for International R&D Projects.* Report Memorandum No. 218, 1991.

————. *National Institute of Advanced Industrial Science and Technology (AIST), An Independent Administrative Organization under the Ministry of Economy, Trade, and Industry.* Report Memorandum No. 01-04, 2001.

————. *A New System for Promoting Science and Technology in Japan.* Report Memorandum No. 01-15, 2001.

————. *Preview of the Second Science and Technology Basic Plan.* Report Memorandum No. 00-18, 2000.

————. *Second Business-Academia-Government Summit.* Report Memorandum No. 03-03, 2003.

————. *The Science System in Japan.* Report Memorandum No. 98-04, 1998.

Vogel, Steven K. *U.S.–Japan Relations in a Changing World.* Washington, DC: Brookings Institution Press, 2002.

Waga, Miwako. "MITI Assesses the Ten-Year Japanese Micromachine Project." *Micromachine Devices* 5, no. 2 (December 2002): 1–5.

Weber, Steven, and John Zysman. "The Risk that Mercantilism Will Define the Next Security System." In Sandholtz et al., eds., *The Highest Stakes*, pp. 167–96.

Westney, Eleanor. "Cross-Pacific Internationalization of R&D by U.S. and Japanese Firms." *R&D Management* 23 (April 1993): 171–81.

Whittaker, D.H. "Crisis and Innovation in Japan." In Keller and Samuels, eds., *Crisis and Innovation in Asian Technology*, pp. 57–85.

Wiesel, Torsten. *The Human Frontier Science Program: Future Perspectives.* Strasbourg: HFSP Organization, 2000.

Yakushiji, Taizō. *Tekunohegemoni: Kuni wa Gijutsu de Okori Horobiru* (Techno-Hegemony: Nations Prosper and Perish Based on Technology). Tokyo: Chūō Kōron Shinsho, 1989.

Yamada, Atsushi. *Neo Tekuno Nashonarizumu, Gurokaru Jidai no Gijutsu to Kokusai Kankei* (Neo Techno-Nationalism: Technology and International Relations in the Glocal Era). Tokyo: Yuhihaku, 2001.

Yamamoto, Kosuke. "Japanese Technology: Industrial Strategies in a Changing World." In *Technology Rivalries and Synergies Between North America and Japan, Symposium III*. Alexandria, VA: Licensing Executives Society, 1993.

Yoshikawa, Hiroyuki. "International Society and the Goals of the National Institute of Advanced Industrial Science and Technology." *Journal of Japanese Trade & Industry* (July 2001).

————. *Tekunogurobu: Gijutsuka Shita Chikyū to Seizōgyō no Mirai* (Techno-Globe: The High-Tech World and the Future of the Manufacturing Industry). Tokyo: Kōgyō Chōsakai, 1993.

Zinsmeister, Karl. "MITI Mouse." *Policy Review* 64 (Spring 1993): 28–35.

Index

Gregory Corning is an associate professor in the Department of Political Science and director of the Asian Studies Program at Santa Clara University. He earned his A.B. from Brown University and his Ph.D. from the University of Southern California, both in international relations. A former Fulbright-Hays fellow at Tokyo University's Institute of Social Science, he has published in journals including *Asian Survey*, *Pacific Affairs*, and *Social Science Japan Journal*.